CW00924523

BE
CAREFUL
WHAT
YOU
WISH
FOR

BE CAREFUL WHAT YOU WISH FOR

SIMON JORDAN

YELLOW JERSEY PRESS
LONDON

Published by Yellow Jersey Press 2012

2 4 6 8 10 9 7 5 3

First published in Great Britain in 2012 by
Yellow Jersey Press
Random House, 20 Vauxhall Bridge Road,
London SW1V 2SA

www.vintage-books.co.uk

Addresses for companies within The Random House Group Limited
can be found at: www.randomhouse.co.uk/offices.htm

The Random House Group Limited Reg. No. 954009

A CIP catalogue record for this book
is available from the British Library

ISBN 9780224091817

The Random House Group Limited supports The Forest Stewardship
Council (FSC®), the leading international forest certification organisation.
Our books carrying the FSC label are printed on FSC® certified paper. FSC® is
the only forest certification scheme endorsed by the leading environmental
organisations, including Greenpeace. Our paper procurement
policy can be found at www.randomhouse.co.uk/environment

Typeset in ITC Galliard by Palimpsest Book Production Limited,
Falkirk, Stirlingshire

Printed and bound by CPI Group (UK) Ltd, Croydon CR0 4YY

To the most precious thing in my life,
my darling daughter Cameron

contents

list of illustrations

ACKNOWLEDGEMENTS

The writing of a book, as I found out, is an extremely difficult task. It's one that requires a great deal of commitment, time and, I feel in the instance of an autobiography, one where you have to dig deep and be honest. I cannot say it was always a process I overly enjoyed, but it certainly was a challenge and one which I did my very best to rise to. Writing a book about your life and experiences requires a certain amount of fortitude, even when you are in the ascendant. Writing one when things are certainly not going your way has an element of masochism to it. But, beyond all of that, it has been an experience, and that is what life is about. There is also a touch of privilege in being published and, dare I say it, if the reader likes what they see, the ends have justified the means. With all of the above in mind I would like to thank the following people.

Theo Paphitis for saying 'write the bloody book' and engendering in me a 'right, I bloody well will' attitude. Without him I never would have attempted it, so it is him you have to blame. Paul Smith, who helped me write the book. 'Smithy' soon realised this was a poisoned chalice as not only did he have to look at me for days sitting across the table in my house in Spain, but he also had to suffer endless abuse every time he dared make a suggestion. In the end I wrote nigh on every word, but the book benefitted from Paul's, at times invaluable, counsel and structuring.

My thanks to David Luxton, my literary agent, for his support, perseverance and the endless hours he spent on the phone to me in Spain. Judy Daish for introducing me to David, which got me the agent and ultimately the publisher. Appreciation goes out to Matt Phillips and Rowan Yapp at Yellow Jersey for having the vision to publish this book, Justine Taylor for her hard work, input and advice and James Jones for his cover design.

Despite extremely trying circumstances – namely dealing with me – I would like to thank my partner Suzanne for being supportive and encouraging throughout this project, always saying things were good even when I knew they were not. And my parents, Peter and Linda, for at times saying the exact opposite, and giving me some much needed honesty and objectivity.

A thank you is due to Nick Moran, one of my closest friends and a talented writer himself, for helping me (hopefully) learn to write. After I had spent two weeks huffing and puffing over two chapters, he also came up with the immortal line 'Well, it's a start,' which pushed me on to be better than some of the initial drivel I had written.

I would like to thank my dear friend Deano, just for being a good friend, Mark Ryan, godfather of my daughter, Cameron, who I know will come through. Also, to that end, all those people who have stood by me during the last few years where things have been difficult.

I would like to thank the following people who have been encouraging and supportive during the process of writing and shown a genuine interest in this book: Jeff McGeachie, Ian Wright,

Mark Bright, Con O'Neill, Richard Keys, Andy Gray, Ian Payne, Anna Panour, Andrew Johnson, Anna Keel, Charles Koppel, Mark Fuller, Johnny and Carol Howard, Neil Warnock, Steve Bruce, Adam Pearson, David Groves, Greg Charalambides (kindest man in the world), my Marbella gang, Simon, Marco and Nicky Dalli, Marco and Carlo Morelli, Ash, Grant, my housekeeper Anna and groundsman Tarik, Graham Donkin, John Alvarez and my dear and brilliant friends stateside, John and Walter Almeida and George Raposa. I could go on.

I would like to thank my brother Dominic just for being a brilliant brother and one who has always watched my back even in sometimes impossible circumstances – we tried so hard, mate, especially with that football club. Thanks to Kevin Watts for being so loyal and committed to me for ten years, Lisa Kavanagh for being a fantastic PA. To Avril and Andrew Hall who, almost literally over the last five months, saved my life – Andrew, your generosity and support has astounded me.

To the Crystal Palace fans who, on the whole, were brilliant with me – I hope you know I gave my best.

To the industry that is football, a bullshit, nonsensical island in its own right, but one that has been a hell of an experience to be involved with and one I have to say I miss every now and then.

To those that read this book, thank you and I hope you enjoy it.

To my surrogate daughter, little Ally Sophie Walker, who is a wonderful big sister to my little girl. And finally to Cameron, who this book is dedicated to, who is the best piece of work I have ever done and who gives me the reason to want to be better.

INTRODUCTION

My name is Simon Jordan. I am the former owner of Crystal Palace
Football Club and the former owner of a string of businesses from
mobile phones to film companies. I am also the former owner of
£75 million, perhaps proving that 'a fool and his money are lucky
enough to get together in the first place'.

In order to tell this story I will show you just what it felt like
in 2000 when, aged thirty-two and listed as the 712th richest man
in the country, with the world at my feet and choices aplenty, I
chose to buy a football club, the youngest person in the world to
do so. You'll see how I felt when, aged thirty-six, I became the
youngest owner of a Premier League club, and what happened
when in 2010 I lost it all. This is a tale fraught with great highs
and devastating lows.

Football is the national game and means so much to so many,
but it's mostly about money now, not passion. I had both the
money and the passion for my club, so with these bed partners I
took a shot at achieving something. A few times I nearly got it
dead right. Rightly or wrongly I spoke my mind in no uncertain
terms and my outspoken attitude launched a thousand headlines.

1

Whether it was taking on the football establishment or fighting for my own club I caused mirth and mayhem in equal measure.

During my time I wrote acclaimed columns for the *Observer* which were said by others to be unique, hard-hitting and informative, but there I had a word limit and a defined subject matter; in this book I have no limits and so I will tell you exactly what goes on behind the running of a football club 'when Saturday comes'. Without bias, prejudice, bitterness or agenda (well, not too much), I will tell you about the real world of football – the personalities, the myths, the players, the managers, the hangers-on, the agents – every facet of this unique business that is not quite bound by the normal rules of society.

Throughout this book you will encounter household names and characters and discover what they were really like, you'll have my take on situations you've perhaps heard about and you'll read things that will make your jaw drop. At points you are likely to laugh or shake your head in disbelief as I bloody did.

But this book is also about a journey, one that I'm still undertaking today: it's the story of someone who has always backed himself to the hilt even when the odds seemed stacked against him. Most of the time this worked in my favour. Ultimately, it didn't.

The legendary Liverpool manager Bill Shankly famously once said: 'Some people think football is a matter of life and death . . . I can assure them it is much more serious than that.'

At 3 p.m. on 26 January 2010 I found out what Bill Shankly meant. Administrators were appointed into Crystal Palace Football Club, ending my ten-year ownership, ripping away my dreams and ambitions, wiping out vast amounts of my wealth.

Losing ownership of a football club has far-reaching effects and given my affinity with my particular club it leaves scars. Whilst this book is not about score settling, rest assured I will lay bare what happens when events overtake you, people betray you and agendas become all too apparent.

This is not a story about Crystal Palace; it's a story of what it's really like to own a football club, warts and all. It is a tale of ambition and dreams coupled with excess, politics, some stupidity, irreverence and humour.

Let's face it: everybody would love to own the club they support. You would, wouldn't you?

1

MIRACLE AT THE MILLENNIUM

May 2004. It's a sweltering hot day and I am standing in this bloody suit I've worn every Saturday for the last three months. I swear the damn thing is going to walk off on its own and I am dying to get it off, but it's my lucky suit! I can't help but pander to my newfound superstition that wearing it makes a difference.

So here we are, the suit and I, slap bang in the middle of the Millennium Stadium in Cardiff, surrounded by nearly 40,000 delirious Crystal Palace supporters, each one drowning in euphoria. It is one of those rare moments when all the shared hopes, dreams and aspirations have finally come to fruition.

I came to discover that moments like these are extremely scarce.

During the previous ninety-three minutes, against resounding odds, I watched the team I owned and loved get promoted to the Premier League. I had pumped my heart, soul and a king's ransom into this club and now they had reached the Mecca, the promised land of top-flight football.

We had just beaten West Ham United, the overwhelming favourites, in the play-off final. Prior to the game I had heard on good authority that the Hammers had already booked their victory party and bus parade through the streets of East London. Oh dear, Mr Pardew.

As luck would have it, fate was inexplicably stacked against them.

Take the hotel, for instance. We were booked into the Vale of Glamorgan, where all the previous play-off winners had stayed. The Hammers also drew the short straw in terms of dressing room. They were forced to enter the field from the south dressing room, which had yet to yield a play-off winner.

Then there was Neil Shipperley.

I had taken the striker off the administrators at Wimbledon Football Club in recompense for failing to pay their cleaning-up bills at Selhurst Park when they were our tenants.

Talk about cleaning up: I had just watched Shipperley bag a six-figure goal bonus for the solitary strike that catapulted us into the big time and instantaneously cleared the entire West Ham end of the stadium.

As a precautionary safety net I had attempted to broker a unique deal with West Ham whereby the losers kept the entire gate receipts as a small consolation prize instead of sharing them. The arrogant buggers were so confident they were having none of it. Their loss.

Did I really care about some minor spoils though?

People never forget where they were at key moments in history. For me, Saturday 29 May 2004 was one of them. I had many doubts during my tenure at CPFC, but this day was one time when I had few regrets.

Here I was, if only briefly, a god amongst men in the eyes of the club's supporters. I had delivered on my promise to bring Premier League football back to Selhurst Park. And I'd done so a year earlier than I predicted when, back in 2000, I rescued the club from administration and an uncertain future.

The almost daily battles, bust-ups and dramas that had ensued since then receded into distant memory that day. It was a phenomenal achievement by my team. In November 2003 they had lain fourth from the bottom of the division and now here they were, taking, in my view, their rightful place amongst the English football elite.

As I was cocooned in my own little bubble my mobile phone went into terminal meltdown as message after message from around the world went unanswered. I randomly answered one call. It was Ian Wright, the iconic England and former Palace striker and a close friend, screaming down the phone in celebration.

As I made my way around the Millennium Stadium, taking in the unprecedented outpourings of emotion, my mind flashed back to a similar occasion marked by widespread tears and relief.

It was another May three years earlier, and took place in rather less auspicious surroundings but it was nonetheless equally important. Dougie Freedman scored a goal in the eighty-seventh minute at Edgeley Park, the home of Stockport County, and catapulted himself into Palace folklore. This minor miracle saved us from relegation to the third tier of English football in my first traumatic season.

Dare I say it: the goal never should have stood. But it was symbolic in a way – as I was later to find out to my considerable financial cost, there is indeed a thin line between success and failure.

How things change. I remember playing Wolves at home in the third game from the end of that campaign and losing 2–0.

The Palace supporters were baying for blood and demanded the head of manager Alan Smith and his assistant Ray Houghton.

With two games remaining I thought we were nigh on dead. I took a monumental gamble and fired Smith and Houghton to replace them with chief scout Steve Kember.

We went on to destroy fellow relegation-threatened Portsmouth 4–2 at Fratton Park and then, thanks to Freedman's minor miracle, won at Edgeley in the final game to preserve our status and escape relegation.

Much had taken place in those three short years. The difference in circumstances was so vast as to border on the obscene.

All the battles, managers, headlines, meltdowns and controversies I had encountered in those three years had led us to this moment.

Previously I had been fighting to stay in the old First Division and pick up the £2 million a year in BSkyB money. Now we had the keys to the Sky vault to plunder.

There was no official invite; we didn't even knock on the door. We simply walked in and helped ourselves to a near £50 million and landed ourselves a place amongst the elite. Billed as the richest game in football and beamed to 160 countries with a global audience exceeding 700 million, the Premier League was a high-stakes poker game where the winner takes all.

We were going to the big time, playing the likes of Manchester United, Arsenal, Liverpool and Chelsea.

Left behind was a graveyard of twenty-three grounds I had no interest in revisiting, in front of us was not one but nineteen theatres of dreams. It felt good to own a Premier League club, I can't deny that.

It was the beginning of a new era. No longer was I an outspoken, controversial owner of a First Division club; I was going to be, well, the outspoken controversial owner of a Premier League club and join the media circus that accompanied the world's most elite league.

At thirty-six I was the youngest ever Premier League club owner, but mixed in with that euphoria was a feeling of wistfulness.

I had done what I set out to achieve. Was this the moment to take a bow, walk offstage and get out of the industry that I had quickly come to dislike for all its falseness and disingenuity, its pressures and disappointments? Should I get out now, whilst Crystal Palace was at its height, or was this the time to enjoy the spoils and try and go even further?

The boy that had travelled a hundred yards to watch his favourite team play had already travelled a lot further in life, and was going to travel a lot further still.

And while the journey had never been a straight line, it was to become an even more crooked path and I would run down it with my customary lack of regard for establishment and protocol.

But as I stood in the Millennium Stadium, all that was in the future. Let's start instead at the beginning.

2

SHOW ME THE BOY

As the saying goes, 'Show me the boy and I will show you the man.'

Childhood is one of those things that you have to address when you are writing a book about your life, but it is also in my view possibly the least interesting part of the journey. What you did as an adult is the money shot, certainly in an autobiographical book, that is.

My childhood wasn't without event, but I grew up in a loving, supportive home. I've found that writing the vague memories of your childhood in some respects lacks integrity. Recreating how you felt as your mind and body was forming; trying to get in touch with 'the child within you' is, in my view, not hugely honest or obtainable.

But, on the other hand, we all came from somewhere, with a background and traits that were introduced by our parents, honed by our friends and changed by life experiences. So I will indulge myself by setting up my childhood as the backdrop to my sometimes fantastically successful, sometimes totally destructive, but always eventful life, so far, at least!

I was born in South Norwood, Croydon on 24 September 1967, sharing that birthday with my close friend Theo Paphitis (he of

Dragons' Den), although it is fair to say my birthdate was many years after his.

I was lucky to have in Linda and Peter two loving parents, and my younger brother Dominic arrived two and a half years after me. I grew up on a friendly street, where back doors were always left open and all your best friends in the world lived next door. In my street all the houses were in the shadow of Crystal Palace Football Club's stadium.

Throughout my childhood I was rebellious and strong-willed. I never sought out confrontation, but I certainly wasn't the sort to avoid it. This trait has stayed with me throughout my life. I rebelled against all authority, starting at home then extending it to the world at large. I was single-minded and believed I could achieve whatever I wanted when I put my mind to it. Reflecting on my childhood, it seems I wanted to do exactly as I wanted when I wanted and not be bound by discipline and rules like everyone else.

Football was my love as a boy; I played it all the time and became accomplished from a very early age. All the neighbourhood houses faced out to a disused field, called the Brickfield, and regularly all the kids would be out until their mothers called them in to dinner, playing football in the most competitive of spirits.

Ironically that field now houses the car park of Crystal Palace Football Club and was the battle ground for my dad and Ron Noades, who owned CPFC at the time. Noades had perhaps rather thoughtlessly done a deal with Sainsbury's to convert the Brickfield into a car park and fence in all the houses. My father, being the tenacious animal he was, became locked in a rather bitter and vitriolic court case with Noades and Sainsbury's to protect our rights. Perhaps if Noades had a bloody great fence stuck at the bottom of his garden blocking him into his house he might have taken umbrage too. At the time, I was too young to really know what was going on, but it probably did colour my dealings with Noades in the future.

My father regularly took me the hundred yards up the road to watch Palace play; he loved football too. As it happened, he had played for the club as a young man and his father and grandfather before him had been Palace fans. I loved going to Selhurst Park, the home of Palace. I loved going so much, I even went when I was not invited, breaking into the stadium on Sundays with my younger brother, kicking about on the hallowed turf and climbing floodlights – amazing to think of now as I am scared of heights – running through lounges and the like. Perhaps not quite the behaviour of a future owner, or perhaps I was marking my turf.

Soon enough I played football in school teams rather than fields. I can even remember my first-ever proper goal aged nine for my school, Cypress Juniors, in a 4–2 win. Recalling my last goal to date is easier as it was the second goal scored during the first game at the new Wembley Stadium in a pro–celebrity match alongside such football luminaries as Geoff Thomas, Graeme Le Saux, Mark Bright and Neville Southall.

As I moved into my teens my parents sent me to an all-boys' school, Purley Boys. It had a fearsome reputation for discipline and its headmaster was a major advocate of the cane. Obeying rules was not my forte so going to a school where discipline was so prevalent was like an irresistible force meeting an immovable object.

Perhaps my only saving grace throughout my school years was my ability at sports, and I excelled in football, tennis and cricket. My father always supported me, and he'd run me here there and everywhere and always bought me the best equipment. My dad's focus on me sometimes bordered on the obsessive but he believed in me and wanted me to be the best. Throughout my life he has remained the same, believing I can do whatever I set my mind to.

My football career blossomed and two professional football clubs, Palace and Chelsea, eventually picked me up and, in the end, put me down too.

My most hated subject at school, although it was fair to say there were a number of subjects in close competition for that title, was design and technology, and I loathed the teacher with even greater passion. He wanted discipline and I wanted to do as I wished: the end result was constant conflict and me being regularly excluded from the lesson and locked in his office.

On one of many lock-ins I decided to exact revenge. His prized cactus, grown from a seed, was sitting on his desk. I sliced it to pieces with a Stanley knife. Mid-mutilation, he came up behind me. The result was my first but not my last encounter with the bamboo cane.

Despite the battles I had with the school structure, at the year-end assembly of my first year at Purley I received at that time a record number of Full Colours awards for sporting achievement. No sooner was that achieved than I got my next visit with the bambooed one.

It was the very end of the final day of term. After the last lesson of double games I had decided to leave my sports shirt on and not change into my proper school shirt.

As I lined up to get on the bus, two arrived and all the pupils jumped on. Suddenly Mr Wright, the deputy head of the fifth year, spotted me not wearing my school shirt and ordered me to go back into school and change. The second bus made to pull away and, assuming it was departing, I jumped on, ignoring the order, safe in the knowledge the bus was leaving and I was going to be on summer holidays for seven weeks. Not only had I disobeyed Mr Wright, I made a cocky comment as well. Unfortunately the bus was not leaving, but merely shuffling forward. So there I was, stood on the bus platform, looking directly into the face of Mr

Wright. My reward for my disobedience and comedic timing was to be ordered off the bus, dragged back into school and caned.

My last year at Purley Boys was to be one long battle, especially with the Head of Year, Mr Wozniak, who had taken a dislike to me and I to him – I don't like bullies. My sporting prowess was what kept me in school; it certainly was not my scholastic application or observation of rules.

As spring approached the cricket season arrived. It was the headmaster's second favourite sport and one I excelled at.

In a game away to Maidstone Grammar, my cricketing teammates and I were subjected to a very fast bowler, bowling very dangerously and hurting several of us. He hit me and then knocked out one of our players. As no intervention and protection ensued I, much to the chagrin of the teacher in charge, walked off and got the game abandoned. It was my first foray into righting the wrongs of sport!

On Monday morning a raging headmaster awaited me. 'How dare you lower the name of the school and disobey a teacher!'

I tried in vain to explain what happened, until Mr Wozniak barged in, took over and suspended me for a week.

As the end of the fifth year approached incredibly I was accepted to stay on to the lower sixth. Since my suspension I had kept my nose clean and worked hard. I was also back in the headmaster's good books and restored to the cricket team.

Mr Wozniak got there in the end by having me expelled. This was due to confusion as to what time I should have arrived for the traditional end-of-season cricket game between staff and pupils. Wozniak insisted I should have been there at one time; I countered by saying I had been told another, the end result was being told I was not playing in the game. This invoked great disappointment in me and ended with me pushing a teacher, resulting in expulsion.

To top it all my exam results were poor and I had no choice. I had to enrol in Croydon College to get more qualifications. It dawned on me that I wouldn't amount to much if I didn't pull my finger out.

College was completely different from school. Education was up to you. You were not forced to attend lectures or put in detention for misdemeanours. My new friend Edward Penrose (son of Barrie Penrose, co-author of the book *Conspiracy of Silence*) and I decided we wanted an in to the student union. There were elections in the winter of 1984. We put ourselves forward and were both elected. Once elected, we did absolutely nothing; sitting in meetings had no interest for either of us. We used the student union supplies and offices as our personal fiefdom, liberating supplies, using the student union phone; eventually our fellow student union reps respectively requested we leave.

Edward and I had identified a business opportunity delivering fresh vegetables to households. We canvassed a hundred houses and ascertained whether they would like such deliveries. Then we went to new Covent Garden and put together a price list. As our enterprise was about to begin, we decided it was too much like hard work and what we should do instead was sell Edward's father's vintage stamp collection at a radically reduced price from what it was really worth. Anything rather than hard work seemed to be our motto.

I coasted through the year. College was barely holding my attention. But I finished my exams and awaited my results. I passed two: English Literature and Government and Political Studies to add to the three I had passed at school. Now, fast approaching eighteen, I had five O levels and was standing at a crossroads.

Croydon was a melting pot of cultures, and like a lot of inner city areas it had its share of violence. There were gangs of all colours and creeds, and I had a brief flirtation with people in that way of life.

I saw many incidents of violence and destructive behaviour. Whilst I was always on the periphery of them, the mindlessness of some of these acts and the outcomes for my 'friends', who had run-ins with injuries, the police and ultimately the legal system, were not lost on even my adolescent, rebellious mind.

The tin lid for me was when I was sitting with a group of lads in a pub and a guy walked in and stuck a shotgun in my face. I had never seen him before in my life and to this day I still have no idea what it was about. But he was waving it in my face and telling me he was going to 'blow my fucking head off'. I seriously thought my time was up. One of my mates even turned to this lunatic and told him to pull the trigger and see what happens to him. For some reason the gunman had a dramatic change of heart and bolted out of the pub.

Whether these experiences brought about a sea change in my attitude, or whether I simply started to channel myself better, I always believed I was going to achieve something in life, thinking I was a leader not a follower. Now, at eighteen, it was time to start doing it.

The National Computer Centre invited applications in the local paper and from 200 applicants I got one of twenty places. My parents were thrilled: finally I was knuckling down and showing in their view my true potential. It was a year-long course of education in computer operating, programming and maintenance and also included two work placements.

This shaped the course my immediate life would take. I studied hard, excelled in my two work placements, passed all my exams with distinction.

I was ready for the big wide world.

3

FIRST STEPS INTO THE BIG WORLD

My first job was at Data Stream International. Fifty candidates had applied for the vacancy and I got it. I was on my way for a long and fruitful career in computing. Or so I thought.

September 1986. I strolled in on my first morning at 7.30 wearing a new double-breasted Prince of Wales check suit from Next. In my mind I looked and felt great. Unfortunately I got off to a bad start. I wore the identical suit to the man that greeted me, Ray Gilman, who was to become a good friend. And I mistook my scruffy boss, Dave Beerman, for a cleaner.

The job was shift operator, working both days and nights providing online information to the City. The most basic part of the job was printing out the information and as the lowest member on the pole you can guess who landed that plum job. I don't think so! I was destined for much greater things. That attitude made me a target for this team of practical jokers.

My first night shift came along and I walked headlong into disaster. The phone rang and I was told to answer it. An unfriendly voice demanded to know my name and informed me I was speaking to Hugh Kearns. It didn't mean much to me so I greeted that with a curt silence. The voice went on to say that I hadn't answered the phone appropriately, and it asked to speak to the shift leader, Dave Beerman.

Dave had a brief conversation with this Kearns and when he put the phone down I enquired who that miserable fucker was.

'You've done it now,' was his swift reply. 'Hugh is the MD and he hates people who don't answer the phone properly.'

The others took great delight tormenting me and goaded me throughout the night, insinuating I was in serious trouble.

The following evening there was a letter in my in-tray. It said that due to the unacceptable way I had answered the phone to the MD, the company were terminating my employment at the end of the shift.

All my cocky bravado disappeared in a millisecond. The blood drained out of my body. I asked Dave to help me and he went off in an attempt to rectify the situation, but to no avail.

Great. There I was, unemployed after just three days in the job. I wanted to burst into tears but was too numb to do so. I spent the remainder of the night consoling myself in the print room.

Come the morning I said goodbye to everyone for the last time only to be greeted with hysterical laughter.

The bastards had drafted the letter themselves; it was a complete wind-up.

With the newfound wealth that came with my first job, I acquired a convertible Triumph Spitfire for £750. It was a complete pile of shit. To my dad's great amusement, on his first inspection the window fell out.

Whilst the job was serious and the work needed to be done, it invariably came second to shenanigans. One particular night we completely overstepped the mark. The underground car park had a massive ramp and we amused ourselves by racing trolleys down it. An accident was inevitable. No prizes for guessing who caused it.

I completely lost control of the trolley I was riding and smashed straight into a brand-new Volvo estate owned by none other than the MD, Hugh Kearns.

To make matters worse it was caught on CCTV by the security guard, who usually spent most of his time asleep on the job, except on the evening in question when I smashed into the MD's car.

As Dave Beerman was the occupant of the other trolley we were forced to give the guard a sizeable bribe in cash and bring him six cans of lager every time we did night shifts in order for him to accidentally erase the security tape.

I may have been having fun at Data Stream, but I also was serious about my career. I wanted to progress and was ambitious and hungry for knowledge. The company hired a freelance computer contractor and when I discovered how much money he was earning I immediately wanted some of that. When I announced my plans to an amused set of colleagues they told me to a man that they had forgotten more than I was ever likely to know, along with a variety of other amusing put-downs – or so they thought.

I spent sixteen months cramming in as much experience as I could. I had come to the conclusion that the more experience I had on my CV, the greater chance I had of going freelance and making some serious money.

With a combination of confidence, bravado and ignorance I landed a job at Thomson Holidays, giving me an extra £4 grand a year. It came in handy, as I was no longer in possession of my car because I had to sell it to pay off a gambling debt after losing £600 in a night-shift card game. You suspect that would put me off gambling for life. Far from it.

The move to Thomson was a bad decision. The job was not for

me and the people I worked with were unfriendly and boring. Despite that I decided the best course of action was to stick it out for as long as I could so I could further fabricate – sorry – add to my extensive CV in the pursuit of a lucrative freelance computer career.

I was young, focused, full of ambition and I had no intention of wasting time.

My next move was to register myself with several computer recruitment agencies providing them with the embellished CV I would need to secure my first contract as a freelancer. Through – how should I say it? – the embellishment of the truth (or perhaps more truthfully, bullshit), I secured an interview for a contract. The interview consisted of me passing off things I had only read about as work I had done. They certainly must have believed me because I landed a plum job with Chevron Petroleum, earning three times as much as I had at Thomson.

Upon leaving the interview I saw a man holding court. It was their MD Mark Goldberg, someone I would become acquainted with in ten years' time.

After twenty-two months' experience I had fast-tracked myself into becoming the youngest freelance computer operative in the UK, with scant knowledge, little foundation and my only real collateral being an unadulterated belief in myself. In fact, I moved on through my early working life flying by the seat of my pants. I had audacity and confidence in spades, and an utter disrespect for authority or protocol.

Having cut my teeth at Chevron I moved swiftly onto my next contract at the Trafalgar House Group, the owners of the famous cruise line Cunard.

Even a little bit of knowledge is an extremely dangerous thing as I was about to discover with catastrophic consequences.

There wasn't a great deal to get stuck into. Bored, I started reading various operator manuals.

Three days into the job I thought it would be funny to execute a command that would prevent certain terminals in the group accessing the main computer. Initially I thought I would get a few calls from users asking to reactivate their terminal; unfortunately my command had more far-reaching consequences when the whole place went into total meltdown.

I hadn't shut down a few terminals – I had shut down the entire worldwide network so people working from Mitcham to Mombasa couldn't access the mainframe of this enormous international company. Undoing my damage wasn't a major issue, it was the incriminating evidence I left behind.

A smart-arse analyst decided to print out the activity on the operator terminal, which clearly showed someone, notably me, had executed a command to shut the entire network down.

I considered blaming someone else, but there was no one else there to blame so they, with looks of disbelief at my nonsensical actions, terminated my contract after just three days.

I wasn't too concerned about Trafalgar House, I was more worried about the agency, MSB, who were getting me good work. Fortunately they knew infinitely less about computing than I did so when I scandalously laid the blame on anything other than me, and appeared to sound like I knew what I was talking about, they accepted my explanation and we moved on.

After a number of contracts I decided to take a three-month sabbatical and travelled to America. During my trip I met one of my best friends in the world, Walter Almeida, who looked out for this somewhat green and cocky Limey. Eventually I returned home and resumed working as a freelance computer operator.

But despite doing very well, I had itchy feet. I wanted to progress my career quickly and at the advanced age of twenty-two, I decided I wanted a new one. I went to a career analyst on Baker Street to ascertain what else I could do. After a day of tests and evaluation, it emerged I was completely wasted in computing. To my horror it was suggested I should be a salesman. Images of Arthur Daley and Del Boy sprang to mind. I was mortally offended and proceeded to argue that there was no way on God's earth I was a salesman; I was a computer professional. But no – according to the career analyst, sales was where my natural abilities lay.

My next computing contract unknown to me at the time was to be my last. I was working for British Telecom at a top security site with all the MI5 circuits running through the mainframe.

Working nights again was hard and relatively boring. Well, so I thought until I made the mother of all balls-ups.

Early one morning the site experienced a power blip, which caused the mainframe computer to crash. Numerous attempts to reboot the system later, I ran out of patience and decided to power down the main CPU and restart it.

As soon as I pulled the switch down on the back of the main-frame I knew I had a serious problem. Without call-out engineer expertise everything was irretrievable and the expression 'get your coat' was never more appropriate.

I was done with computer contracting. My friend James Wright had set up a company selling mobile phones from an office at his father's home. It was a small business and the retail explosion in the industry hadn't yet manifested itself. Within a week I'd done a deal to become his partner. I was taking on a sales role, the very thing three months earlier I said I would never do.

We were selling maybe twenty phones a month, making a profit of around £3,000, which hardly satisfied my ambitions for world domination. I worked tirelessly and educated myself about selling the product and technology and then set about expanding the business. We rapidly moved up to selling fifty units a month and turning over £20,000 with £7,500 in profit.

As our company grew we changed the name, rented offices and employed staff. Fairly soon we were up to 150 connections a month, which was about £70,000 turnover with gross profits of £25,000 per month. Our first year's turnover was in excess of £1.2 million.

We had the makings of a good business, but unfortunately our ambitions were not matched by our business nous. Overheads were becoming excessive and trading fell, which put enormous pressure on us.

James wanted out and took extreme action to make that point. After I had been out securing a sizeable deal I came back to discover he had made a rare excursion to the office, taken all the stock and then used it as leverage to get me to buy him out.

Believing in myself I bought him out, but in the weeks it took to do this, the bank froze our account and the damage to our trading relationships was beyond repair. Six months later I was forced to close the business.

What the hell was I going to do now? I had squandered all of my money and all that was left was what I was standing up in. I cleared out the office the next day, took the remaining stock and sold it for £1,200.

I needed to get away and rethink my life. Despite all my mishaps, I had had a potentially good career in computing and had built the makings of a good business, but through bad luck, bad judgement, youthful impetuosity and stupidity I was now on my arse.

I called my old college friend Edward Penrose, who was working in America. So off I went to share Edward's apartment in Greenwich Village in New York with dreams of starting new businesses in the

States, oh yes and to wait tables! Edward said I could stay with him rent-free for as long as I liked. He was working as a waiter in an Italian restaurant on the Upper East Side and had arranged for me to have an interview.

I started work the following morning.

My bed at the apartment was a pull-out sofa next to a window that overlooked the street. I was introduced to Edward's dog, or should I say horse. This dog was a huge beast, unruly and disobedient. It jumped all over you, slobbered and mauled you whenever you were anywhere near it. I also had to take the damn thing for regular walks – or drags, as the thing was so powerful. And as it was New York I had to take plastic bags to pick up the brontosaurus-size shits that came out the horse's, I mean dog's, backside.

Whilst I lived in Greenwich Village I had some good times. It was a hive of activity.

I was a regular in a famous place called The Temple Bar on the corner of Lafayette and Broadway. I became friendly with the actor Matt Dillon. He was a very cool guy and part of the Hollywood brat pack. He was a New Yorker and enjoyed living and drinking in the city. We frequently met up, got drunk and chased women. It wasn't as much fun as it sounded: he was an internationally recognised film star and I was a waiter so no need to guess who got all the girls.

I was not a great waiter: taking orders and serving people was not something I relished. One thing I did learn was never piss off someone who serves you in a restaurant. I saw some pretty unpleasant and disgusting things done to the food of rude and complaining customers.

I got to experience the very dangerous side of New York City. Late one night I was hungry and went out for food. I walked out of the building and when crossing Broadway, I noticed three guys looking at me very suspiciously. Call it intuition but I suspected something was wrong.

I turned on my heels quickly and as I entered our apartment building the main window to the right of me shattered. One of them had tried to shoot me. Thank God he was a bad shot. Later on in life I was to pay a fortune for people like that.

I managed to save $2,000 quickly at a time when my relationship with Edward and his horse was in rapid decline. Things were so strained that I had to look for somewhere else to live on a very limited budget.

I eventually found a motel way up town in Spanish Harlem. I had a small room with a sink and there was a communal bathroom shared with ten other rooms.

Things were also strained at the restaurant. Udo, the German assistant manager, thoroughly disliked me. I had no respect for him and did very little for Anglo-German relations with my constant dam-busters impressions; he wanted to fire me at every opportunity. He didn't have to wait long to get his wish. A few months into my restaurant career he started on me for no apparent reason, and not being able to help myself I verbally took him apart and got fired.

I walked out of the restaurant into the cold November night feeling numb. I now had no job in New York and I was living alone in a complete shit hole. How much lower was I going to go?

New York wasn't turning out to be the city of opportunities that I had hoped it would be. I hadn't been able to give any of my business ideas the attention they deserved as I spent all my time and energy in a series of jobs. I worked in Wilson's, a restaurant owned by Brian Wilson of the Beach Boys, and waited tables in a café called Lalo where Madonna, Woody Allen and the Baldwin brothers were regular customers.

Then two bright lights appeared on my immediate horizon. One of my new friends, a Dominican guy called José, asked me to share his apartment overlooking Broadway and I played semi-professional football for a team in New York for $200 a game. But it was small beer compared to what I really wanted to be doing.

I was now not earning a great deal of money, and failing in New York was taking its toll on me. My best friend Walter Almeida insisted I come and stay with him. My journey from New York City to Providence, Rhode Island took about three hours and gave me ample time to think and reflect.

Part of me was sad to be leaving. I felt that New York had chewed me up and spat me out. And failure never sat well with me. But I did learn a great truth: the only safety net you have in life is your own arse.

I took a number of jobs in Rhode Island but I never felt settled there. One morning I woke up and decided I'd had enough. I'd been away from home for eighteen months and it was time to get back into the real world and make something of myself.

I was so broke I had to sell my gold ring and bracelet to a jewellery store to buy a flight home.

I arrived back home without a penny. But help came when my younger brother Dominic offered me a job as a labourer on a building site he was overseeing.

My skill set was now becoming very impressive, from computing to businessman to waiting tables and now labouring. Most people work their way up in their careers; with all due respect to those two professions, I was going in the opposite direction.

Dominic was a senior site agent for the building firm DJ Higgins and was responsible for a site undergoing restoration work at the London Hospital Museum. Seeing Dom at work took me by surprise. I had always viewed him as my little brother, but on site he was a powerful, confident and forthright person, working with people who didn't like being told what to do and who often resolved their differences with their fists.

As I was Dominic's brother I was given a bit of latitude, which I totally abused. Labouring was damn hard work and not something I excelled in. What I was good at was being first in the tearoom for breaks and the last to leave, great at looking busy at knocking-off time and always at the front of the queue for my weekly pay. Most of the time I found myself telling the lads on the site stories of my past business exploits. After initial and understandable scepticism some of the lads started to seek my advice on financial matters like mortgages, pensions and benefits they could claim.

So there I was, on a building site knee deep in muck, and leaning on my broom like Andy Dufresne out of *The Shawshank Redemption*, dispensing financial advice to a bunch of hardnosed labourers and tradesmen. I even filled out their SC60 tax assessment forms for them. My brother would just shake his head and mutter 'unfucking-believable' whenever he found me holding court.

My career as a labourer-cum-tax-accountant was to be short-lived. Within weeks I was to make a call that would change the course of my life.

The Carphone Warehouse were advertising for a salesman for their rapidly expanding company. I spoke to their Sales Director, Ricky Elliot. I was well aware of the company from owning my own mobile phone business, the one good thing to come of my relationship with James Wright.

I was stunned to discover how the industry had expanded in two years. CPW had twenty-odd branches and ambitious growth plans. Despite having been out of the business for over eighteen months, it was immediately apparent that I knew more about the mobile phone business than Ricky did. I played it down though to secure an interview.

The day of my interview arrived. I was greeted by Andrew Briggs, a very large guy who, as it turned out, was one of their first ever members of staff. He would be interviewing me with Ricky Elliot. There was nothing to give me the idea that Andrew and I were going to be so pivotal to one another's lives in the very near future.

Interviews were something I enjoyed as they gave me a free-range opportunity to talk about my favourite subject: me. I got on well with Ricky, but not so well with Andrew. I was confident and perhaps a little cocky. At the end of the interview, Ricky said they would be in touch.

As I made to leave, Andrew just stuck his hand out in a disinterested and dismissive way. I sensed that his opinion of me was vital in whether or not I got this job; I figured I had better try and create a better impression with Mr Briggs. I needed this job. It was time to sell myself!

I asked if they minded if I stayed in the showroom for a short while, promising not to get in the way. Looking back it was a smart move. I read brochures, looked at phones and feigned interest in customer sales. Eventually I got a chance to speak to Andrew. I went into full-on contrite mode. I apologised if I had come over as cocky, and explained that I had been nervous and I hoped that he hadn't taken a dislike to me. I thanked him for his time and wished him success in the new Fleet Street branch that he had interviewed me for. Barely hours later I was called and informed the position was mine. I had gone full circle and was back in mobile phones, albeit working for others this time.

I arrived for my first day at Carphone Warehouse's head office on Marylebone Road. This place was busy and there was serious money to be made! There I met some of their hierarchy including Charles Dunstone, the MD. He was quite a pleasant, low-key guy. David Ross, the finance director, couldn't have been more different. Over a period of time I found him to be one of the most difficult and unpleasant people I have ever worked with or for. Although, astonishingly, many years later when I bumped into him in Puerto Banus I did share an enjoyable drink with him.

Once the new Fleet Street branch was ready, Andrew, Gerald (another new guy) and I moved in. It was a small branch and had just enough room for three desks. It looked crowded if you had four customers in it. So I was a little dismayed. But it turned out to be great, and was where I had some of the best times of my life. The three of us became very close friends and the atmosphere in the branch was a very happy one, but more importantly we were selling a substantial number of phones.

The pecking order was established very quickly. Andrew was the boss, I was the self-appointed number two and Gerald was at the bottom of the pile, i.e. he was the lunch and tea getter. It was a friendly environment but it was also dog eat dog and I was here to sell and progress my career.

I am a great people studier and I listen to what people say, especially in the work environment, and I picked up sales techniques from all manner of sales people I worked with. If I say so myself I was pretty damn good at selling mobile phones. I understood the technology well from previous experience, and had a way with customers that didn't make them feel like they were being sold to.

As I would say at many a sales meeting in the future, the biggest decision a customer made was walking into the shop. After that it was your decision whether he or she bought something from you. And whilst many sales people seemed to be pleased with just selling phones, I tended to sell/push everything that came with them, in order to increase my commission.

Andrew used to roll around laughing because my sales pitch was ballsy, to say the least. I knew the products, the accessories, all the services we offered inside and out. I would push everything with such confidence that the customer felt that they would be stupid not to take me up on the deal I was offering. If they walked out with only one extra, I would be mildly upset, if they had the front to not take any, then I would feel real indignation, much to Andrew's amusement.

The branch was obliterating its targets and I was doing 60 per cent of the branch sales on my own. I was golden, so Andrew let me get away with murder.

Poor Gerald suffered, as I grabbed every sale I could. If a customer walked in with a complaint or a fault, then I would immediately direct them to Gerald's desk. If a buying customer walked towards his desk, I would be up out of my seat directing them to mine.

With my performance my profile in the company was rising. Just five months into the job I got a call from Ricky Elliot. The company had signed a concession deal with Staples, the American office superstore, and he was putting me forward to head up the first one in Swansea. The partnership with Staples was a big deal. There were massive expansion plans to open up as many as a hundred stores across the UK. I was happy in Fleet Street but my father always told me to say yes to every opportunity, as you never know where it may lead.

So I accepted the job. Andrew was extremely upset. Not just because we had become close mates but also because they had failed to tell him. He sent Charles Dunstone, the MD of Carphone Warehouse, an email. Andrew did this all the time if he was unhappy with anything. Most of the emails began with, 'Frankly, I am

astonished . . .' They pissed Dunstone off no end and would ultimately cost Andrew his job.

I wanted a big pay rise to go to Swansea. Company car, big
commissions, expenses. Let's just say my wish list wasn't small.

David Ross just said no to everything, but as I had been introduced to the Staples management team and they had liked and
wanted me, he was pretty much on the back foot. I said that if
I didn't get what I asked for, I wouldn't go. After an hour of
abuse from Ross I got what I wanted and departed with a cocky
smile and thanking him for his support and belief. Smart arse?
Maybe.

Landing in Swansea, I was horrified to find I was expected to
wear a Staples uniform and my concession was a four-foot stand
at the back of this aircraft hangar of a superstore in the middle of
nowhere. They even wanted me to go on a Staples in-house course,
so I kicked off, resulting in a very uncomfortable and unpleasant
few weeks. Eventually accord broke out. I got some of the things
I wanted but my biggest saving grace was my performance.

Whilst I was down in Wales I spoke to Andrew every day. I
could sense that he was feeling more and more marginalised, yet
he continued to ping off his emails to Charles Dunstone on anything
and everything that pissed him off.

I was selling more phones on my own without support than a
lot of the standalone Carphone Warehouse stores, and Staples was
seeing a significant return. They began to take it very seriously.
The next Staples store was coming on-stream with others to follow
quickly and I was asked to hire someone for that, as well as for
one in Wales. The job was finally the supervisory role I had signed
up for.

I established the protocols, set up the procedures and got the
sales off and running. The Staples stores were now a phenomenon

and both businesses were making a significant amount of money out of these small concessions.

Meanwhile Andrew had sent off one too many 'Frankly, I am astonished' emails to Charles Dunstone and was fired.

He was distraught so I calmed him down and told him to get straight onto the phone and ring CPW's main competitor Intercell. They had poached a number of CPW's staff. Andrew called them and within twenty-four hours he was running their store in Swiss Cottage. He also wasted little time trying to persuade me to leave CPW and join him.

You would think that it would have been easy to have said no to Andrew and to stick with Carphone Warehouse. Under my leadership, the Staples concessions were doing brilliantly. We were selling hand over fist and the commission levels being paid to my staff went through the roof. Some earned over £10,000 a month. Other sales teams in the group envied my staff. From being considered a bit of a canker sore, the Staples stores concessions and their staff now had an air of elitism about them.

But David Ross became agitated and unhelpful. He didn't like paying the commissions we had earned. He had to sign them off each month and he did everything in his power to hold up the process. In the end, my reward for making the Staples concessions one of the most profitable parts of CPW was a pay reduction by Ross, who slashed the commissions because we were earning too much.

My departure was inevitable. When Ross refused to pay commission on a phenomenal deal that secured them £130,000, I took the decision to leave.

I knew Intercell wanted me. They were expanding rapidly, had big ambitions and clearly needed my expertise. I met their joint MDs, Harry Ramis and Andy Demetriou, and negotiated myself a nice little deal, including a £15,000 golden hello. They wanted me to replicate for Intercell what I had achieved with Staples. No problem.

When I submitted my resignation, Ross demanded I went immediately. But they still owed me £2,000 in commission as well as expenses so I went up to his office and demanded my money. He became bolshie straight away. 'You will get your expenses in due course.' So I explained he would get their company car in due course as well. He started to shout at me and was getting up out of his seat when all the months of his uncalled-for behaviour just got to me.

'Don't get out of your chair and threaten me,' I bellowed at him. 'I have put up with your nonsense for nine months and if you get out of that chair I will throw you out of that bloody window. Give me my money now!'

Everyone in the building was aware what was going on and Martin Cox, the sales director, came flying up the stairs to calm things down. One way or another I got my cheque.

As I went to hand Ross the keys to the company car I looked out the window and saw it being clamped. I laughed my head off.

Joining Intercell was like jumping out of the frying pan and into the fire. CPW knew what they were doing and, on the whole, were professional. This outfit was like the Wild West headed up by two guys who gave the impression of playing at being gangsters and businessmen and falling short in both areas. All fast cars, big suits and threatening attitudes. They were not funded properly and they were not well set up. They had also employed a DTI consultant called Spencer Fox who was guiding them in everything. I quickly gathered he knew as much about mobile phones as I knew about colonic irrigation, although I would have gladly found out more if I could have applied it to that charlatan. I was straight on a collision course with him from the get-go.

Within weeks I got them their concession deal. I had agreed a deal with the managing director of Office World, another big office supply company and a direct competitor of Staples, and set about opening the first one in Colindale in London, which was quickly followed by another in Portsmouth. Although both Ramis and Demetriou were delighted by the swift delivery, Spencer Fox was getting himself involved in the area of business I had been brought in to do. I had a very low opinion of him and I didn't stop short of telling him that. I was very vociferous about the shortcomings of this business – as was Andrew – and this grated on the MDs. Within three months I knew that this place was not for me.

Sure enough I had one fierce row too many with Spencer Fox and was summoned to the head office. Clearly I was far too much for these people; I challenged the whole politics of their business. Despite doing exactly what I said I would do, and despite having set up a concession operation for them, they wanted me gone.

I was going to be paid £15,000 to leave, the same amount I was paid to join. It came in very handy as I had ideas for that money and it didn't involve working for incompetents like Demetriou and Ramis.

It was May 1994 and unemployment was upon me again. I suspected Andrew Briggs, who was equally as dissenting as me, was going to be fired so I called him. He had already been informed the HR Director was en route to his store.

I arranged to meet Andrew the next morning as I had something specific on my mind I wished to discuss with him.

This was the beginning of something very special, but even I didn't envisage the magnitude of it.

4

BUILDING THE EMPIRE

The PocketPhone Shop started its life in a Chinese restaurant on the Finchley Road in London, over lunch with Andrew Briggs. It made sense to start up on our own – I considered us to be two of the brightest, most experienced guys in the mobile phone industry not to own our own business. After that auspicious lunch, it took me less than a week to pull together a pretty good business plan, and Andrew came up with the great name, The PocketPhone Shop, or PPS, as it was soon to be known.

Starting a business is much easier than making it grow into a success: anyone can start up their own business and meet with failure, as I had proved earlier in my career. I may have been just twenty-six, but I had come through a lot, and was older, wiser, had accumulated a great deal of experience and knew this business very well. One of the keys to being successful is a bloody good knowledge of your industry.

My gut feel was £50,000 was a good start-up figure. I had the £15,000 I just got from Intercell and suggested to Andrew that he should match it. Somehow, I persuaded my father to put up his house as collateral for the remaining £20,000. He also arranged for us to meet his bank manager Andrew Spence at Lloyds Bank in Norbury, where we stayed for two years until we were taken into the corporate world of Lloyds. I will be for ever grateful to old Spencey for the support he gave us in those early days.

Obviously, we had a list of things as long as your arm to do. Near the top of the list was putting together a computer system, and early on we brought software designer David Goodman on board, who was going to hit the jackpot with us. We wanted to imitate the sales system we had used at the Carphone Warehouse and, as chance would have it, I just so happened to have a copy of it on disk.

Our banking relationship had been sorted with Lloyds, but prior to completing the account Andrew wanted us to meet with the bank his late father had banked with, NatWest, 'the listening bank'. After sending in a business plan, we attended a meeting.

Straight away, I knew this was a complete waste of time. They stuck us in a room and handed us a loan application form as if we had walked in off the street. As we waited for the privilege of a meeting with the bank manager, we ruminated on what we were doing there; clearly they hadn't read our business plan. Eventually we were taken through to the bank manager who sat behind a big desk in an austere room. Very pompously he crossed his fingers under his chin and in a most condescending way asked, 'How can I be of help?' following that with 'if you need banking facilities, they are unlikely to be available'. This was going nowhere. The discussion turned into a farce and I reduced this arrogant, dismissive bank manager into a stuttering wreck.

Andrew wrote one of his 'frankly I am astonished letters' to 'The listening bank'. We got a written apology, a cheque for our parking expenses and an invitation to come back in for another meeting, which we never accepted. In time, Andrew regularly sent annual accounts to them for a few years to show them what an opportunity they had missed.

On signing the concession at Office World for Intercell, I recalled their MD, Simon Fox, telling me their busiest store in the country was in Slough. So on a rainy day in May 1994 we drove into Slough town centre and almost immediately found our ideal shop. It had everything we needed – big frontage, parking and on a busy road, it was available – and the rent was only £15,000 per annum. This was to be our first store, and it would launch our success.

During this time Andrew's mother died and his world fell apart. I tried to console him but all I really could do was offer him support. I ploughed on regardless, unsure of Andrew's future plans. He was brilliant, though. Following his mother's funeral, he decided that to get past his grief he would need to be busy, and within a week he returned to work.

My business plan was very detailed, incorporating forecasts, margins, stock levels, expansion plans – I took the experience I had crammed into my relatively short period of time in the mobile phone business and distilled it into one document. What we wanted was to be a retailer, not a dealer. Dealers are small time, and we wanted to compete with the big boys on the high street. Scratch that, we wanted to be one of the big boys on the high street. To do this, we knew that we had to have a good relationship with your airtime provider as it was through them that you connected customers to a network. I identified five of them, but only one, Astec Communications based in Cheltenham, showed any interest.

After a series of fruitful meetings with Edward Eve, the sales manager at Astec, we had a deal, or so we thought. We had negotiated all aspects of the commercial relationship, commissions, equipment provision, shop fit monies, all the nuts and bolts of the deal. Just as we were ready to sign, all of a sudden they asked for a meeting in Cheltenham. David Savage, their chairman, wanted to change the parameters of the deal.

Astec had their own retail outlets called Buzz Shops and Savage decided he wanted us to brand our shops the same way. I flatly refused. My view was we were going to be an independent retailer, not a bloody Buzz Shop, and I wasn't going to budge on that. I could see Andrew physically sink into his chair. We had no other airtime provider and this deal was in danger of falling through if I refused to give in to their demands.

Savage insisted it was a deal breaker but, whilst Andrew panicked on the journey home, my gut told me different. By that evening, Edward Eve called me and the original deal was back on. We were ready to sign the agreement.

We hired two staff for our first branch, which would open in August, three months after our lunch in that Chinese restaurant. We decided on stock, price lists and an opening promotion, launching with an incredibly aggressive price point selling phones for just 99p. We were the first company to hook customers with the deal of an extremely cheap phone.

We hired Sharon Carlisle, who we had worked with at Carphone Warehouse, as the branch manager. Sharon started immediately and set about pre-selling phones from Andrew's kitchen so we could get a good head start. Employing her was an inspired decision: she was an outstanding character and the heartbeat of our company, had a wonderful way with people and was instrumental in the success of the first store, which over the ensuing years would be our headquarters and the springboard for all the successes that followed over the next five years.

Opening day arrived, 6 August 1994. We had most things in place, but Andrew and the shop fitters were panicking as our sign for the front of the shop hadn't arrived – without it, above the door was just an empty light box with all its gubbins. We had booked the mayor to officially open the shop, and had contacted the local press to take pictures. As the mayor got out of his car, the sign was being erected behind him. We started PPS as we were to go on – getting things done by the skin of our teeth!

The showroom looked great and our first customers came through the door, had drinks and purchased phones. By close of business we had connected around thirty phones.

The next day people were waiting outside when we arrived and we sold an incredible hundred phones on the day, which was no mean feat, given Astec expected us to do 100–120 connections a month based on the performance of their 'fantastic' Buzz Shops, and we'd done it in two days. The first three weeks flew past, and we had sold 257 phones, and in month two we sold a similar amount. Slough was proving to be successful from the get-go.

I moved to Berkshire into a small two-bedroomed flat next to the train station. It was hardly the most luxurious of surroundings but better than staying in my father's spare room and my next-door neighbour was David Kemp, a former Crystal Palace player and now a coach at Stoke City.

With any business that has a small start-up capital and big plans, cash flow is king. The analogy I use is that lack of profit is like cancer and will get you in the end, whereas lack of cash flow is like a massive heart attack and will shut you down immediately. In order to get our cash flow, well, flowing, I negotiated getting paid the commissions for connections in two weeks and paying for stock in four. Getting paid before paying out was critical to the advancement of this or any cash flow-challenged business.

Soon Andrew had located a second branch, Epsom in Surrey. Our first shop had been open for just eight weeks, and we only had the princely sum of £7K in the bank, but such was our ambition and drive opening another store seemed the natural thing to do. Logically, perhaps it made more sense to establish ourselves before expanding, but we had big plans.

My eagerness to succeed knew no bounds. Using my stored away knowledge from my past in computing I even managed to override the online computer credit check system Astec provided for putting customers on air, increasing the pass rate by 30 per cent. This information was not best shared with Astec but proved very fruitful as we were able to connect so many more customers than other retailers.

The plans behind our ambitions were laid as we moved onto our second store.

We decided very early on that we were going to have to punch our way into this market. Using Wal-Mart's legendary model of 'stack 'em high and sell 'em cheap', which was very successful in the US, we created our platform on price, as well as offering tremendous value and service to the consumer.

Having been on the shop floor, I believed it was incredibly important to trust your staff and treat them like professionals. I gave them information on margins and their commissions were paid on profit, so they knew what their performance meant to them and the business. This approach was very different from our rivals, and of course was open to abuse, but it was the way I wanted to work. We were not a citizens' advice bureau where people casually strolled in, browsed through the tariffs and handsets, and left, clutching a handful of leaflets. We were a business and our job was to sell to every customer that walked through our door. I went to great lengths to have the business run the way I wanted, making each branch operate as if I were personally in it.

Once Epsom opened in the first week of November 1994, we now had all networks, including 121 and Orange, alongside the traditional networks of Vodafone and Cellnet, and were truly an independent dealer. We opened with a belter of a promotion, pricing the new highly rated Ericsson 237 phone at £49.99, a hundred pounds cheaper than anywhere else in the country. Epsom opened with a bang, although we did get complaints from Ericsson about our pricing. Epsom would never be as successful as Slough, it did OK but it was not phenomenal. Despite this our plans for expansion continued.

At Christmas, having only really been in operation since August, we had two shops, five members of staff and sold 500 phones in that month, which was not bad!

After New Year we were off again, planning our third shop – in Aylesbury, which was to open that April. This was to prove a landmark opening. It would be our first inside a shopping centre, and became our blueprint for stores. We were very creative in our approach, because this was a counter, not a shop. The rent was virtually nothing but we had a prime location next to the entrance doors. As part of the process before we opened each store, we worked out how many phones we would have to sell to make a profit. In most stores it was sixty, in Aylesbury it was twenty, and there we were selling 150 a month.

Andrew came up with the idea of using a celebrity to open stores so we signed up 'Mr Blobby', the popular character from *Noel's House Party*, and used him first at the Aylesbury store. He was very popular and drew big crowds. When we changed to another television personality it sparked the headline in the *Sun*: 'Mr Blobby loses his Jobby', giving us some unexpected exposure.

The force behind the company's expansion and progression was my direction and drive. I negotiated the commercial deals and made all the key decisions. It was never planned that way; Andrew just wasn't as driven and confident as me. Nevertheless, his contribution was vital in the success and growth of the company. When we started the company we made ourselves joint MDs. But almost a year on, I felt that should change. A business invariably has one leader and that clearly was me.

I became the sole MD and Andrew became chairman, without relinquishing his 50 per cent shareholding in the company. Andrew saw the logic behind it and rather liked the idea of a statesmanlike role, overseeing the business. For me, this change needed to be made so that I could get about running the business and making the decisions that would benefit us both. Additionally Andrew's health was not great. He suffered from the chronic fatigue disease ME, which I have to confess at the time I had little sympathy for; I merely deemed Andrew's lateness or absences from work as him being lazy. Knowing more about the disease now, I realise my reaction to Andrew at times was terribly wrong.

As our first year of trading came to an end we had a turnover of a million pounds, profits of £75,000 and had opened our fourth store – in Newbury, the hometown of Vodafone, the world's biggest mobile phone network. We had always been on Vodafone's radar, but now we were clearly in their sights.

Vodafone was buying out Astec and things were changing. Our relationship with Astec altered as our agendas diverged. At this stage we began to develop a direct relationship with Vodafone's marketing team and especially Chris Tombs, who was the head of Vodafone's channel marketing and someone who could provide the key for significant funding going forward.

In September 1995, we held the first of what would become an annual summer ball, which was attended by twenty staff. These events became bigger and more glamorous. The last one we held in September 1999 catered for 2,000 people, cost in excess of £350,000, and was held at the Royal Lancaster Court Hotel with entertainment that included Ben Elton. The balls were a way of rewarding my staff, but they also illustrated to the outside world how well we were doing.

During recent months I had pushed direct relationships with manufacturers. I had managed to open an account with Mitsubishi, and was working on one with NEC. This was what the big players did, and was a unique and aggressive strategy for a fledgling company.

As well as developing relationships with manufacturers we bought from wholesalers. Caudwell Communications, one of the biggest in the country, gave us competitive prices but wanted cash on delivery, cash we didn't have. I found a way around this by dumping the cost on a relative's American Express gold card, and because we were putting over £100,000 a month on it, it soon became a black card. Strictly speaking, we were in breach of rules and regulations governing the use of the card, which prevented you from buying items for resale. Caudwell's sales team never should have authorised these payments but they were on commission. We paid the bill and everyone was happy, especially my relative who had more air miles than anyone in history.

These creative ways of thinking were critical to advancing our business, enabled us to gain more margin and allowed us to force the prices of stock down. Only big dealers had the clout to have direct relationships with manufacturers and wholesalers, yet we were doing it inside a year of trading.

By November 1995, we were up to 800 connections per month. And 60 per cent of those were Vodafone connections. We were now a respectable dealer in volume terms, but as I have said previously I had no desire to be a dealer, a dealer was a small business that only had a small amount of shops. I wanted to be a retailer and I wanted us to be the biggest retailer in the country.

As Astec was being bought out by Vodafone, they were trying to reduce costs. Connections from a third party like ourselves cost more money, and they also were not overly keen on our rapid expansion plans as they were part funding us. At the end of 1995, they terminated our contract, which meant we needed to find a new airtime provider. They had given us a period of time to find a new home for our business, not out of the goodness of their hearts, but because it was Christmas and they wanted the additional volume before completing their sale to Vodafone.

I negotiated a deal with another airtime provider, Unique Air, and then switched all of our connections immediately, ditching Vodafone in favour of Cellnet. I was furious that Astec let us down and extremely disappointed that Vodafone, despite our loyalty, had offered no help or support. This was a strategic move at the busiest time of the year to show that I could control our destiny. Effectively, I had stuck two fingers up at the biggest network operator in the world and with our store slap bang in Vodafone's hometown, Newbury, signing customers up to their main network rival had political ramifications.

My audacious move had the desired effect. In early 1996, Ivan Donn, a Vodafone director, called me and hastily arranged a meeting with their airtime provider Vodacall. Ivan was keen to see us back in bed with Vodafone and recognised the fact that, although we were only sixteen months old, we had significant potential and a burgeoning reputation.

I secured an incredible deal with Vodacall. We received significantly more money than we had at Astec, we were given direct marketing and store funding, our commissions were to be paid weekly and they supplied stock on ninety-day terms. They also agreed to pay for the two stores that we had just opened. Sign the contract? I nearly broke their arms off. By a combination of skill and balls we had landed on our feet. We now had two airtime provider relationships: one with Vodafone and one with Cellnet.

At the end of our second year, our turnover had doubled to over £2.4 million. We opened a further four stores in very quick succession and were now up to ten, opening Reading, Harrow, Southampton and Uxbridge in quick succession. The spirit we had in the early days was replaced with achievement and massive growth, but the company changed, I changed and, despite all the gain and achievement that was to come, something was lost.

We were now cutting a bit of a swathe through the industry, ruffling the feathers of some of the market leaders. One was our old employers, the Carphone Warehouse, especially when we opened a store next to them in Guildford. We didn't respect their self-appointed position as market leaders; they viewed us as upstarts.

Opening a store directly in competition to them in a very affluent town showed enormous courage and confidence. It illustrated that we felt we could compete with them at a time when most of the other mobile phone companies avoided going toe to toe with CPW. Quite frankly, I couldn't care less. I wanted to have a store wherever it was profitable to have one.

Going into the lucrative Christmas market at the end of 1996, a war broke out between Carphone Warehouse and us over pricing. We now had fifteen stores, and CPW tried to squeeze us out of Guildford, lowering their prices to an unreasonable level. We followed suit. The networks tried to intervene as Carphone Warehouse went whining to them, but when Vodafone approached me I suggested that this was a conversation we should not have as it could lead to the thorny subject of price fixing and the matter was dropped. Christmas came and went, and we had a successful one, despite annihilating our margins in Guildford.

We now had a significant marketing spend so we employed a specific marketing manager to work alongside Andrew, and after opening another five stores brought in Mark Hodgson as our sales director, who had been at Astec Communications and instrumental in us getting our initial deal with them. Mark's appointment saw us take on our first board member and probably marked the beginning of the deterioration of my relationship with Andrew as it was no longer just the two of us at the helm. For some time Andrew had gently mooted that he wanted to sell the business and now his overtures were becoming even stronger, but I told him to sit tight.

Mark and I set about restructuring the sales team bringing in a new raft of management – area managers. Over the last two years I had pushed, cajoled and driven my staff, making stores phone and report their sales figures to me on the hour. This had made the staff very focused. By bringing in area managers I would, via Mark, concentrate their minds on driving the stores even further forward.

In my all-out pursuit of growth I woefully under-resourced the finance department. We had twenty outlets and pushing towards a hundred staff on the payroll and were doing 3,500 phone sales per month. Simply speaking our accounts were in a mess and the inaccuracy of financial information was beginning to affect the business. I put Steve Maddocks, the poor bugger, who was working pretty much on his own, under tremendous pressure, which on more than one occasion reduced him to tears.

By the end of 1996 we had a cash balance of £1 million but

our account lurched dramatically as we had to pay big stock bills, a sizeable payroll and an ever-increasing quarterly rent bill. Opening stores was now not only about increasing volume, it was about keeping the snowball of cash flow building.

In early 1997 in an attempt to get a bit closer to Cellnet, we binned Unique Air and signed up with Cellular Operations Limited, a Cellnet-owned airtime provider. At the same time we were being transferred to the biggest airtime provider in the Vodafone Group, Vodafone-Connect, as we had outgrown Vodacall. This put us into the same arena as CPW.

Chris Tombs at Vodafone was trying to get more money to support our expansion and arranged a meeting with Vodafone's marketing director Mike Webb. It was a complete waste of time, as Webb showed no interest and asked me questions he already knew the answers to merely as an exercise to see what I knew. I intensely dislike people humouring me and like even less being patronised. I became so agitated by his behaviour I completely lost my temper, called him a wanker, and brought the meeting to a swift halt.

Tombs phoned me afterwards and said, 'What the fuck did you do that for? It has taken me ages to get that meeting and you call a main board director a wanker.'

The story did the rounds over the coming days and I got some pretty good kudos out of it. It may have been that a few others in Vodafone shared my view and subsequently I got their extra money although I never dealt with Webb again.

Having now spent just over two and a half years with our head down and running, it was time to make some fundamental changes the business needed. Firstly we acquired a proper head office as we could no longer use the back of the Slough store as our headquarters, and created new departments like Human Resources and Customer Care.

It became apparent to me Mark was not running the sales team, I was. Mark was better suited to dealing with the marketing side of the business so I moved him out of sales and into heading up Marketing.

Coupled with our expansion and evolvement we enlisted the services of Ulrika Jonsson for the 'nominal' sum of £500,000. We planned to open a further fifty stores in 1998 and Ulrika was to be the face of the company. By the time we moved into Eton View House, our new head office in Slough, we were up to thirty-seven stores, opening twenty-two in 1997 alone, and selling over 7,000 phones a month.

Cash flow, given the level of expenditure and costs increases, was becoming a nagging worry as always, so I increased our bank overdraft. We had never used or even gone into it but as our status increased I felt we should take advantage of the situation and have access to money we might need at a later date. The thing that amused me about the bank's attitude at the time was the security offered by us for the overdraft was a charge against stock and cash; of course if you are using an overdraft you have no cash and the first thing that often goes if a business were to fail would be stock.

Martin Cox, my former boss at CPW, had left them and I took the decision to appoint him as the new sales director. This didn't go down well with Andrew. After all Martin had been the one that had sacked him at CPW. While he trusted my judgement and took on board the fact that Martin now worked for him he was very unhappy.

We also needed a real-time online point of sale computer system and, using my computing background again, I sat down with David Goodman and designed one. Until that point we were still using the sales system based on our unlicensed copy of the Carphone Warehouse's system.

By the final quarter of 1997 we were ready to fully launch our new computer system. It was online, real time, tracked every single transaction and I could get sales figures from all the stores at the push of a button. I now had cyber control of my business, not relying on phone calls every hour from area managers but getting figures from locations all over the country by the second. The investment into this system was significant, with Goodman on a retainer of £20,000 a month, with an expected total cost of in excess of £1 million.

The new computer system was sometimes brilliant, but had teething problems, at times it crashed for no reason but worse than that . . .

The system worked on unique telephone IP addresses for each store that dialled up the server, got the information and logged off. What we didn't realise was that once it went online at shops in the morning it stayed online until they closed.

I had fifty stores logged on for nine hours a day, six days a week for three months. Before then, our quarterly phone bills were coming in at around £60,000, so you can imagine what happened when one arrived for £400,000 – I dropped short of having a heart attack. We eventually resolved the issue with new software, but it still left us with a major financial headache.

Sales for our fourth year were over £24 million, with forecast profits of £1.2 million. But the disaster with the computer system wiped out a large percentage of them.

By now we had seventy-one stores and needed additional working cash. Financing this massive growth was always going to be bloody difficult, and with the whack we got from the telephone bill we needed more cash. I had a brainwave: approaching 121 I offered them a guaranteed 200,000 connections the following year. In exchange I wanted £3 million to finance our expansion and to increase our marketing. I knew they would bite my hand off as this kind of volume was what they were missing and would help their market share.

I met John Barton, their MD, and secured an additional £3 million, paid in four instalments. I was hedging my bets that we could deliver, we were only currently doing 15,000 connections a month on all networks – i.e. 45,000 a quarter, not the 50,000 per quarter required to just service this one deal with 121. But as I projected we would be opening a further forty stores by the middle of 1999, I gambled on delivering.

As we signed the agreement, John Barton said to bear him in mind should I ever think of selling PPS.

Problems started to surface with Vodafone Connect, who cut our commissions. So in a counter-measure, I decided to switch connections to 121. Within days connections to Vodafone were down 90 per cent. Once again, I was flexing my commercial muscles, but this time I had eighty stores so the message was even clearer. Within a week Andy Smith, the sales director from Vodafone Connect, was on the phone. He wasn't impressed and wanted the connections back; after a few weeks the Mexican stand-off abated and we had commissions reinstated.

After winning the battle with Vodafone Connect over commissions I agreed to restore their level of connections. However, there was one small problem: the 121 deal. The fact that we had a falling-out with Vodafone had half-suited me, now it was back to my mouth writing cheques that my business couldn't cash. I was spinning plates trying to balance cash flow, open stores, give volume back to Vodafone and give 121 the 50,000 sales per quarter I had promised them. The first quarter we did 29,000. My argument was that it was still a significant rise and they agreed to pay the second of the four £750,000 instalments, thus feeding PPS's rumbling belly with its dietary requirement of cash.

As we were powering towards our one hundredth store, I now took a greater interest in our cost base. We had been spending £30,000 on each shop fit. I employed my brother Dominic as Operations Director, which led to a considerable saving. He recruited his own workforce in house, mass-produced all counters and shop equipment, which ensured that all future shops were built the same way, and we saved a million pounds over the next raft of shops.

Opening a new shop took time, as there was always a lag between agreeing a location and doing the necessary legals to obtain leases. Dominic, when surveying shops, took the keys from estate agents and unbeknownst to them cut copies. As soon as I gave him the nod on a shop, he would use his newly cut keys, go in and start fitting shops before we had even signed leases. We amazed everybody when days after completing a lease we had a fully fitted shop and were open for trade.

By now Andrew and I were enjoying the spoils of the business. We were paying ourselves £250,000 each per year, plus all our expenses. I had two cars, a Jaguar convertible and a Ferrari, and Andrew had an Aston Martin, but despite all this he was still banging on about selling. We had a company Mercedes S class and we also had a fleet of expensive cars for department heads, area managers and directors alike. In fact, our car park at Head Office was like a showroom for German luxury car manufacturers.

We had over 500 staff and were growing daily. We employed a new HR manager and started our own training academy. Training courses were mandatory for all new employees. They were required to attend for a week and pass exams to commence employment. On average between fifteen and twenty-five people would attend the course and I spoke passionately on every one to instil confidence, belief and drive in my staff. Besides, I was only thirty, and I'd been where they were not so long ago, so they could relate to me. I wanted them to have my passion, determination and desire to succeed; I wanted them to be the best.

Stock management was becoming a major issue. Criminals were now targeting vans picking up stock. Three times in the space of two weeks vans with tens of thousands of pounds' worth of stock were held up at gunpoint. And, as if I didn't have enough on my bloody plate, the police informed me they had intelligence to suggest that I was being targeted as a kidnap victim. I had to hire security to accompany me everywhere until the police dealt with this information. I viewed this as slightly comical and laughed it off but eventually the police arrested a crew they strongly believed had targeted me.

Having spent several months looking for a finance director I employed John Davies at the start of 1999. For the first time I had someone on board who went through the finances like a forensic accountant and gave me a proper financial picture, yet it irritated me as I was used to my word being law. As I didn't take kindly to criticism, this led to some early disagreements and almost John's departure, which would have been a disaster at a time when we were projected to do £60 million in business and make £2.4 million in profit.

Andrew now had little day-to-day involvement in the business and had plenty of free time on his hands. He wanted to sell the business and he employed Arthur Andersen's, one of the 'big five' accounting firms, to represent him in his desire to find a buyer.

I was up to my eyeballs in managing this monolith of a business that was now in excess of 110 stores. I humoured Andrew by reluctantly agreeing to meet his people. It was in the early part of 1999, and the moment they walked into my office on a Monday morning, all pinstripe suits and pinkie rings, I knew it was not going to go well. Their ringleader, who looked like a Giles so we'll call him Giles, regaled me what I had to do. I listened to his self-serving nonsense and, after a deliberate pregnant pause, sent the aforementioned Giles and his mute cronies fleeing back to the City with two words ringing in their ears, and one of them was 'off'.

Andrew extracted a solemn promise from me that I would seriously think about selling, but as soon as he left I filed it in miscellaneous and got on with the real business of building the company.

My determination and single-minded focus to make PPS successful was relentless. I was accused of being a control freak and a hard taskmaster. I think you have to have elements of the two when you are building a business.

I was driven crazy by stores' inability to answer the phone. So I instructed every branch to answer the phone within three rings, and set up a team of customer care girls to ring the branches four times a day for a month to ensure they did – and woe betide those that didn't. It led to a fair few verbal warnings but after a month or so everyone answered the bloody phone promptly.

Punctuality was also an issue. I wanted stores open for business at 8.45 a.m. and it wasn't happening. I could monitor what time staff arrived through the activation of each store's alarm, and got reports electronically produced. Stores that were late got a phone call from their MD, and if they persisted they got a call from HR terminating the staff's employment. One store, in a shopping centre in Uxbridge, got the shop next door to open the store for them and deactivate the alarm. So one morning I turned up, waited for them to arrive at 9.30 a.m. and sacked the entire staff on the spot.

I wanted professionalism and excellence and I would damn well do what it took to get it.

For two quarters we failed to hit the level of connections we had agreed to do with 121, and the last quarter we did 40,000 of the 50,000 required. This meant that 121 were reluctant to pay the third tranche of £750K. In fact, their finance department tried to reclaim some of the monies they had paid, but our increase in volume was still so significant that I managed to cajole the money out of them. I just kept spinning those plates!

In the middle of 1999 Time Computers approached us about a concession deal. We settled on twenty concessions and jumped up to 150 stores. We had moved into London, opening three stores in key locations. It was the last time we were to use Ulrika Jonsson. She failed to turn up on time to open one of our stores and we missed the chance to gain some serious publicity. As a result I went ballistic and when she refused to meet her legal obligations we sued her (subsequently, due to ensuing events, incredibly this action was dropped). Later, when I purchased Crystal Palace, liberty-takers being paid and failing to honour performance obligations became the norm.

Due to our size, it was becoming incredibly difficult to control what was sold in the manner I had so rigidly been able to in the past. I had eight terminals on my desk and each one monitored twenty stores. I watched sales figures religiously and when they weren't to my liking, called meetings with the area managers and, shall we say, focused their minds in no uncertain terms. In an attempt to get figures up to an appropriate level I used all kinds of incentives, including the use of my Ferrari 355 Berlinetta to area managers with the best sales. Stephen Hargreaves, who managed our stores in the north-west, was the first winner. He drove thirty miles in the car and had an enormous crash – so much for incentives.

By the last quarter of 1999 cash flow was beginning to become critical. Again, we needed a serious cash injection to keep the business afloat. By now we had a £3 million overdraft, which we had never used, but our forecasts predicted we would eat into it and require at least another £1 million on top imminently.

My brainwave was to arrange another deal. This time the agreement was with Vodafone. We had nearly 300,000 live customers on Vodafone's airtime and growing and were paid 3 per cent of their call spend, which roughly meant about 0.25p per customer per month, paid to us on a monthly basis. I convinced Vodafone to pay the next two years' worth to us in one lump sum. Hey presto! £2.7 million, and the end of the cash flow crisis . . . for five minutes. How many plates was I spinning now? 121, Vodafone, cash flow, Andrew, stores opening . . .

Speaking of Andrew, he was becoming impatient and again wanted to sell the business. So, after some deliberation, in a strategic move, I offered Andrew a figure for his share of the company upon completion of the sale of the business, and after careful consideration he accepted my offer.

So on the eve of a new millennium, as everyone else was preparing for the beginning of a new era, I was preparing for the end of one. I had decided to put The PocketPhone Shop up for sale.

In December 1999 we topped 50,000 connections. We had done in a month what had taken us the first two years to achieve. We were now the second biggest phone connector in the country and one of the fastest expanding businesses in the UK. The remarkable growth of this company in the space of just five years was almost beyond comprehension.

After I agreed a price with Andrew for his share in the company, his lawyers drafted up a formal agreement, stipulating the price for

Andrew's stock out of the proceeds. Other stipulations were made, notably that any offer over £30 million had to be accepted!

Andrew again brought Arthur Andersen's into the fray and this time I decided to use them, albeit different people from the irksome 'Giles' I had thrown out of my office a year earlier, but on my terms. I met Andersen's, who were aware of the proposed agreement between Andrew and me and its stipulations. I spoke in detail about the market and who I believed would be the likely buyers. I discussed their fees and made it clear that the bigger the sales price they achieved, the bigger percentage they would get. It meant that I could be in breach of Andrew's stipulation that the business must be sold at offers over £30 million. But I didn't care, and neither did they.

Selling a business is a protracted and often nerve-racking process. And whilst I had made my mind up to sell, it felt strange: I was selling something that I had put my heart and soul into.

Andrew and I barely spoke. He never came into the office again. Our conversations were short and to the point, sometimes flaring into arguments. As far as I was concerned, Andrew was in no position to make demands. As long as he got what he wanted, everything else was academic. I had done pretty much all the bleeding work building the company for the last five years and was not going to engage in petty conversations and arguments with him.

In February 2000, once the polished sales document was complete, I suggested Andersen's should approach Orange, Cellnet and 121, leaving Vodafone for another day. A quick timetable was mapped out. Documentation with interested parties by middle of March, indicative offers end of March, and final offers mid- to end April. There would then be an exclusivity period to allow the preferred bidder to perform due diligence, and completion by end of May 2000.

As the documents went out, I then told the Andersen team exactly who would buy it and for how much. I predicted it would be 121 and for north of £60 million. I told them of the conversation with 121 fifteen months earlier, when John Barton wanted me to tell him if I ever decided to sell.

In March we got three offers: Cellnet for £35 million; Orange for £40 million; and 121 for £40 million. We were now in play. All three exceeded the £30 million I was obliged to accept under the agreement with Andrew. As these were indicative offers, Andersen's and I decided not to accept them. We also agreed that this was something that Andrew did not necessarily need to know at this stage.

Andersen's went back to the bidders with a risky strategy to demand more. It was a gamble I was prepared to take because I strongly believed the business was worth more than what was on the table and Andersen's agreed. Of course they did – their commission structure told them to.

Cellnet dropped out, to no surprise to me – we never had much of a relationship with them. Orange came back with £45 million and 121 with £50 million.

I decided to inform the other directors where we were at with negotiations, as individually they would profit from the sale. This was a mistake as, with the exception of my brother Dominic, at least two of the other directors lost their focus. I had heard of people when a business is being sold going into the 'departure lounge' but some of my directors were sitting on the plane sipping fucking mai tais.

At this stage Andersen's started to panic and wanted to involve Vodafone. Their concerns increased when Orange dropped out, leaving one bidder at the table, 121. I had had a phone conversation with 121's MD John Barton, who wanted a steer. I told him to get serious. Days later they came back with an increased offer: £60 million.

Time was against me doing this deal because the agreement with Andrew expired on 30 June 2000. Andersen's wanted to take the offer but I said let's go again. We unbelievably had 121 bidding against themselves.

When they upped the offer to £70 million and I still refused to sell, Andersen's almost went into meltdown. But the way I wanted to sell PPS was indicative of how I ran the business, pushing the envelope on every deal.

My apparent disregard for what 121 were offering made them want it even more. Eventually they got to £88 million and refused to go a penny higher. It was somewhat remarkable, given that they had been bidding against themselves from £45 million onwards.

I eventually phoned Vodafone and told them we wanted £90 million for the business or we would sell it in twenty-four hours. They required less than an hour to say no.

So, on 27 April 2000, I instructed Andersen's to accept 121's bid of £88 million. We entered into a period of exclusivity with a timetable of completing in May. This is where the dynamics changed and the fun began.

When Andrew was finally informed what price I had accepted, the silence was palpable. His lawyers demanded to know how we got to this figure. I metaphorically shrugged my shoulders.

121 came in and brought a massive team of accountants and experts to go through all aspects of our business. This was a painful and arduous process. And the balance of power had shifted in the negotiations: since I had accepted their offer, my façade of being reluctant to sell had been destroyed.

I soon discovered that due diligence was Gaelic for get the price down. They wanted to go through the computer system and the stock, two prospects that concerned me, to analyse every financial agreement and document, and interview key staff in the business without my presence. They wanted to understand every commercial deal we had ever done. I didn't want 121's people sniffing around behind my back; I wanted to be present at every meeting they held. They tried in vain to circumnavigate me.

But 121 and their due diligence were not my only problem. I had two others that almost broke the deal: Andrew Briggs and David Goodman. Andrew was communicating only through his lawyers and trying to make other demands to indemnify himself against this and that.

And then there was David Goodman. The computer system had been sold as the best, which it was – when it was working! 121 wanted the intellectual property rights, and I believed I held them. But it turned out I was using it under licence. Goodman was a prickly little bugger who had got up most people's noses. I was probably one of the few people that tolerated him. I demanded the IPR but he wanted big money for them. I couldn't believe it – I had paid him untold amounts of money and swallowed the £400K in BT Costs because of his software balls-up and now this.

There was also the added complication that he had been diagnosed with a very serious illness; thankfully he was to make a full recovery in time. The treatment he was taking made him even more difficult to deal with, and while I tried to be sympathetic to his plight, at times it proved very difficult. After all, this was a computer system designed to my specifications and he was holding a loaded gun to my head. When he demanded £10 million for the IPR I was consumed with rage. And all this was going on without the knowledge of 121.

The cash flow at PPS was creaking again. No, more to the point, it had reached a critical stage. During my absence, my fellow directors had failed to hold things together and had let the business drop. As PPS balanced on a knife edge of cash flow, a couple of months of bad trading put us under extreme pressure.

Back at Head Office it was one meeting after another. 121's guys went out to stores and the warehouse without my knowledge, precipitating a massive outburst from me. In a fit of pique I threw their guys off site. John Barton called me to complain. I told him they either coordinated through me, or they could piss off. John Barton reminded me of the size and importance of this deal, and told me to calm down and let them get on with their jobs, but he assured me that they would extend all courtesies.

Then I discovered a hole in the stock to the tune of £700,000 and had to call in a favour with a wholesaler to get a million pounds' worth of stock and to arrange to pay him after the completion of the sale.

121 wanted a demonstration of the computer system and on the day they turned up it only bloody crashed. I made the decision to go ahead with the demo, but I had to create an illusion of it working using a back-up system, a mobile phone and a guy who would know what store I was logging into in advance. After going through this routine of what pre-arranged store I was logging into, my in-house IT guy, Suresh, downstairs, would log into the said store and I would illustrate how transactions were going in Liverpool, Newcastle, Dundee, Croydon. It was smoke and mirrors, but I pulled it off – they loved the real-time system and went back to their headquarters raving about it.

We were reaching the end of May and 121's due diligence and legal meetings were still ongoing. Their legal people were getting right up my nose and Andersen's were invaluable at keeping things together.

Briggs' absence caused unnecessary concern with 121, who thought the deal would break down because he was not on board. I showed John Barton the confidential agreement between Andrew and myself so he understood there was no issue in the sale, just Andrew being tetchy about the differences in what we were both getting. John understood immediately and brought some order to the fraying nerves at both ends.

121 now started to chip at the price. They had discovered that the contract for the Time Computers concession was not being renewed and attached a £10 million valuation to it. That was nonsense and they knew it; they had seen the volumes we were shifting weren't that great. So a £10 million reduction was a try-on. They also had a raft of adjustments, which caused much argument and nearly broke the deal on a daily basis.

More pertinently, I had decided that I was going to buy Crystal Palace Football Club and as much as I had tried to keep it under wraps, John Barton was aware of it. He tried to knock the price down to £65 million, we horse-traded, negotiated and beat each other up until we eventually settled on the final sale price of £77.8 million.

Right in the middle of this I had to fly to America as I was best man at my best friend Walter's wedding. I was writing a speech for that, whilst juggling calls between lawyers and accountants representing my sale of PPS for £78 million, and another set of lawyers and accountants for my purchase of Crystal Palace Football Club, which I was buying with money I didn't even have yet.

On returning from America I discovered our cash flow was completely shot to pieces. I pushed to close before the shit really hit the fan. David Goodman finally agreed a figure of £1 million for the licence, not the IPR and no software support contract.

Adding insult to injury two of my directors refused to sign standard non-compete agreements. That was it for me. I had held this thing together by duct tape, whilst they had taken the foot off the pedal. These two difficult sods were about to get more money than they had ever seen and they were arguing about the ability to sell accessories or some such crap in the future. I took both of them outside and said they either signed or they would get fuck all. Let's say it had the desired effect.

121 were cooling and I sensed the deal was falling away. I suggested we complete on Monday 18 June in a hotel in Borehamwood and drove there first thing Monday morning. 121 were sticking on wanting the IPR for the software and a maintenance agreement.

Even so, we couldn't complete the paperwork, as Andrew's lawyers were not ready. The following day we tried to sign the completion paperwork again. Andrew had signed a power of attorney overnight with his lawyers after Andersen's had intervened and read him the riot act. His lawyers signed for him, completing his end of the agreements and providing the bank account details of where he wanted his share of the sale proceeds sent.

All day I worked on Goodman. Eventually I got his assistant to provide a third-party software maintenance agreement but I couldn't get the IPR. In the morning I had no choice but to go with what I had: a third-party service agreement and an irrevocable licence to use the software.

I called John Barton into an alcove next to a vending machine outside the room, and after a few words he finally shook my hand on the deal. I went in, signed document after document in triplicate, and also signed my own resignation.

I had wanted to stay and oversee the takeover, but they wanted to put their own footprint on the business straight away so I agreed to go, and that was to prove a very costly decision.

On 20 June 2000, ten days before my agreement expired with Andrew and probably a matter of weeks before the cash flow ground to a halt, I signed away my ownership of the company. It had been five years and ten months since we had opened the doors to that first shop in Slough on 6 August 1994. This brilliant business built out of acumen, alchemy and bloody single-mindedness was now in my past. I had swapped passion, drive and immense achievement for a big bag of cash. Was it an equitable swap? I wasn't quite sure, but it did give me the opportunity to look after my family.

And who knew what else would come of it?

5

HOW TO BUY A FOOTBALL CLUB

I'm often asked how I bought a football club.

And more often than not my glib response is: 'I wrote a cheque for £10 million.'

That's the simple answer, and of course you have to have the funds to cover that cheque, which fortunately – or unfortunately – I did. Obviously the reality is much more complicated and convoluted than that, so I think the bigger question should be: why would you buy a football club? And, more to the point, why buy an ailing south London club – as cynics would say – like Crystal Palace?

People buy football clubs for many reasons but there is always an element of ego involved. Some simply have the means and want to show it off, for some it's the kudos that comes with being the owner of an iconic British institution; others, especially those from foreign shores, buy clubs to gain instantaneous legitimacy and credibility. I know one chairman who bought a big club in the north-east that he had no affiliation with whatsoever just because his best mate was vice-chairman of a perceived top London club. And I've heard it said that one big west London club was bought as the world's biggest life insurance policy for its owner! None of these motives has much to do with football itself, and none of these motives applied to me – OK, maybe there was a bit of ego in there – but my agenda was more about building something meaningful.

When I was younger, most of my friends abandoned their local clubs. Even my own brother claimed to support Tottenham at one stage, though he didn't know one end of the Tottenham High Road from the other. I put that down to the trendy Admiral kit that Glenn Hoddle was wearing at the time rather than a treacherous defection. But I wasn't one of those that subscribed to supporting a fashionable club. Otherwise I would have moved to Hertfordshire and become a Manchester United fan!

Palace was the team I supported as a child, the team my father played for, and a club that was perceived to have vast if unrealised potential. In fact, at the time I was looking to buy Crystal Palace, I could have bought Leicester City – it was a far better deal for me financially – but Crystal Palace was the club I wanted.

In the previous five years I had overcome every adversity and turned it into success, built a business from virtually nothing and sold it for a vast amount of money. At the ripe old age of thirty-two, I had the world at my feet. I didn't need to work another day in my life but given my personality I needed a challenge. Running a football club was that challenge, one that I believed I was more than capable of rising to. Turning potential into reality was something I was good at.

That covers the why. If you asked me now what owning a football club is like, I'd say I imagine it's a bit like being a drug addict. You indulge yourself in something you enjoy, knowing it's bad for you, and after the initial rush of pleasure it gives you a headache and sucks all the money out of your bank account.

*   *   *

In the summer of 1997, as a token of appreciation to my father, I spent £10,000 on what Crystal Palace laughingly described as a 'luxury box' so he could watch his cherished football team out of the cold.

To some extent that is where it all began.

The following year I received a call from the club's extremely pretty marketing manager.

'If you're ringing me up to renew that scabby box at Palace the answer is no,' I said cheekily. 'If you're calling me to go out on a date with you, the answer is yes.'

Whilst the company of a charming and beautiful woman is priceless, after dinner not only had I spent £10,000 on the executive box, I had also coughed up £100,000 for a PocketPhone Shop marketing campaign with Crystal Palace Football Club, an expensive evening out by anyone's standards! Was the date worth it? I think I'll keep that to myself.

In truth I was showing off to impress her, but there was also an underlying interest in becoming involved in the club in some way, which appealed to my ego. So not only had I had a charming evening, but I also had the promise of an introduction to her boss, the new club chairman.

In the autumn of 1998 I met Mark Goldberg.

Mark was a personable, energetic character – a small chap, with slicked-back hair and braces – who struck me as being a little guilty of style over substance. He had recently paid £20 million – a vastly overinflated price – to acquire the club from its previous owner, Ron Noades, the same Ron Noades who had been locked in a long-running legal battle with my father.

Mark's hugely expensive deal hadn't even included the purchase of the stadium, leaving Noades with some feeling of tenure over the club. Rather like a noisy ex-wife, he felt this gave him the right to expel his opinions. In what was his charmless way he'd spewed out one of them at the time: 'Goldberg was stupid and he wet his knickers when I agreed to sell him the club.' In my opinion, Noades was a thoroughly dislikeable man, who had used the club to make money for all it was worth and showed no respect for Mark and, more importantly, the club. Rather than disappear into the ether with his huge bounty, he had the audacity to ridicule someone who was prepared to put their hand in their own pocket. This made me gravitate towards Mark.

But all this did not detract from the fact that right from the start of his ownership Mark was in serious financial trouble.

He had arrived in a blaze of publicity, appointing the former England coach Terry Venables as a marquee manager following relegation from the Premier League. He talked about signing Paul Gascoigne and Ronaldo, invested heavily in the playing side and support structure and overpaid for players. His plans were unsustainable in the division they were in and the club was haemorrhaging money.

Mark wanted investment and wasted little time before instructing one of his sales staff, Phil Alexander, to invite me to a corporate club event held at the Selsdon Park Hotel in November 1998. It wasn't my thing but I decided I would attend out of sheer curiosity.

The whole evening was a non-event. I knew I was only being buttered up for money and lo and behold found myself sitting next to Terry Venables.

I had mixed feelings about Venables. On one hand, there was the childhood memories of him as the young, energetic and flamboyant Palace manager of the eighties; on the other there was the apparently disinterested person I had seen standing in the dugout in some of the games I watched early into Mark's ownership.

Unfortunately, for me, Venables wasn't particularly good

company. He only laughed at his own jokes, which frankly I didn't find funny in the slightest. He really was no comedian, although I dare say a fair few supporters of certain clubs around the country may disagree with me on that.

In late 1998 Mark's financial problems were reaching a critical level, so I suggested I might consider putting some money into Palace. PPS was at full tilt at the time and, as I've said before, cash flow is king, so most of the money was going back into my expanding company, but – in a way that is typical of me – I thought I would agree a deal with him and work out how to fund it afterwards. But, aside from the financial leg-up, an incident in January 1999 convinced me Mark needed some real support.

Palace had bought Lee Bradbury for £1 million and Mark was attempting to unload him for as much as he could get. Ironically he was attempting to do a deal with Trevor Francis at Birmingham City, someone I was later to employ at Palace. I was in his office when Mark took a call from Paul Walsh, the ex-Liverpool and England footballer, who was Lee Bradbury's agent.

Walsh was on speakerphone and the way he spoke to Mark stunned me. He was yelling at him about how the player wouldn't do this and wouldn't do that and that was how things were going to happen. 'If he doesn't like it then he can fuck off.'

Once the call was over, I felt compelled to comment to Mark about the way Walsh had spoken to the chairman and owner of a football club. He just shrugged resignedly; he was prepared to listen to that shit in order to get things done.

I saw it differently. Surely the player was Mark's asset to sell and Walsh was most likely to be working and being paid by him so where did he come off talking to him like that?

On reflection, Mark's conversation with Walsh probably influenced the regard I held agents in and determined how I was to handle a large proportion of my negotiations with them in the future.

Very shortly after that incident, Goldberg rang and asked if I was prepared to invest £250,000 in CPFC, which would give me a certain amount of equity and say.

I mulled this over and told him that in exchange for a seat on the board, I would. As I said earlier, like drug addiction, football has a habit of pulling you in like that.

Mark arranged to come over to my head office and brought his team of sycophants and lickspittles with him. We negotiated a deal and I wrote him out a cheque for £250,000, with the condition that it was secured against something. One of his cronies piped up with some comment about Mark being good for the money.

I just ignored him. I wasn't prepared to sink £250,000 into Palace without insisting on some form of security. I asked Mark what he could offer and he suggested a charge on his home Holroyd House, a stately manor in its own grounds in the leafy well-to-do suburb of Keston.

I agreed, provided that there were no other charges on that property. I left the funds and an order to set up a charge with my lawyers because I was flying off on holiday to Miami Beach with my girlfriend for a well-earned holiday.

A few days later, whilst I was sunning myself and preparing for what was to be my biggest year at PPS, my lawyers called with a problem: it transpired that everybody from the dustman to Venables had a charge on Goldberg's stately pile.

After discovering these charges I realised just how desperate he must have been and in later years I had a better understanding of his desperation. But at the time I took a dim view of it.

As far as I was concerned Goldberg had lied to me. I had a personal rule that I always believed everything anyone told me until they lied and then I never believed another word they said again.

Goldberg phoned me up some time later and apologised profusely, and reluctantly I agreed to meet him. He was full of his nonchalant confidence. Brimming with half-baked ideas, he was going to get a huge Chinese marketing and advertising deal as one of the Palace players was the national team captain. As often was the case with Goldberg, he detached himself from the reality of the problem and operated in a cloud above it.

In my view he was a dead man walking. 'Mark, you are living in cuckoo-land,' I told him. 'Your problems are on the ground here, now, and your head is up in the clouds, with dreams that are not realistic.'

I pushed him hard on the true financial position. Crystal Palace's financial situation was all over the papers and I deduced he had wanted that £250,000 from me to help pay the players' wages for that month. Goldberg took a moment and then said the club was on its knees; both he and it were staring into the abyss. My God, this was after only nine months of his ownership. I advised Goldberg that he would need to seriously consider insolvency and administration advice. Whilst writing this book, it's occurred to me that in the last months of my ownership, as I was pouring money into the club and desperately trying to prevent it from going into administration, I really needed someone to lay it on the line as I had with Goldberg. To be honest, I probably wouldn't have welcomed it. But Mark had something that towards the end of my tenure at Palace I lacked: necessary, if harsh, advice.

Back to 1999. Some months earlier I had met David Buchler, who was a board director at Tottenham and one of the leading insolvency guys in the country. He had a history of dealing with football club administrations. I told Goldberg that he should go and see Buchler and see what, if any, options he had.

Goldberg went along to this meeting still in a jaunty state of mind, illustrating that the gravity of his circumstances hadn't fully registered for him. After listening to Goldberg explain the situation, it didn't take long for Buchler to tell him that his only choice was administration. Goldberg was determined that whatever happened he was going to come out the other side still chairman of Crystal Palace. Buchler had to put him straight: unless he was going to buy CPFC back and fund administration himself it was unlikely he would retain any kind of control.

Finally the reality of Goldberg's situation hit home. But instead of heeding my advice to keep quiet, he went off, talking to fans at prearranged public meetings and got himself unfairly vilified. Goldberg's only real crime was the naivety that led to the destruction of his own personal wealth in less than a year.

The next thing I heard Palace had gone under and Simon Paterson of Moore Stephens was appointed as the administrator. Perhaps the reason why Goldberg didn't engage Buchler as administrator was because he didn't like his advice, but I also suspect Buchler was just too expensive for him.

Aside from reading the occasional snippet in the media, that was the last time I was to really pay attention to the plight of Crystal Palace for the best part of a year. My focus was on the small matter of running and selling PPS.

In the middle of 1999 I met the well-known DJ David 'Kid' Jensen through 121's MD John Barton. David's son, Viktor, was a racing driver and was looking for some corporate sponsorship. Given 121 had just done the marketing deal with me at PPS, John Barton gave me a strong indication he would like me to talk to the Jensens so I agreed to provide some sponsorship money for him. I also knew that he was a huge Palace fan. During our discussions Palace inevitably came up and I told David that I had tried in vain to help Goldberg.

Nearly twelve months had passed and the sale of PPS was in full flow when David Jensen contacted me again to see if I would renew his son's sponsorship deal, and of course we talked about Palace. At that time Crystal Palace had been in administration for fourteen months and had sold a large number of their players and laid off a lot of staff to fund the administration. The club really was in desperate straits.

They had a potential buyer in the mysterious Jerry Lim, a Malaysian businessman who had been negotiating for some time with the administrators to secure exclusivity and do due diligence, but was not coming up with the money, despite promising via the media time and again to do so. From my outsider's perspective, I got the impression he was not the real deal!

Given that now I was on the cusp of selling PPS and rather than having the ever-present issues of cash flow I was about to have a significant amount of money, I had decided I would look very closely at the possibility of buying CPFC as my replacement for the business I was about to sell and told David Jensen just that.

He was very surprised and I think somewhat sceptical; I insisted that I was deadly serious. In return for my benevolent sponsorship of young Viktor, I asked David for his public support when I made a move to buy the club. Until that time, I wanted him to keep this conversation between us. A slightly bemused David Jensen left my office with his cheque for the sponsorship and a secret.

Towards the end of April, while I was settling on final offers for PPS, I made a formal approach to Crystal Palace's administrators with a view to making a bid for the club. I used Andersen's again, and their guy Charles Simpson approached them, representing my interest on a no-name basis.

Surprisingly, Simon Paterson rebuffed the approach, saying they were near to a deal and exclusivity with Lim, and didn't want to ruin it. This struck me as commercially stupid, as two factions expressing interest in buying the club was a godsend.

The bloody-mindedness of the administrators' response strengthened my resolve. When I am told 'no' for no good reason, it's like igniting a blue touch paper. I make it my mission to turn that 'no' into a 'yes'. I stepped up the interest, insisting via Andersen's they disclose the purchase price and what was required to put forward a legitimate bid.

As Andersen's were at that time one of the biggest accountancy firms in the world, just the fact that the new bidder was being represented by them should have carried significant weight. But for some reason Paterson was not interested, insisting that he had a deal with this Lim.

This struck me as odd behaviour from an administrator whose sole purpose in life was to sell the club for the best price and to ensure the creditors got as much of the money they were owed as possible. If nothing else, having two bids was an ideal way to achieve this. Lim was hanging around like a bad smell, continuing to play the media, but he didn't seem to be able to back up his bid with cold hard cash. And all the time the club was sinking further and further into the mire.

I decided to do two things.

First I contacted David Jensen to put me in touch with the Supporters' Trust. The Crystal Palace fans had galvanised around their ailing club and formed a trust to see if they could help in any way. Their head guy Paul Newman came to see me in my office in Slough. He was well informed and also concerned about the future of Palace. He also had genuine reservations about Lim and informed me that the trust had collected somewhere in the region of £1 million, which they were holding to see if it could be of help.

We discussed our various experiences of Palace and he quickly understood I was a genuine fan with means. Not that it was a glowing endorsement as Goldberg had peddled the same story before he crashed and burned at Palace.

I explained to Newman the strange stance Simon Paterson was taking by stonewalling me. Newman knew Lim and suggested he would contact him and put us in touch, to see at my suggestion if there was something we could do between us. And the thought of getting Lim to step aside was starting to germinate in my mind.

In return for facilitating a meeting Paul Newman wanted, if I did buy Palace, a seat on the board for a trust member. Everybody had an agenda! I didn't want to commit to this as it seemed to me that fans can be too passionate about their club to be able to make unblinkered decisions, with respect with your money! However, I never ruled it in or out but I did categorically say that in the event I did indeed buy the club, I wouldn't be taking any of the Supporters' Trust money. The focus was to ensure this club got bought and did not die.

Next I instructed Andersen's to make sure Paterson understood that he was putting the club in grave jeopardy by not engaging with us and relying on this Jerry Lim character to come through.

Eventually Moore Stephens relented under pressure from Andersen's, saying they wanted a name and proof of funds to the tune of £10 million. That wouldn't be a problem once PPS was sold but technically I couldn't provide that, so I went to Lloyd's and leant on my bank manager, Nigel Gibson, who had been working with me on PPS for the last two and a bit years. It was testament to the strength of my relationship with the bank and the regard that I was held in that Nigel gave the Palace administrators a letter saying I was good for £10 million and more.

Andersen's now gave my name to the administrators under strict confidentiality.

Despite getting what he asked for, Paterson still refused us access to the books, claiming there was insufficient time to do due diligence and complete the purchase by the date the Football League had stipulated for Palace to come out of administration. This was utter crap: the Lim deal was not done, and there was nothing to lose by giving me access. I knew the timelines and if I felt that we could do enough due diligence in that time to convince me to buy the club then it was my money that was going to be at risk.

By now I was completely pissed off. Paterson was standing in my way for no good reason that I could see. So I upped the ante. I instructed Andersen's to phone Paterson to tell him that I wanted access and I was going to get it one way or another.

Up to now we had avoided the media but, given the complete wall we were running up against, we told Paterson that if he didn't cooperate immediately, we would go to them and say how obstructive he was, how he was risking the future of the club and how if the club failed we would ensure he was held responsible through whatever means or authority it took.

Paterson came across as a belligerent individual, rotund in appearance, phlegmatic in conversation and seemed to revel in his fifteen minutes of fame as he presided over the future of CPFC. Regularly popping up in front of cameras resplendent in his Palace tie, he was intransigent. 'Do what you want,' was his response.

So I laid it bare to the media. I had the motivation, the means and the intent to buy this club and was being blocked by a fee-generating administrator who in my view could ruin the club.

This provided the pressure we needed. After an outcry from the

2,000-strong Supporters' Trust and the adverse media attention, I was reluctantly allowed access to do what turned out to be a very limited form of due diligence.

At this time, John Barton, 121's MD and key driver in the purchase of PPS, invited me to the England v Brazil match at the old Wembley on 27 May 2000. I went along to ensure that I was well in touch with John as the sale was coming to its critical stage. Now that my interest in buying Crystal Palace was common knowledge, Barton attempted to use that information to his advantage by chipping the price of PPS down. He knew I would be buying Palace with money from the proceeds of the PPS sale, and I hadn't yet agreed a final price.

During this game I met Theo Paphitis for the first time. He was big friends with John and was also the chairman of Millwall FC. He spent the entire afternoon saying it was madness to buy a football club. Perhaps it had slipped his mind that he himself had bought one, although Millwall can barely be described as a football club. He gave me his oracle-like view of football at the same time as ridiculing Palace as they were Millwall's big south London rivals. It wasn't the first time I heard Crystal Palace referred to as 'Crippled Alice', nor would it be the last.

Sometime at the end of May, Jerry Lim walked into my office in Slough. He was far from mysterious or mythical, in fact, he was a bit of a caricature. No joke – he looked and spoke like he had jumped off the set of a Charlie Chan movie. Just five minutes into the meeting I was struggling to take him seriously. He was an excitable little fellow with a pronounced accent and a rhetoric that would make a sailor blush – and that's coming from me! He was going to 'fluck this person up', 'fluck that person up', he had 'big flucking plans', and 'Won' Noades was every flucking name under the sun – on this point we did agree. He was talking about building bowling alleys, nightclubs, multiplex cinemas and a luxury hotel. Quite where he thought he was going to build all this and quite why anyone would want a luxury hotel in an unglamorous suburb of south-east London seemed to have escaped him.

There was nothing about football – sorry, excuse me, he did touch upon it, advising me of his plans to bring his close personal friends the Gurkhas to be stewards at the club. I remain unconvinced to this day that he ever had the money to go through with this deal or even that Lim was his name.

And this was the guy that Paterson, the administrator at the club, was telling me was the reason I could not make a bid for Crystal Palace.

This made no sense to my advisers. Surely this stance didn't stack up. Maybe I had missed something!

After wading through Lim's initial claptrap, I suggested that perhaps I could buy the club and use him to work up the remainder of the deal. He jumped at that. I bloody knew it. As I thought, he had no money and I had just given him the out he needed. From that point he was my fiercest ally; smelling money and an earning opportunity, he snuggled up close to me. I also had the added benefit of having the Gurkhas as extra security if anyone ever threatened to kidnap me again.

It was now 20 June 2000 and the sale of PPS had been completed.

That evening I had drinks in the suite I had rented in the Dorchester. Arthur Andersen's people, the ones who had sold PPS and the ones that were acting for me on the CPFC deal, joined me, along with my brother Dominic.

Charles Simpson of Andersen's put pressure on me about doing this deal and all of a sudden, I felt like I was drowning.

My brain went into a meltdown. All the pressure of selling PPS came to the fore and within hours I was moving into another problematic high-pressured deal.

All my instincts said, 'Don't do it.'

I walked into the bedroom to get away from everyone. I had a deep sense of foreboding, and paced up and down the room muttering to myself, 'I don't want to do this, I don't want to do this.'

I had worked myself into a bit of a state and was getting quite distressed when Dominic came in and was understandably concerned.

'Jesus, Dom,' I said. 'I'm not sure I'm ready for this. I'm being pushed into something that I'm not sure about.'

'Don't do it, you haven't got to do anything,' he replied. 'Just tell Andersen's to piss off and stand down.'

I got myself together and we all went out to dinner at Daphne's in London to celebrate the sale of PPS. The conversation turned to Palace and my brother got quite irritable with Andersen's, indicating I was having second thoughts and that they should slow things down.

Overnight, despite the grave reservations I had, I changed my mind again. My father had told me once that buying Crystal Palace was my destiny, and his words were ringing in my ears. So, for want of a better expression I called myself out. I said to myself: 'You have sold PPS, you need and want a new challenge, and here it is, son. What is the worst that can happen?' Bloody understatement of the year right there!

So I committed myself mentally to this deal and the following morning informed Andersen's that I would be proceeding with the purchase of CPFC.

I met Jerry Lim again, this time with Charles Simpson of Andersen's in tow, who also scratched his head at this strange little character.

A deal was agreed with Lim that I would buy CPFC 2000 Ltd, the company that had been set up by him to buy the club and take them out of administration. This was to be done in complete secrecy. Lim had negotiated all of the deal to date and I wanted him to complete the process on my behalf in the strictest confidence, whilst ensuring all aspects of the deal came as close to my satisfaction as possible.

One key area concerned me: the stadium. There was no way I was dealing with Noades. I knew he would try and take me like he had taken Goldberg. Ridiculously he demanded £12 million for a stadium that was actually valued nearer £6 million.

So, via Lim, I resisted the Goldberg trap of paying option fees on freehold purchases or ninety-nine-year leases, Instead, I opted for a ten-year lease, believing it would enable me to be fleet of foot if ever there came an opportunity to move to a purpose-built stadium in the borough. I was not going to let myself be taken in by Noades. I later said that I did not need to deal with Noades on the stadium – given that he was getting on I could deal with his estate. It wasn't the most tactful remark, but in my view there was no dealing on a reasonable level with this man. Ironically the fact I only wanted a ten-year lease put me in breach of Football League rules after my first day of ownership, as you needed to have a minimum of ten years' tenure, but, as I was to find out later, there was no surprise in the lack of diligence exhibited by the governing bodies of this business.

I wanted Lim to deliver these things for the money he was getting out of the deal. At the time I believed he had the deal in the best shape but later I was to find out that that was not in fact the case and certain parties, namely Noades, might not have received monies if I had had the time or opportunity of dealing with it myself.

The transaction was now ready according to Andersen's, which in any other deal wouldn't have been true: we had limited access and did limited due diligence purely because the drop-dead date from the Football League for the club to exit administration or face liquidation was virtually here. But I was in the deal now and I took what can only be described as a fly. By making this somewhat reckless call, I backed myself to have the means financially and logistically to make up for any parts of the deal that fell short.

I transferred the money for Lim to complete the deal on my behalf and also had legal documentation drawn up between Garrets, my lawyers, and Vincent Brown, who was representing Lim, that would transfer the ownership of CPFC 2000 from Lim to me immediately after he acquired it.

The completion meeting was set for 5 July 2000. The newspapers had phoned me to ascertain if I was out of the deal now that Lim had confirmed that he was buying CPFC. I played along, confirming that if Jerry Lim said that he was buying Crystal Palace Football Club, then he was buying it. I didn't want the papers running stories that could potentially threaten the deal.

In those days there was no such thing as the, frankly laughable, fit and proper person test for ownership of a club as there is now. Not that it would have been an issue for me personally. But if those rules and regulations had been in place at the time it would have prevented me from doing the deal this way.

So with my money Jerry Lim would buy Crystal Palace Football Club and all its assets through his vehicle CPFC 2000 and no sooner was that done than I would buy CPFC 2000 from him.

What needed to be paid was the administrator's sale price for the ownership of the club. I also had to put £1 million into the fully paid-up share capital, which was a requirement to get the Football League share, and then pay Lim his fee.

All in all I put £10,175,000 into Vincent Brown's account held to my order and agreed to meet him on the morning of 5 July at the offices of Denton Wilde Sapte, the solicitors handling the legals for the administrator.

I was not invited to their party, so I crashed it.

On 5 July I met Charles Simpson and my lawyer Jeff McGeachie and we made our way to Denton's.

We rocked up there and somehow or other Andersen's got us into the floor where the signing was taking place. Just as I was about to enter the room flanked by my team, I walked straight into the irritating Paterson, the administrator. His face said it all but he still had to ask, 'What are you doing here?'

'You'll find out in a minute.'

It was clear that he knew from the moment I walked through the door why I was there, but he couldn't help himself.

Over his shoulder was a room full of people. Lim's lawyer was there and I made to go past Paterson into the room.

He blocked my path – as he was quite rotund this was not overly difficult for him. 'You can't go in there, the room's full.'

'You're right, full of my bloody money. Now get out of the way,' was my frosty response.

Pushing past him, I entered the packed room. Very quickly the penny dropped and everyone realised what was going on. Vincent Brown had just signed on behalf of Jerry Lim and he now signed everything across to me.

A Football League representative was there, a perplexed expression on his face. I would get to see that look on the faces of League officials many times over the years.

Andersen's took over the show and within five minutes Crystal Palace had a new owner. Actually, in point of fact, it had two new owners in the space of those five minutes: one that lasted for approximately one hundred and twenty seconds, and yours truly.

Fifteen days after the protracted and difficult sale of PPS I was now the youngest owner of a football club in the world.

I was told the expectant management team of CPFC were sitting in another office waiting for Lim to come in and announce his purchase. They had been working with him for a long time on his takeover and clearly thought they were going to be part of a management buy-out and would be free to run the club in their own way whilst Lim ran around hatching his hare-brained schemes to build hotels and bowling alleys.

The silence in the room was palpable when I walked in and announced to Phil Alexander, Steve Coppell and Peter Morley – chief executive, first-team manager and acting chairman respectively – that I was now the owner of the club, thus dashing all their hopes.

Alexander, being the animal I know him now, disguised his disappointment and said, 'Great, what do you want me to do?'

Steve Coppell just looked at me sullenly, although as I got to know him sullen was his normal expression, whether ecstatic or miserable.

And Peter Morley looked at me imperiously, remarking: 'I guess you won't be needing me any more.' He was wrong in that and was later to become a great friend and ally.

I told them I was heading straight over to Selhurst Park to meet the staff and I would see them later. I would have loved to listen to their collective comments in their car on the way back to the ground.

The next morning would see the beginning of a new dawn and a complete change of culture for Crystal Palace FC.

6

LEARNING THE HARD WAY

So what had the drive to rid myself of £10.5 million no sooner had I got my hands on it really bought me? Well, let's find the right words. If some people's palaces are luxurious and opulent, my Palace was a bloody toilet.

In August 1994 I had invested £15,000 and turned it into nigh on £80 million; here I had invested 700 times that amount not in a shiny new showroom and big new dreams, but at first glance a bloody eyesore fraught with problems.

As I sat in my office that first morning – and when I say 'office' it was a Portakabin, an actual Portakabin, a testament to the investment of previous owners – I looked out over the threadbare pitch and at the derelict building fraudulently passing itself off as a stadium, not quite with my head in my hands but certainly with some vigorous shakes of the old noggin. Had I bumped it a bit too hard when I had made the commitment to buy CPFC?

I had arrived on my first day at 8.30 a.m. to familiarise myself with my newly owned surroundings and eager-to-impress workforce.

At 9.30 my staff trickled in an hour later than I had expected, not quite the start I was anticipating. Within hours I realised there

was a vast difference between my version of hard work and professionalism and that of the incumbent staff.

And a warm welcome wasn't exactly awaiting me online either.
I made the mistake of logging onto one of the fans' websites only
to read, 'Let's give Jordan a chance until he makes his first mistake.
Then we can hammer him.' Bloody charming, I thought.

At lunchtime I walked out of the office I was using, which was
considerably smaller than the one Phil Alexander the CEO was
occupying, and found the office virtually deserted. I asked my
inimitable PA Sara Warren where everyone was and she said they
had all gone to lunch at the pub over the road.

I immediately marched over there and told them I wanted them
back in the office now. When they returned I made it simple: 'You
don't all piss off to lunch at the same time, and from now on no
more drinking at lunchtime.' The second point went down like a
lead balloon. These people needed a major wake-up call.

This football club was in a shambolic state from top to bottom.

With a few exceptions, the commercial staff I inherited were an
unmotivated and unenergetic bunch nobody else wanted and who
were cheap enough for the administrators to keep on.

All manner of wonders that I had been unable to uncover in
the limited time I had to do due diligence were becoming apparent.
It was dawning on me that my typically cavalier approach to the
gamble of buying the club might just take a big bite out of my
not-so-clever arse.

During his ownership, Ron Noades had raised £6.5 million
from advance season ticket sales to build a new stand. Unfortunately
those long-term season ticket sales were now impacting on one
of my biggest income streams, meaning in effect in a perverse
way I was picking up the tab, without the benefit of the £6.5

million! The spend on the stand I was told was £3 million but it was a shell, all fur coat and no knickers, and one on which the manufacturers had refused to give a warranty because someone hadn't paid the final instalment of money he owed them. That can't be right! I mean, £6.5 million had been raised to build it and only £3 million had been spent. So where was the rest of the money? As I gazed out on to the football ground, I reasoned that the £3.5 million must be bound up in the facilities somewhere. But where?

The stadium was in an absolute state of disrepair. Virtually everywhere you looked it was almost coming down and the lounges were like the inside of an Indian restaurant that hadn't been redecorated since the seventies. The training ground, if you can call it that, was a series of paddy fields located in the grounds of a sports club. So clearly the excess money hadn't been invested there; no one had invested in the facilities for twenty years. I had an inkling of where the money had gone, and it was nowhere near Selhurst Park.

The state of disrepair was typified by some news I received less than a week after I had bought the club. The roof on the Arthur Waite stand, which had been there since the sixties, was unsafe. Given that it was predominantly the away supporters' stand, my initial response was 'And?' but joking aside, I had a obligation to fix that roof. The safety council for the Football League told me I had three weeks to do it or close the stand for the season.

So I brought in my brother Dominic, and £200,000 and an age later, that stand had a new roof for the new season. Quite why it had taken forty years for anyone to provide one and quite why I had it dumped on my lap a week after buying the club I don't know – oh yes, I do: the administrators didn't have the money to do it; Goldberg barely had a chance to get an office before losing

Palace; and Noades . . . do I really need to spell out why he may not have fixed the roof?

After my first few hours of pleasure at the stadium I was off to meet the fans' hero and irrepressible football manager, Steve Coppell, who, it turned out, was bloody difficult to communicate with. As I said earlier his demeanour was sullen whether unhappy or exhilarated. And the group of players I inherited, and I use the word 'group' very loosely, seemed totally uninterested. Even the training and playing kit was falling apart and we were tied into a deal with a second-rate manufacturer of cheesecloth-like kits for another twelve months.

The new season opened in just over a month and I had the bare bones of a team, facilities that were falling apart and no commercial activity, Palace had no shirt sponsor, ground advertising, executive box sales or significant season ticket receipts, it had bare minimum training facilities and not even travel arrangements or plans for the imminently approaching season. It frankly had a piss-poor attitude that reverberated throughout the entire business.

This was all to change within four short weeks; with a complete dose of Jordan focus and finances all of the above were rectified. All executive boxes and advertising boards were sold. For the first time in two years we secured shirt sponsorship – a major brand in Churchill Insurance – and a busy industrious environment was created. Of course all this was with an incessant background hum of 'it can't be done' or 'it's not done that way'. I don't think so, was my attitude. To me it was simple: sell these things or get new jobs. I impressed upon Phil Alexander that we were now not in administration and he was accountable to me and his staff would deliver – and despite themselves they did.

The two major but very different and distinct parts of the

business that make up a football club are the commercial operation and the playing side – the youth set-up was a third part that considered itself a different business. I felt that each part of the club had significant importance and I would set about treating all facets the same, whether it be a steward on match day or a multi-million-pound centre forward.

The team were heading off to China for a pre-season tour, paid for by Dalian Shied, a Chinese team. Palace had purchased the national captain from them two years beforehand. The tour made no commercial sense – it was a legacy of Mark 'Head in the Clouds' Goldberg's time – but the club was committed. I had neither the time nor the inclination to fly to China, so I decided to stay back and set up my stall for running this new business.

Peter Morley, the chairman through administration, came in to see me. Peter was a charming man, with an austere demeanour. He was small in build and imperious in an unassuming way. He had been involved with Palace for a long time. His wife, Paula, who had a fearsome reputation, had been Noades's secretary when he owned the club. Peter also had the impressive background of having been a main board director at Tesco's.

For some reason Peter had taken a dim view of me, and once in my new office he wasted no time letting me know his opinion. 'Young man, you may think you are special, but I have met many people like you and you are not special.'

Laughing, I said, 'Peter, I want to build a club we can all be proud of and I would really like your help with that.'

That stopped him dead in his tracks. I think he expected some cocky response and I deliberately didn't give him that. I knew he wanted to go to China, so I asked him would he please go for me. He sniffed at it and said if it would help the club then he would of course consider it. Peter and I over the years developed a very good friendship. He became one of my biggest supporters and I was always grateful for his wise words. In fact, I wasted no time in making him the club president.

Before they departed, Steve Coppell and I had a number of conversations about the playing squad and his coaching staff. Clearly they both needed investment, but Steve was not the easiest man to talk to. We attacked his coaching requirements first.

He needed a new first-team coach so, feeling like some eager-to-please new pupil, I asked who he wanted. That was Bobby Houghton, a well-respected coach who was working abroad with Malmo. I took Steve at face value and asked how much he would want. Steve came back with 'Two hundred grand a year.'

Coppell was on £125,000. I was confused – was that the right money for his assistant? Apparently not! In fact, the right money was £50–60,000. I sighed inwardly. 'So why did you suggest him then?'

'Because you asked me who I wanted,' Coppell replied.

'So what do you want me to do then?' I persisted.

'Nothing, as Houghton wouldn't come anyway.'

I looked at Steve Coppell, bemused by this totally pointless conversation. Was he being clever with me?

After that enlightening chat, we moved on to players. He liked two boys at Arsenal on the periphery of their first team, Tommy Black and Julian Gray, ideally both but certainly Black. I promised to look at buying them, asked for a steer on the price and got a big fat helpful 'No idea!'

I wished him a successful trip to China, thinking it was an appropriate place for him after the Chinese torture of a conversation I had just had with him.

I immediately arranged to meet David Dein, the Arsenal vice-chairman, at their London Colney training ground. Dein greeted me with manager Arsène Wenger, and I think this was designed to impress me, but frankly I have never been over-impressed with anyone and I certainly was not happy to have to put blue bags over my feet to see Arsenal's 'wonderful' training ground.

I listened to David Dein do his best Fagin impression of wanting to help, as he put it, any new boys coming into football. Almost straight away I worked out that you didn't want Dein to do you any favours – he would sell you a player with a real foot and a wooden leg if he could. We got down to business and after much haggling Dein did me one of his wonderful 'favours' of selling me two young players for £500,000 each.

I had just spent a million pounds on two players who had no first-team experience on someone else's say-so. I knew we should have got more information on the boys but I wanted to show Coppell I had faith in him. Quite why, I'm not sure, but that's the thing about not knowing your business or people within it, you do things differently and learn the hard way.

Signing these two players was my first experience of dealing with agents and I wanted to make sure from the get-go that agents knew I was not an idiot who would pay them for doing absolutely nothing. The two agents in question became well known to me over the years: Tony Finnigan for Julian Gray and David Manassi for Tommy Black, and these first negotiations were terse to say the least.

Let me tell you how signing a player works, so you can see the absurdity of the situation.

You agree a fee with the selling club for the player. Ironically, that's the easy part. You are then contacted by the player's agent, who arranges to come and see you and negotiate a deal for his client. In principle, this is fine and for young boys early on in their careers pragmatic advice from an agent is perhaps appropriate; grown men later in their careers should be man enough to negotiate their own deal and I always had a big regard for players who did that. Players always knew exactly what they wanted, more often than not all agents achieved was a feeling of bad will and additional fees.

Upon meeting, the agent's aim is to achieve the optimum amount of money he can get for his client and of course there is always going to be a difference of opinion on that subject as you negotiate.

The key factor for them is the player's basic wage, his 'guarantee', but once that is achieved suddenly everything else becomes just as important.

Firstly you have sign-on fees, a golden hello every year for the player agreeing to be paid a basic wage. Then there are appearance bonuses for the player turning up – but isn't that the very thing his basic wage and sign-on covers? Then you have goal bonuses for forwards – but hang on, surely that is what you pay them a weekly wage for? You also have the same for clean sheets for goal-keepers. The list goes on.

Agents ideally like to write in staged increases so if you sign a four-year contract with a player they want a pay rise every year irrespective of performance and, if they can, a pay rise after a certain number of games. Then there are loyalty bonuses, typically paid annually, which are for the monumental thing of the player turning up for a year, and on top of that they want win bonuses. Win bonuses? The fact that we are paying a basic wage, sign-on money, appearance money, etc., etc., on the expectation of them securing wins seems to be lost in all of this.

But that's not all. Irrespective of where the player lives, you pay a relocation fee of about £10,000, then their medical insurance, and 90 per cent of the time all of these costs are greater than you want to pay.

With a straight face, the agent then tells you that he has worked for you, and it is hardly fair for the player to bear the costs of his fees. So after you pick yourself up off the floor you have this to consider.

Someone who is purporting to work for you, who has got a deal for his client that is worse for you than you could have got yourself, is now demanding to be paid or he would be unable to recommend this deal to his real client – who is not, of course, paying him, that is your job. Confused? Clear as mud, isn't it!

How this business had got like this was beyond me. Greed, I suppose. The alternative is to not sign the player, but then you are in a public domain situation and the rules are different. Managers, supporters and results put pressure on you and in the end you have to bite down.

I soon developed a reputation as someone who didn't pay fees to agents, which had good and bad ramifications. Over the years the controls and regulations over agents have changed, but they still get their money come what may. For the record, I would always be perfectly happy to pay agents who clearly work for me, and I did on many occasions.

The team arrived back from China. Coppell appeared to be pleased about signing Gray and Black, although he could have been unhappy, I couldn't really tell!

I was more established in my new environment. Phil Alexander came back to find me sitting in 'his' office, having removed his stuff. He wasn't best pleased. Mind you, I wasn't best pleased about some of the unacceptable behaviour that had gone on in China either, notably from Phil. Phil Alexander, incidentally, was the only person to be in a business that went into administration and come out better off. He went in on a certain wage and came out on a much bigger wage, with all kinds of perks like the fees paid for his children's schools and a one-year notice period. As I was to learn, 'The king is dead, long live the king' is Alexander's mentality.

The pre-season was drawing to a close and there were four games left to play. These would be the first I was to see under my owner-ship and, oh boy, what joys awaited me.

I had been trying to develop a relationship with Coppell. He was a hero to the Palace fans. He had presided over the team's most successful period, the 1990 FA Cup Final and finishing third in what is now the Premier League. More recently, his hero status had been elevated further as he managed Palace through the period of administration and kept them in the division, which was all fine to me, so of course I wanted to try and galvanise the euphoria surrounding a new owner with the popularity of the manager, but this relationship wasn't really there. We seemed to be speaking different languages.

One evening he mentioned he was going scouting at Southend. I had heard he had been scouting with former chairmen, and I thought that this might be the ideal opportunity to start building a relationship with him. I asked if I could join him. Silence. Undeterred, I asked, 'What time?'

'Seven thirty at Southend,' was the disinterested response.

I mooted the idea of going together and was greeted with silence again, so I changed tone. 'OK, Steve, I would like us to go together,' I said and set about arranging a time and location to meet. We must have spent five minutes with me saying one time, him another, me suggesting where we met, him wanting to meet somewhere else . . . After losing the will to live, I decided no more debate. We meet at Selhurst Park at six, and go in my car. I had my driver, John, so Coppell and I could discuss business on the way to Southend.

I wish I hadn't bothered. I sat in the back of the car trying to strike up some form of rapport with him. It was like talking to the Grim Reaper. Everything was doom and gloom and very quickly I found it quite annoying. I had just spent £11.5 million and counting in three weeks, to listen to this negative, dour, unresponsive football manager do me a favour and sit in my car grunting at me.

As the journey continued I persevered, just to receive more of the same. In the end I remarked that he was so negative he was interfering with the signal strength on my phone. That raised a rare reaction, a smirk, and we discussed a few things like centre backs and was I prepared to spend £1.5 million on Jody Craddock at Man City etc., etc. I felt like I was being challenged and almost as if he wanted me to justify myself to him. So this fun-packed evening of bonding and bonhomie dragged by, and to top it all the game we watched was crap.

When we dropped him off later that evening, my driver John looked in the rear-view mirror and said, 'Excuse me, boss, but fuck me that was hard work.'

The excitement of watching my first game as owner against non-League Crawley Town, at the time only some 120-odd places below us in the football pyramid, as part of a pre-season schedule was tempered by a 5–1 thrashing. It was embarrassing.

When I asked Coppell afterwards what that was, 'I told you the deficiencies were deep,' was his reply.

'Are you joking, Steve? They are a non-League side, for crying out loud.'

All I got for my answer was a dismissive shrug.

And there was more to come. The following Wednesday we played Reading behind closed doors at the training ground. Reading were a league below us and managed by an ex-Palace player Alan Pardew and his assistant, Martin Allen. I remember hearing Pardew and Allen saying Palace had no arsehole and Reading should beat them up.

That offended everything I stood for as I did have an arsehole. Unfortunately my new team didn't, and we got thrashed 4–0.

Again, that oh-so-endearing shrug of the shoulders from Steve Coppell.

It was evident further strengthening was required and someone suggested the signing of Neil Ruddock from West Ham United. Ruddock had been a good player and a big name, and even Coppell thought it was a good idea. On approaching West Ham, I discovered he was a free transfer, although he did have a weighty salary – which was not the only weighty thing about him. West Ham were very helpful. Harry Redknapp, the West Ham manager at the time, told me to put in a weight clause. 'If his weight was right, he'd be right.' So I decided to put a 10 per cent penalty on the contract we were proposing to offer him if he was over the recommended weight of 99.8kg, which by the way was still frigging huge. At the time I was grateful to West Ham for being so helpful and open, but soon realised they could not believe their luck, and would have driven him round in a cab, or possibly, in his case, a bus.

I phoned the ever-enthused Coppell and asked him to come to the meeting with Ruddock, thinking the weight clause issue was better coming from the manager. I should have known better.

'I can't come,' he told me. 'I have a previous engagement I can't and won't change.'

'So, Steve, I am signing a player that costs ten thousand pounds a week and you can't come?'

'No, I can't.'

'OK, Steve, thanks for your help.'

I put the phone down, this guy was beginning to get on my nerves.

The raison d'être for Ruddock's signing was a statement of intent. He was an experienced ex-England player, a good leader and I hoped he would be an example to this young squad we were assembling, and what a fine example he turned out to be.

The next warm-up game was away to Millwall, one of Palace's biggest rivals just five or six miles down the road. Getting out of my car at the New Den I was greeted by a bunch of their supporters and for the first time I learnt my full name: 'Simon You-are-a-fucking-cunt Jordan'. It was to change over the years to 'Simon you blond-headed wanker' or 'Jordan you fucking poof'. Going to Millwall was always a pleasure.

So with that warm welcome I was looking forward to shutting up their fans with a resounding victory.

We lost 6–0!

And Ruddock didn't even play.

After getting the ringing of laughter out of my ears from the Millwall fans, I went down to their manager's office and saw Coppell in there. I declined to ask what the hell that was as another shrug might have resulted in the death of one of us. I just said: 'Where was Ruddock?'

'We didn't have a pair of shorts big enough for him and he would have looked like a right cunt out there,' said Coppell.

'Would have fitted in nicely with the rest of them, then,' was my response.

The silence that followed pretty much said it all for both of us.

The next morning my phone rang. It was Steve Coppell.

'Not working out, is it?' he said.

'Nope,' I replied.

'Shall we call it a day?'

'I think so,' disguising my enthusiasm for his suggestion.

And that was that. No massive blow-out, just two people who didn't gel. In hindsight, I think Coppell had been used to doing what he wanted and without having to answer to anyone. I was irritated by the lack of help he was prepared to give me in a whole new industry where I had no experience. Anyway, the reasons for our lack of chemistry were academic – we were parting company. It was a sure-fire way to lose some shine: appear to get rid of the fans' hero.

With the season less than two weeks away, things had just got a little more difficult. I had a brainwave that was to make life even harder. I decided to approach Alan Smith, the ex-Palace manager. Smith had led Palace to the Premier League in 1994 and they only got relegated when the League dropped an additional team for the first and only time in their history and Palace went down with a record forty-nine points.

He also fell out with Noades, which was always a plus for me, and knew his way round the place. He was currently running Fulham's youth academy and as Palace had a lot of young players, he seemed to be the ideal candidate.

I rang my newfound pal Peter Morley for his thoughts and advice. He had scant sympathy for Coppell. Reading between the lines I think Pete had found him difficult during administration and quite liked the idea of approaching Smith. He furnished me with his number. Thanks, Pete, you could have said you didn't have it . . .

That evening I met Alan Smith at the Selsdon Park Hotel, intent on offering him the job to succeed Coppell if he didn't say or do anything ridiculous. In my previous life I spent weeks, sometimes months, making senior appointments, but in this game, I did it at a hundred miles an hour and on the back of a fag packet.

We got on well and he asked if there was money available for players as he thought the squad needed significant strengthening. He asked what I expected, and naturally I said success. He also wanted to employ his own staff: Ray Houghton, the former Palace and Liverpool player, as his assistant and Glenn Cockerill, the ex-Southampton captain, as his first-team coach.

I have to say he was not quite what I expected, having spoken to him earlier in the day. In that call he came over as self-effacing with an edge of self-belief and cockiness. Yet on meeting him I could see he was more than enamoured with himself, but at least he was positive and talked a bloody good game.

We spoke for a couple of hours; I told him I would remove the existing first-team coach. Coppell had employed Brian Sparrow on his return from China. He had been in the job for about a week and was about to lose it. I learnt very quickly that football people walk around expecting this situation so the only reaction is 'What am I getting paid?' Paying someone for failing to do their job was one of the many things about football that was to perplex and irritate me.

Coppell came in on Monday morning and a statement was issued that said he was leaving by mutual consent. We agreed a figure to settle his contract. It was the first and only time I would pay a football manager what they wanted on their departure, which was a good thing as I went through my fair share in my unrelenting determination to bring success to this club.

Some fans were disappointed with Coppell's departure and maintained that I had forced him out. I was to find out that football fans and the media often believe what they want and don't let the truth stand in the way of their opinion.

After Coppell's departure I wanted to give the players the courtesy of an explanation. I soon learnt that wasn't time well spent.

On the whole, the players couldn't care less and were only concerned with things that directly affected them, such as how much they were getting paid and what cars they drove. Departure of managers was part of the territory and, more often than not, down to the performances of the players.

I took this opportunity to have a chat with Neil Ruddock about the importance of the example he would be setting and impressed upon him that I wanted him to lead the younger players. Neil said all the right things but I was to discover he was just a flash Herbert and was exactly the opposite of what I required.

I then phoned Fulham and spoke to their MD, Michael Fiddy, and informed him I wanted to speak to Alan Smith about the manager's job. It was football etiquette to ask permission. In real terms that is utter rubbish, but I did it. I found the concept of 'tapping up' slightly ludicrous as what was the point of not sounding someone out before approaching the club they worked for? Fiddy said no problem and good luck with him. That should have been a warning sign right there, a complete lack of concern about keeping Alan in what was a key role as academy director.

The next day the press conference was called and I introduced Alan Smith, Ray Houghton and Glenn Cockerill as my new management team. I also introduced the world to my bright red Ozwald Boateng suit, a fashion faux pas I was to regret for years to come, and proceeded to rattle on about my ambitions and my belief I had brought together a team with a 'winning mentality'. Because football is such a public business you get to say things in haste and repent at leisure. By now I had done lots of press and attracted a lot of attention being so young and, to be blunt, seemingly irreverent about everything.

Alan set about supplementing the squad or, let's call it what it actually was, spending my money. We had already secured Mikael

Forssell on a season-long loan deal from Chelsea and goalkeeper Stuart Taylor from Arsenal. We then signed Jamie Pollock for £750,000 from Manchester City and Craig Harrison from Middlesbrough for £250,000. So that was £2 million in four weeks and seven new players. All these signings were done in complete faith on my part, as this was the world I was now in and money kept it spinning. The key was to spend it wisely, again, learning the hard way.

The Sunday before the first game of the season the club had its annual open day where supporters got to tour the ground and meet all the players. It was my first experience of meeting the fans en masse. I pulled up in my 'trademark Ferrari', as it was now being called in the newspapers, and I was immediately surrounded by hundreds of fans. Two or three thousand people showed up that day, and for most of the afternoon I was signing autographs, which was a new experience but one I was soon to realise was part and parcel of the world of football.

On the whole I think we quite liked one another, the fans and I, despite my alleged treasonous removal of Coppell.

So after a somewhat difficult pre-season, with abhorrent results and now a new management team, we were to play our first game. We were playing away to the recently relegated and red-hot promotion favourites Blackburn Rovers, managed by the enigmatic Graeme Souness.

It was my first visit to a boardroom and Phil Alexander was drooling over the Blackburn directors and their facilities, like it was some kind of honour to be there. My attitude was, yes, it was impressive, but so what? I grabbed him to one side and said, 'For God's sake, Phil, stop walking around like we are lucky to be here.'

Blackburn as expected beat us quite comfortably 2–0, but it was bloody better than what I had seen to date.

After the game Graeme Souness, who I came to like very much, popped into the boardroom and made a point of saying hello. 'Welcome to the madhouse,' he joked.

'Well, if it's a madhouse, I should fit in nicely,' I replied.

I left quickly after the game, scowling at Phil Alexander for being such a flake and heading back to London.

Our opening home game of the season was the live televised game against QPR and so there was a fair degree of excitement. My friends from Rhode Island, USA, Walter and George, came over. It was also a busy media week. I did a big interview on Sky, and a radio phone-in with the late great Brian Moore, in which I was very verbose, stating I intended to put Palace back in the Premier League in five years. I even went as far as to say that in potential terms Palace were the fourth biggest club in London, which endeared me no end to the Premier League Charlton supporters.

On the day of the game I was walking my two pals George and Walter around the stadium. I had a message put up on the electronic scoreboard and drew their attention to it. 'To Walt and George . . .' They started to take pictures of the scoreboard before the message finished '. . . a right pair of wankers'. Well, if you own a football club and you can take the piss out of your mates, why wouldn't you?

We drew the game 1–1. After nearly six weeks, I had seen my team not get beaten – progress at last.

I had brought in two very important additions to support me. The first was my brother Dominic, initially as operations director, to look after all the logistics, starting with stadium maintenance and getting on with the remedial work, which it desperately needed.

Dominic's work became far-reaching as we uncovered so much abuse in every facet of the business – the culture was just rotten. We were being ripped off in every conceivable way: programme sellers pocketing monies; stewards signing one and another in for games when they were not there; merchandise being stolen by staff or given away; turnstile operators letting hundreds of their mates in per game for free. All of this – and more – cost us thousands of pounds.

I then brought in Kevin Watts, my human resources manager from PPS, as I knew that I would have to go through the staff with a dose of salts and would need a good HR guy.

On the commercial side, people's standards were low, their discipline was poor, they were generally quite sloppy and after about six weeks of being in there I set about changing things.

First thing every Monday morning at 7 a.m., which was a shock to their systems, we had a management meeting consisting of all the department heads. These management meetings were for them to put forward ideas on how to improve the business and they were told that if they didn't have any ideas, not to bother to come and work out how much longer they would be department heads for.

In the first meeting I was going round the table for their ideas and got to the academy director John Cartwright, head of our youth set-up, who said that the grass in the morning was a bit wet and we could get a machine to dry it. Well, at least he came up with something, I suppose!

For me, the youth development side of the club was of paramount importance. We had an academy, which was the real jewel in any club's crown, and was bloody expensive to run, but it was worth it. There were only twenty-odd academies in the country and hardly any of them outside of the Premier League.

Producing home-grown players had two great benefits. Fans

loved to see players coming through into the first team and the economics of producing your own players rather than buying them from other clubs was significant. I would rather have a young player come through our academy, get into the first team and see it as an honour and achievement to pull on the Crystal Palace shirt rather than sign players for £10,000 a week who do you a favour by just showing up.

John Cartwright was a former England Youth coach and a man with a big reputation. Coincidentally he had trained me as a young man at Palace so I was really looking forward to working with him. But my illusions were shattered very quickly. He was a very difficult, bitter and negative man.

Cartwright was not only on twice the money of most other academy directors in the country, he was also solely responsible for deciding which youth players got a pro contract. As a result of those contracts he would get a £5,000 bonus per player, so as you can imagine a fair splattering of young players each year were signed on pro contracts; none of them I might add went on to any great levels of success, with one notable exception, Steve Hunt, who is now at Wolves. It was a gravy train that was just about to get derailed. I was not having someone decide his own bonus with no accountability.

You would have thought given all of this that he would have been helpful but he was downright divisive from day one. He objected to being in management meetings and having to provide any information to someone like me – i.e. his boss and paymaster – and had no desire to form any dialogue with the first-team manager. Basically, Cartwright didn't want to be part of a regime that was dynamic, supportive, wanted best practice and good order. Kevin Watts concluded that he was trying to bait me into firing him so he could get a big pay-off.

In one meeting Cartwright asked: 'Does anyone else think the morale is low?' This was clearly directed at me and after the meeting I dealt with him in no uncertain terms. It was disappointing to me that he was so negative and so destructive. He just basically wanted to make things difficult and was a major exponent of the sentiment of 'we don't do things that way'. The academy was too important for me to play these kinds of games.

Despite my gut reaction to just fire the destructive, disrespectful Cartwright, he was managed out of the business by Kevin and paid a smaller amount of money than he wanted. But we got rid of an extremely bad apple. Unfortunately he was not alone and I was to go very quickly through a lot of the staff I had inherited as this mentality existed in a lot of them.

As if I was not having enough fun it wasn't long until I experienced my first example of football's internal bullshit and the nonsense that goes on inside this self-serving, make-the-rules-up-as-you-go-along industry. The club was being taken to the football tribunal by a player, Craig Foster, an Australian who hadn't got his work permit renewed due to failing to meet the necessary criteria. Nevertheless, he was expecting to be paid up for the rest of his contract, which was for another two years.

Every year Foster was required to have his work permit renewed. To do this he had to have been a key member of the team for the club he played for and also play in over 60 per cent of the available international games for his country. Foster qualified on neither front, and without a work permit he couldn't legally play professional football in this country.

At tribunal the case advanced by the PFA, the players' union, and his lawyers was that even though he was not able to work or be paid legally under the laws of the land in this country, he should still be paid two years' money – around £600,000 – for doing nothing according to the 'laws of football'. Foster's interest level was so great he couldn't even be bothered to come back for his work permit hearing, let alone attend this kangaroo court. He just wanted to be paid.

The tribunal was made up of my first experience of so-called 'football people'. You had a Football League representative, an FA council member, an ex-manager, Frank Clark the former Nottingham Forest boss, and you had a chairman who was a QC. And guess who got to pay for them attending? Muggins.

It was a complete try-on. It was the football establishment closing ranks around a newcomer, which believe it or not is how football really works, self-interest at all times.

Before Coppell left, the subject of Foster had come up and he had said in no uncertain terms that he didn't rate the player and he would rather not have him back, preferring to use the money on someone better. So it came as a surprise to see Coppell as one of his key witnesses, and I was outraged when he got on the stand and told the tribunal that Foster was a major player and part of his squad plans if he had remained in charge. I nearly choked.

It was clear that the tribunal wanted to make Crystal Palace, or more pertinently me, pay Foster, even though the law of the land said differently. When I went on the stand I launched into a diatribe. I said that I didn't recognise the authority of this tribunal, and pointed out that if they awarded the player this money they would be breaking the law and I would take this into the public domain. I also launched a scathing attack on Coppell, quoting exactly what he had told me. All of which I am sure endeared me to the establishment no end.

In one of the breaks I bumped into Frank Clark, who had the damn audacity to tell me this is how football was, I should accept this and just pay it. I erupted with fury and we had to be separated.

My legal team really cranked up the legality of it all. Despite their best endeavours the tribunal knew they couldn't find a basis that wouldn't be challenged outside of the football world, although they bloody tried.

Most people accepted the internal self-regulation of football. From the get-go that was not me and I put the football establishment on notice very early of that.

The decision was begrudgingly given: we didn't have to pay Foster's wages but had to pay his signing-on fees of £100,000, which they argued could have been paid at the start of his contract. This enraged me. I had to pay £100 grand to a player I had never even seen, as well as £10,000 worth of costs for the comic tribunal. Taking the damn thing to the High Court would have been uneconomical so I had to get on with it, but not before telling the tribunal exactly what I thought of them.

This was my first experience of how everybody else, bar the owners and funders of the clubs, seemed to be looked after. Everything appeared to be geared to the well-being of players, agents and managers and tough shit on the club owners – how can that be right?

Then, and over the years to come, I listened to what was, in my opinion, supercilious rot from Gordon Taylor, the head of the PFA, a man who ran the smallest union around but had the biggest salary of any union leader, who talked about players' wages and how they have a short career. If you are earning £5,000, £10,000, £50,000 a week it can afford to be a short career.

Also players were insured for injuries, which most of the time was paid for by the club, so if their career finished then they would get a huge pay-out.

Managers had fixed-term contracts and if they were fired for doing a poor job, they got paid up to the end of their contract or part of it. In other words: paid to fail.

Despite our first point, the team had started poorly, winning only one of our first five games. Alan Smith was having trouble with certain players and struggling to get control over them. One particular player was getting up his nose, Jamie Fullerton, a Scottish international and a barrack-room lawyer. Every club had one, apparently, and Alan wanted rid of him. So I did it for him, which should have set off alarm bells for me as the manager should be able to deal with these things himself, but again I was learning the hard way.

I sent Fullerton a letter about his conduct and he ignored it. So I had Kevin Watts remove him from the training ground in front of all the players. Within hours I had his agent on the phone, demanding he was either reinstated or paid off. That call was quickly followed by one from the PFA. I told them all to go forth and multiply.

The next day he returned to training, and again I had him removed. I warned him I would call the police and have him arrested for trespassing. I knew I couldn't but I wanted him to realise I was serious. We also served him with a dismissal notice. His agent and the PFA were up in arms demanding meetings; I refused.

At the time this was controversial behaviour. The PFA were powerful and used to getting their way, but not with me. Players were under the impression they could do and say as they pleased – perhaps they could in other clubs but not here. After a short war of attrition the penny dropped and Fullerton was moved out to Dundee on a free transfer.

I wanted to support Alan as much as I could, so as well as ridding him of troublesome players, I supported him with purchases. He wanted a goalkeeper and an attacking winger. The two players he identified were in the Latvian national team managed by Garry Johnson.

Allegedly we scouted both of them. I say 'allegedly' because at later times when I looked into the actual scouting and research behind buying players and multi-million-pound investments of my money there was not a lot, another thing I learnt the hard way and set about changing.

They both played for Skonto Riga in Latvia. I bet the club couldn't believe their luck when we paid £650,000 for keeper Aleksandrs Kolinko and £1.5 million for winger Andrejs Rubins. I spoke to Gary Johnson whose words were: 'You can stand on me on these two players' and I can assure you there were many times later I wished I had stood on Johnson from a great height.

Their agent was Phil Graham. Physically he reminded me of a cross between Ming the Merciless and Dick Dastardly. He wanted a large commission for getting them to join the club, but I was not prepared to pay him a fee as he was working for the players negotiating their contracts.

An avaricious man, Graham said he would be able to reduce the players' wages to a figure I was comfortable with if I paid him. This was the first example of how disingenuous agents were and how much they really cared about their clients, although the players would never believe it.

At the end of September we had played ten games, had the princely sum of eight points and were third from bottom of the league. This was despite having brought in nine players and spent over £5 million on transfer fees, as well as taking several highly paid Premier League players on loan. It was not quite the start I had envisaged. Coupled with the investment in the team, I was buying a new eight-acre training ground for £1 million. I was certainly putting my money where my mouth was, but getting scant return.

Alan decided that during the international break he wanted to take the players away on a five-day trip to a training camp in Jerez in southern Spain. This was supposed to boost morale and help the players bond.

So in the first week of October this bunch of ingrates were ferried off to a camp to train and get themselves together. I joined them at Alan's request; the surroundings were absolutely first class. I watched a couple of training sessions and played some golf.

Over the first few months I had had little contact with the players, preferring as much as possible that the manager deal with them, but of course I knew who was who. I also got the impression they eyed me warily. One of our more talented young players was Clinton Morrison, who had a rather unfortunate attitude, so I had formed a dim view of the little rat bag. I later christened him the 'Pest', which was how I always referred to him. He was a belligerent little runt and on one afternoon in this luxury training ground in gorgeous Spain he sauntered past me with some of his teammates. I went to acknowledge them and was greeted by Morrison with a scowl and a kissing of his teeth. No, Clinton, not at me.

I called Morrison over and let him have both barrels. 'Listen, you, I have had about enough of your shitty little attitude. Next time you kiss your teeth I am going to kick them down the back of your throat.'

This shocked him and his teammates: it was not how the chairman was supposed to speak to his players.

From that day forward I never had another problem with Clinton. He was a good lad underneath all his bluster and I became one of his major supporters, awarding him a new contract later that season. I had a very good relationship with both him and his mother, who was very important to him – just ask Rufus Brevett of West Ham, who had a scrap with Angela Morrison in a players' lounge.

Whilst I was in Spain I found the atmosphere to be a little too carefree and easy. Certain players and management were going out at night to some local bar, which I soon found out doubled as a knocking shop.

The last day comes around and the players are having a drink in the hotel bar so I decide to join them. Sitting in the corner was Andy Linighan, last year's player of the year. He was a brooding character and it was obvious that he had been drinking heavily; I made the mistake of trying to engage him in a conversation. He wasted precious time airing his grievances, claiming the trip was 'shit', questioning why he wasn't in the team and demanding to know why Steve Coppell had been sacked, although apparently he had never liked Coppell anyway. Rather than quit whilst he was ahead, which incidentally he was not, he then turned his verbal attentions to me, being quite provocative and confrontational. I tried to calm the situation but Linighan was having none of it, finally overstepping the line by saying I knew 'shit about football and should stick to selling mobile phones'. All of this was listened to by the other players.

I kept my temper through gritted teeth, said goodnight to the other players and left the room, raging. The assistant manager Houghton and the rest of the coaching staff were sitting at a table in another part of the hotel as I burst in. I gave them a rundown of the conversation I had just had with Linighan. 'I want this drunken imbecile dealt with,' I said.

Houghton and Cockerill went out to see him as he was staggering out of the toilets. Houghton was the first to speak to him.

Linighan snarled back, 'You can fuck off too, you little cunt' and then headed for the door and went out into the night.

That was it for me. I got Alan Smith out of bed and my PA on the phone and told her to book Linighan on the first flight out of Spain. Then I told Cockerill and Houghton to go into his room, pack up his stuff and wait for him.

About 5 a.m. the phone rang.

'Chairman, it's Andrew.'

'Who?' I ask.

'Andy Linighan, why am I being sent home? I'm sorry. I love this club, chairman.'

'I don't care, Andrew, you don't get to abuse me in public and apologise on the QT.'

'I am not going, chairman,' he said weakly.

'Oh yes you are, if I have to physically put you in the car,' and I hung up.

Linighan caught his flight and the rumour circulated amongst the players that there had been retribution for Linighan's unacceptable behaviour.

I flew back from Spain to headlines in the *Sun* that there had been a fight between the player and myself. Once back I wasted little time terminating Linighan's contract. Another bad egg gone, but I was far from impressed with Alan's control over this trip.

As if I didn't have enough on my plate I became embroiled in a row with Terry Venables. After Kevin Keegan had walked out on England, the press were speculating about who should be the next England manager and I was asked my view as Venables was a former Palace manager and was heavily tipped to succeed him. I don't know what the big deal was. I just said if Venables was the only name on the list for England manager, then it was a very poor state of affairs for English football.

This provoked a furious response from Venables and his agent Leon Angel called me, demanding I make a public apology.

I told Angel where to go, as I was just saying what I thought. This was the first of a few altercations with Angel over the years.

During my first season I joined the team on Friday evenings on away games staying in the same hotel. I noticed that the players were put to bed early but the management team and other back-room staff would stay up drinking quite heavily, on expenses of course! This struck me as strange the night before a game, but looking back for some reason I stupidly accepted that this was part and parcel of the management team bonding. In fact, it was them taking liberties, and after seeing them getting on the team coach blurry-eyed and hung over one time too many, I banned them from drinking the night before an away game.

Soon we were in the papers again. This time the story was about Ruddock, the player I had personally asked to set a shining example for the rest of the team. He had taken the players out after a game (which they had lost!) to a swish London hotel for a night out and the papers claimed they were drunk, singing 'going down going down'.

Naturally, when I confronted Alan Smith and Ruddock, they denied the story was true.

In my desire to make the players proud of their club and for us to look the part one of my not-so-bright ideas was to get all the players and management to wear club suits. Not just any suits. I wanted them to wear suits made by the celebrity tailor Ozwald Boateng. I wanted the suits to be handmade and I wanted the lining of the jackets to be red and blue, Palace's team colours.

It turned out to be a nightmare as footballers come in all shapes and sizes and not all are suited to the designs of highfalutin Savile Row tailors, especially the kind of suits that Boateng produced, which were fine for lithe – OK, skinny – people like myself but not so good for strapping young footballers and slightly pot-bellied coaching staff.

Our next game was at home to Grimsby, a team we would expect to beat. The performance was dire. Looking back it was no wonder, given the leadership from Alan Smith and his team and the example they were setting. After this game I took an action which followed me for many years and shaped people's perception of me. For the first and only time, I went into the dressing room to talk to the players about their performance. Smith was talking to them and, in the middle of his speech, Andy Morrison, a player on loan from Manchester City, stood up, bent over and farted.

That was it for me. I'd had enough and exploded with rage at the players. You have to accept the industrial language, as this was how they spoke and anyway was the only language this fucking lot understood.

'How fucking dare you think you can behave the way you are and put out fucking performances like that? You are a fucking embarrassment. If you are under the impression you are going to get this manager the sack, you are very fucking wrong, and you will all go before he does.

'If you don't want to be here then you can all fuck off and form an orderly queue outside my office and I will get you away from this club. Have some pride.'

Surprise, surprise, there was no response. They were all looking to the floor like little boys.

I walked out, taking Alan with me, and sat in his office.

'Get a hold of this, Alan. Whether I was right or wrong to come into the dressing room I have done it because you are not dealing with it. I want you to take a stance and put Mullins, Morrison and Jamie Smith on the transfer list tomorrow.'

This was shock tactics. Mullins and Morrison were amongst our star young players and Jamie Smith was considered to be a strong character. The next morning, much to the surprise of their team-mates we transfer-listed them – ironically we received no offers, giving them a touch of reality – and Alan Smith went and did a massive interview in the papers, and the headline was, 'Players are lazy, sloppy overpaid whingers who only care about what they look like.' This sort of outburst was unheard of at the time in football, especially from a manager.

My mentality was to support my manager, and to build a club on a foundation of respect. I didn't deliberately seek controversy or confrontation, I just didn't avoid it. I wanted the players and management to behave as winners and role models, not this sham-bles, but because of my determination and single-mindedness and, at times, ignorance, I was building myself a reputation in the media.

My programme notes were also attracting attention. I wrote them for every game. I didn't pull any punches and was very stri-dent in my opinions. Within a year, segments of my column were being lifted by lazy journalists and put in match reports, which put a stop to me writing in the programme.

My attitude towards other football clubs had also not gone unnoticed. I was not overly interested in going into boardrooms: I went to games to win, not to fraternise; drinking Chardonnay with the 'enemy' didn't interest me. I expressed this sentiment quite openly, which I suspect made the owners of other teams think 'Who is that cocky arrogant bastard?' But frankly I didn't care about their opinion.

I had walked out of a couple of boardrooms as they would not allow my guests in, preferring to go in the public bar instead; I had been refused admission in one boardroom as I was not wearing a tie. The trend of not going into the boardroom was to continue over the years. I much preferred eating a hot dog in the car park outside away grounds than eating prawn sandwiches in the board-room, although my outlook softened as time went by.

As if a light had been turned on, the team suddenly clicked.

It started with an away game at Leicester in the League Cup. They were the cup holders. The Premier League outfit put out a full-strength side to defend their trophy and were expected to win with relative ease. The team performance was outstanding and we trounced them 3–0.

Around this time I allowed Alan to supplement the squad even further and we took Steve Staunton on loan from Aston Villa and attempted to sign James Beattie from Southampton. Glenn Hoddle, the ex-England manager now at Southampton, accepted an offer for £1.5 million, but then the Southampton chairman Rupert Lowe got involved. He wanted £2 million. I told him that we had already agreed a price with Hoddle and Lowe told me that Glenn had changed his mind.

'Well, that's not very Christian of him,' I remarked, referring to his much publicised religious beliefs.

So I offered £2 million, but then Lowe wanted £2.5 million so I made that offer. He hiked it up to £3 million, and once again I offered what he asked for and then he came back with £3.5 million.

That was it as far as I was concerned. Alan still wanted another striker and I suggested Dougie Freeman, an old favourite. I bought him back from Nottingham Forest for £750,000, little realising that it would prove to be some of the best money I would spend at the club.

After the cup win the team went on a great run, winning a succession of games that fired us up the league. Our cup run continued and we beat Sunderland again from the Premier League to reach the semi-finals, where we faced Merseyside giants Liverpool.

After six months of turmoil we seemed to be in a period of harmony. The only exception was Ruddock, whose performances and conduct at the club had been far from exemplary. Alan was fed up with him. He had been sent off twice, had been at the heart of off-the-field nonsense and was fined eight times for being over-weight.

My patience finally snapped and I summoned him to Selhurst Park. Sheepishly, Ruddock came into my office and I proceeded to give him a tongue-lashing. I told him he was a disgrace, calling him a fat slob and to my amazement he broke down. Ruddock was sat in my office whining about his weight and moaning about his personal life. This cut no ice with me. I warned him that if he wasn't under the weight level in forty-eight hours I would find some way to fire him.

He weighed in underweight for the first time for two months and stood on the scales celebrating like a boxer, in his case a bloody heavyweight. The point was made but it was the beginning of the end for him at Palace.

Players seemed to think they lived on an island on their own where the normal rules of society or employment didn't apply to them. I did an interview around this time, cryptically saying that 'I cared about players as much as they cared about me.' Daniel Sugar, Lord Sugar's son, phoned me to say that my comment had greatly amused his father as he knew exactly what I had meant when I said it. The culture of football revolved around taking liberties, and players were the biggest exponents of it.

Three examples sum up the culture of a large number of foot-ballers. The first was the squad training kit. No sooner was it shipped to the training ground for the players to wear during the season than it was reported lost, as certain highly paid players were stuffing it in the boots of their cars and selling it as knock-offs. Then there was the married player on loan who was staying in a hotel on his own and complaining about not seeing his wife for weeks, but putting condoms on his expenses claim. Lastly there was the player who came into my office with his agent, clutching four match reports from the *Sun* where journalists had given him a high performance rating. This he saw as a reason for me giving him a fat new contract. Pillars of society? No. Just young boys being paid a lot of money by people like me and afforded sometimes far too much leniency in the scheme of the world.

January came around and we played Liverpool in the first leg of the League Cup semi-final at home in front of a full house; the atmosphere was electric. I had invited John Barton, a devout Liverpool fan and the MD of 121 who seven months earlier had sanctioned the purchase of PPS, giving me the money to waste – sorry, invest – on football. We pulled off a sensational 2–1 victory with goals from Rubins and Clinton Morrison. Liverpool got a goal back with ten minutes to go but the headlines were about how Morrison's performance and Alan Smith's management had turned Palace around.

But of course there was some controversy that had been stirred up by the papers. Morrison was asked if he had as many chances as Michael Owen would he have expected to have put them away? Clinton of course said yes, which the papers turned into Morrison considering himself better than Owen.

'The Cocky Face of Division 1 puts the Premier League Mighty in their place' was just one of their headlines and set up a spicy return leg at Anfield.

Alan had started believing his own press, and had become a little bit difficult to deal with. He loved seeing himself in the papers. I remember around this time taking him for a drink at the Fifth Floor Bar at Harvey Nichols. He was carrying around a copy of the *Evening Standard* as it had a big picture of him on the back cover.

I will always remember Alan walking down the road outside Harrods and some guy coming up to him with a magazine. Alan must have assumed he had been recognised and took the magazine and signed it. The guy just looked at him in total amazement, as he was a *Big Issue* seller and wanted Alan to buy one, not give him his bloody autograph.

The eagerly awaited Merseyside return leg arrived, and it was a media circus. I came into Anfield with the team and as we walked through, Gérard Houllier, then Liverpool manager, was waiting for us, insisting on shaking everybody's hand and wishing them luck. This annoyed me intensely as it was clearly just a mind game, so I ignored him and walked past.

But this was nothing to what I was going to get in their boardroom.

Before going upstairs I went in and wished Alan and his staff good luck and told them how proud I was of them, irrespective of the result.

I only went into Liverpool's boardroom because my best friend Mark Ryan was a big Liverpool fan and had brought his dad along. We were roundly ignored by their chairman David Moores, but one of the Liverpool directors handed me a plaque, saying, 'We like to give the smaller teams a memento of their visit to Anfield.'

I responded in the only way I knew: 'You are fucking kidding me.'

I turned away handing my coat off to one of the boardroom

attendants to hang up. Unfortunately it wasn't a boardroom attendant, it was Chris De Burgh the singer of 'Lady in Red'.

How embarrassing. But in fairness, he did hang it up for me.

I looked at the famous Anfield chairman's room. It was the size of a broom cupboard with a big chandelier in the middle of it that almost touched the floor.

As Moores refused to even acknowledge me my only thought was, 'God, I hope we beat these arseholes.' That was another prayer that went unanswered: we were trounced 5–0.

Alan Smith had made a rousing speech before the game, telling the players they needed to hold Liverpool at bay for the first fifteen minutes and we had a chance of pulling off a major shock. That worked. Fifteen minutes into the game we were already 3–0 down.

Liverpool had moved Steven Gerrard to right back to stop Rubins and in the first five minutes he crunched him with a welcome to Anfield message. Rubins was never the same after that game.

So we were brought down to earth with a bang, and that light, which had suddenly come on for the team, was just as suddenly switched off. The team went into complete free fall and failed to win in the following twelve matches.

We dropped down the league like a stone. I went out and signed more players, including Matthew Upson on loan from Arsenal and agreed to cover his £10,000-a-week wages. I was later to find out that was one of those favours David Dein liked to do for you, as he was only earning £5,000 a week at Arsenal.

We also signed Ricardo Fuller and Gregg Berhalter, a US international, and Aki Riihilahti, who had just scored for Finland against England in the 2001 World Cup qualifier at Anfield.

Then I went and spent a further £1.5 million bringing Palace hero David Hopkin back from Bradford. Hopkin was on £16,000 a week, which was huge for the then First Division, and didn't even want to come back to Selhurst Park. So I flew up to Bradford with Ray Houghton, who had played with Hopkin at Palace and went to meet the Bradford chairman Geoffrey Richmond. I always liked Geoffrey. He was a huge man and reminded me a bit of Bernard Ingham, Margaret Thatcher's press secretary. There was quite a bit of the dour blustery northerner about him, but I warmed to him because he had a great sense of humour.

He was desperate to sell Hopkin as they needed the money and were about to be relegated from the Premier League. For some reason I had convinced myself we were desperate to sign Hopkin as our plight was now pretty perilous.

Richmond called in Hopkin and after a preamble where the player expressed his views, namely he was quite happy where he was thank you very much, an instantaneously incandescent Richmond announced, 'I don't like you and I have never liked you. If you want to stay then by all means stay, but I promise you I will make your life a fucking misery.'

Hopkin was stunned, and stammered, 'But I have never met you, chairman.'

Undeterred Richmond boomed back, 'I don't care; I don't like you.' Geoffrey was a huge man and clearly used to intimidating players.

Hopkin left the room to talk to Houghton and Geoffrey winked at me. 'Fuck me,' I said, 'I thought I could bang a bit.' Within minutes Hopkin came back in and agreed to sign.

The next game we lost 2–0 to Preston, plunging us into even deeper trouble.

No sooner had we signed a midfielder, than another one fell out with the club, Alan and ultimately me. Jamie Pollock had been difficult for Alan Smith to manage all season. He was a bright lad, with a slightly inflated opinion of his own importance. He had clashed with Smith on a number of occasions. He had been sent off in an earlier fixture and missed the Preston game through suspension, but had taken it upon himself to go on radio and criticise Alan and his team selection. This resulted in an ugly altercation between Alan, myself and Pollock and us shipping him out the door on loan to Birmingham.

Rather than shoulder the blame for the team's failing, Smith looked to deflect some of it on to the coaching staff he himself employed. As a result, he fired the first-team coach Glenn Cockerill, who probably was the weakest link in the chain between himself and the assistant manager Ray Houghton. Smith then brought in Terry Bullivant as first-team coach. Earlier in the year he had rehired Stevie Kember, who was a Palace legend, making him reserve team manager. Without knowing it, Smith had hired his immediate successors.

We finally reached crisis point on 28 April, losing 2–0 at home to Wolves.

The fans were in an uproar. Alan Smith had been getting a hard time from them in recent weeks but this loss looked more than likely to have guaranteed relegation.

I had spent £8.75 million – a huge sum in the First Division in 2001 – on players and quadrupled the wages bill and we were staring at relegation. A unified crowd booed Alan off the pitch. Ironically, the same crowd who three months earlier had proclaimed him a hero turned on him with absolute vilification.

I made a decision after the game. It was time for him to go.

What choice did I have? He had lost the support of the fans and the dressing room and if we were going down, I wasn't going down without a fight.

I walked into Alan's office and with great sadness, the only time I ever really felt it, I fired him. I think Ray Houghton was expecting to take over the team but I fired him as well.

From the fans' point of view, it was too little, too late, but I had done it and took the monumental decision to put Steve Kember and Terry Bullivant in temporary charge for the final two away games.

Over the years my relationship with the Palace fans was very important to me. In all football clubs, fans are the lifeblood of the game. Without fans you have empty stadiums and the air football breathes is made up of the fans' fervour. For the ten years that I owned the club, I enjoyed a very good relationship with 95 per cent of the fans. Of course, there was always a vociferous minority on websites, and for them, even if I had bought Lionel Messi, built a brand-new stadium and halved the ticket prices, they still would have said the hot dogs were shit. But I enjoyed a unique relationship with Palace fans and over the years that was to extend to fans of a lot of other clubs who liked the fact I was prepared to stand up for what I believed in.

Early in my tenure I went into the fans' end in an away game at Norwich and was picked up and lifted in the air and thrown from the front to the back of the stand for ten minutes as their way of saying hello to their new chairman. Whilst that was fine, sitting with the fans is not usually the right thing to do. Fans want to know you are funding and running your club, not necessarily sitting next to them in the stands.

I had a particular affection for away fans as their passion and fervour was something to behold and I admired and respected them for their commitment, so much so that during my first season I refunded the entire away support their ticket money for one particularly inept performance in an away game to Barnsley. Nothing like this had ever been done before, but I felt it was the right thing to do.

*   *   *

Back to the last two games. We needed to win both of them and then rely on other results going our way to avoid relegation.

Steve and Terry were very calm and confident. I suspect they felt they had nothing to lose.

They changed the team around and we went to Portsmouth three days after that shocking display at home to Wolves.

Portsmouth were also in a relegation battle so this was a must win game for both sides. We destroyed them, winning 4–2.

We had given ourselves a chance. We needed to win away on the Sunday against Stockport and hope other results went our way. It appeared relegation was between Portsmouth and us. The game on Sunday was televised and we took 3,000 fans down to Stockport.

I sat up in the stand watching the game unfold with the chief scout Barry Simmonds.

Less than a year ago I had been sitting in my offices at PPS selling a business for a vast amount of money, now I was sitting at a football match watching a club I had owned for less than a year that I had pumped £20 million-odd into, and we were facing relegation, which would have huge financial ramifications.

The game was not a pleasant experience as we huffed and puffed and at half-time it was 0–0. Portsmouth were winning their game, and it looked like we were going to be relegated.

We had chance after chance in the second half. When we missed one chance I kicked the structure in front of my seat, putting my foot through it in exasperation. I had to pay for it later.

The game was coming to a close and out of the blue with three minutes to go, we scored.

David Hopkin, who ironically hadn't wanted to play for Palace, blatantly handled the ball on the edge of our box and the referee completely missed it.

He cleared it upfield to Clinton Morrison, who put Dougie

Freedman through on goal and he scored, catapulting himself into legend status at Palace.

Cue pandemonium from the fans who burst onto the pitch. It took two or three minutes to restore order. Portsmouth had won and appeared safe but Huddersfield, who went into the last game two points clear of the relegation zone, were losing at home to Birmingham. If we held onto the lead they would be the club to drop.

We did just hold on and waited five minutes after our game for the Huddersfield result to come through. They had lost when the Birmingham goalkeeper made a wonder save in the last minute. We had avoided relegation by one point and were celebrating narrowly avoiding failure. Said it all, really.

The journey home was riotous as myself and Dominic travelled back on the team bus and celebrated with the team. At the time, the avoidance of failure felt like winning. God, I was so bloody naïve.

The next night I took the players out for an end-of-season dinner at Quaglino's and then to the lap-dancing venue Spearmint Rhino's in London. I gave the players £5,000 and told them to have some fun – not something I suspect most chairmen would do. Well, I suppose that's what happens when your chairman is aged thirty-two. The next morning my phone rang. It was one of the red-top news-papers, alerting me to the fact that my players had been out last night en masse and had been in a lap-dancing bar. I said, 'I know, I was with them.' That stopped them in their tracks.

I had learnt so much during that season. I never meant to have all this aggravation, it just followed me because I wouldn't accept things as they were. I was a proud man and wanted a club to be proud of and I would stop at nothing to get it. The narrow escape at the end of the season convinced me that fortune favours the brave and I was golden. But I was to learn that life affords you both good luck and bad, and I had just used up a large slice of my good luck.

7

ITV DIGITAL: THE FOOTBALL LEAGUE ARMAGEDDON

The irony of the launch of ONdigital in a blaze of publicity at Crystal Palace in November 1998 will never be lost on me.

The omens weren't exactly great when ONdigital decided to use Ulrika Jonsson to host their lavish launch party. After all, this was the same Ulrika Jonsson who failed to meet her financial obligations to me when I owned PPS, so – although at the time I was looking at it all from an outsider's perspective – I should have suspected that there was a good chance the company she was representing wouldn't deliver either.

From the outset ONdigital's business plan was doomed.

The first chief executive, Stephen Grabiner, declared war on BSkyB with aggressive bids for movie and football rights, while principal shareholders Carlton and Granada decided to withhold the ITV service from BSkyB subscribers in an attempt to lure them to ONdigital.

But they had a formidable enemy in Rupert Murdoch. They just didn't have the wherewithal to take him on. And of course, they crashed and burned – everyone could see it coming. ITV Digital

– which had been rebranded from ONdigital in a failed attempt to reinvigorate the company – held the broadcasting rights outside of the Premier League, so their collapse would see the Football League face the biggest crisis in its history.

And this crisis would bring me very much to the fore in the game as I wasn't prepared to sit back and say nothing. It would lead to me being categorised as a dangerous commodity by football's powers-that-be. I unnerved them as I was determined to bring into the public domain those that were culpable for perpetuating the wrongdoings, hypocrisy and bad practices in football.

In the summer of 2000 the Football League had signed a new broadcasting deal with the newly rebranded ITV Digital. It was a three-year deal for £315 million, representing a phenomenal increase in money for the League and its clubs.

Since its inception in 1992, the Premier League had a broadcasting partner in Sky, which proved massively lucrative for them. In comparison, the broadcasting revenues available to Divisions One, Two and Three were pitiful. These leagues watched powerlessly as the Premier League got richer and richer.

As a result of the massive increase in rights monies from Sky, the players' salaries were hugely increased in the Premier League. This had a trickle-down effect on clubs in the Football League, where salaries went up without the associated TV income. The new deal with ITV Digital was an attempt to redress the financial imbalance between the Football League and the Premier League.

The deal was negotiated by a team that included David Sheepshanks, former chairman of the Football League and also chairman of Ipswich, which – fortunately for them – had just got promoted to the Premier League in 2000. He disappeared into the

Premier League, patting himself on the back for brokering this supposed ground-breaking deal.

ITV Digital and Sky were in direct competition for the satellite and digital market. But one of ITV Digital's major problems, and they had many, was that they would need to use Sky's broadcasting platform. Understandably, BSkyB were not overly keen to help them with this. Added to this, ITV Digital had made a vast investment in order to secure the Football League rights, which made the commerciality of this deal difficult to understand as ITV Digital were going to need a hell of a lot of subscribers to make this work. And Sky's TV packages were just more tempting to the consumer.

It's worth mentioning at this point that the Football League was comprised of seventy-two clubs with very different backgrounds and outlooks, which made its structure antiquated and unwieldy, unlike the Premier League, which only had twenty members, and a common agenda: money. The Football League meetings were dull and listless and more about discussing small-minded business, and on the whole attended by each club's CEO, unlike the Premier League meetings, where the owners tended to be in attendance. In my experience, a lot of the CEOs of Football League clubs were either ex-footballers or people who had somehow drifted into football but who would never occupy such positions of prominence in any other industry. So I had long since stopped attending these fruitless meetings. I had, however, found solidarity with a few of my fellow chairmen, notably Theo Paphitis of Millwall, Geoffrey Richmond of Bradford, and Charles Koppel of Wimbledon, with whom Palace shared a ground. These men were all to become my firm friends.

Back to the deal. In commercial terms, for the Football League clubs it meant there was £105 million of additional revenue per year. The bulk of the cash – some 80 per cent – went to Division One clubs, which would receive £3.5 million per season for three years, quadrupling what had been available previously. The money was paid out in various tranches and clubs obviously factored them into their cash flows and expenditure. The clubs in the lower divisions, unsurprisingly, although in my opinion unrealistically given the main interest from the broadcaster was Division One clubs, greatly resented the way the money was allocated.

Keith Harris and David Burns, the new Football League chairman and CEO respectively, picked up the deal from the likes of Sheepshanks with a view to completing it.

What had not been done was the long-form agreement, and it had not been signed off at Granada and Carlton's end. More importantly for everyone concerned, ITV Digital was essentially a new business, which meant that there was no indication that they could pay the £315 million contract they were committed to.

There were no bank guarantees in place for this money.

What there was supposed to be were parent company guarantees from Carlton and Granada, who were very financially well established, but these guarantees didn't exist. In layman terms, it was like selling a complete stranger your car and allowing them to drive off with it, leaving you with an IOU drawn up on the back of a fag packet. You wouldn't do it. The only difference here was you had supposedly competent and credible representation – i.e. the Football League Board – assuring you your money was fine.

Between Harris and Burns, the deal descended into a farce, and to make matters worse on the few occasions they were asked if everything was in order, they assured everyone that it was.

Given the Football League hierarchy had lauded this deal and applauded themselves for doing it, and assured their clubs that the money was guaranteed, the clubs of course spent it accordingly, thus being exposed to the foibles of a start-up business that could fail, and fail it did.

Harris and Burns were guilty of shocking naivety in not under-standing the importance of tying up the guarantees, but more pertinently were culpable in not volunteering critical information, as clubs simply assumed that if their paid and elected heads assured them that a deal was good, it was.

In the second year of this deal, late in 2001, all manner of rumours began to circulate about the health of ITV Digital, from a contract renegotiation to impending collapse. As a result, people like Theo Paphitis, Geoffrey Richmond, Charles Koppel and myself were asking some serious pointed questions. In a meeting, out of the blue and almost as an aside, David Burns announced that the parent company guarantees hadn't been signed and very quickly the horrific potential of this information dawned on the clubs.

If ITV Digital failed and went into administration, the clubs wouldn't receive the balance of their monies, which most had budgeted for and spent accordingly. As these ramifications were digested, the temperature amongst the chairmen of Football League clubs, especially those in Division One who stood to lose the most, became red-hot.

Outside the meeting room, it became a furious media circus, with me, Theo, and others such as Karren Brady, railing against ITV Digital quite publicly.

It was soon clear that Burns and Harris had allowed this mess to escalate and attempted to cover it up while – I assume – they tried to resolve it. They may have inherited it, but they allowed it to continue. Their decision now was to try and force ITV Digital by public pressure to honour their obligations and pay this money, which stood at £180 million. They also sought to get political intervention. But the government was never going to get involved, so this was an absurd tactic.

We had to negotiate a deal, we would have to deal down, but our 'leaders' did not do this and in any case ITV Digital didn't have the money. Their business model was failing.

The Football League meetings were now definitely worth going to. Rather than mundane crap this was potential financial Armageddon and the bloodletting was starting.

Burns continued to ludicrously assure the clubs they would get this money. In one of the meetings I stood up and accused him in no uncertain terms of failing to do his job. But also, given that he was a lawyer, there was only one place this was going to end up, and that was in a courtroom, and the clubs would have to bear the cost of the action, with no certainty of any beneficial outcome.

At this time discussions began about the formation of a Phoenix League, a breakaway league similar to the Premiership, with some Division One clubs and a few outside resigning from the Football League and doing our own broadcasting deal.

It was discussed in a private meeting in London between certain clubs including Wolves, Wimbledon, Birmingham, Bradford, Palace, Portsmouth, Man City and Notts Forest, and plans were laid for a potential breakaway.

Unfortunately the media got wind of it, and again others and myself were caught up in the controversy. At the next Football League meeting all hell broke loose. We were roundly condemned for getting together and having such meetings. I felt not the slightest iota of remorse or regret. The clubs that moaned the loudest in Division One moaned because they hadn't been included. I kept on having conversations with my colleagues, and eventually the media, about breakaway leagues.

It didn't come as much of a surprise when ITV Digital eventually went into administration.

So much for taking on Murdoch.

The regulators had wanted to prevent the pay-TV market from being dominated by Murdoch but ironically made him even more powerful. He mounted a ruthless campaign to undermine the competition, which only ended when the ruined ITV Digital staggered, exhaling its last few dying breaths, up the steps of the High Court.

With ITV Digital teetering on the brink of disaster, what was there for the clubs to do? The Football League Board's response to the crisis was to organise a humiliating march of the entire seventy-two Football League chairmen down Chelsea Bridge Road to the broadcaster's head office, holding placards lambasting ITV Digital's executives, camera crews in tow.

When I say 'the entire Football League chairmen', I mean all bar three: myself, Theo Paphitis of Millwall and Charles Koppel of Wimbledon. None of us went on this demeaning, ludicrous and pitiful march.

I was phoned by the media and asked if I was marching and I informed them I was. 'I am marching into San Lorenzo's for lunch with Charles and Theo.'

By now there was anarchy amongst the ranks of the football clubs and I was leading the charge.

The problem in football was that people agreed with you in private but didn't stand up in public and be counted. When I was asked about the Phoenix League and who supported it, I named the clubs and the papers printed them. Then straight away Mark Arthur, chief executive from Forest, was on the phone whining to me about mentioning them.

In another instance, I believed we needed to change the personnel at the top of the Football League as clearly David Burns was not effective in negotiating with ITV Digital. In fact, I believe he antagonised them, and I put it to my fellow clubs in a private meeting that he should go. My proposal was roundly supported but when I stood up in the main meeting and called for David Burns to resign I was greeted with silence from behind me, except from people like Charles and Theo.

I pursued this theme and took it up with Keith Harris in a meeting held at Birmingham's ground. I told him Burns had to go and he agreed. I also told Harris that he should go too, given he was supposed to control Burns; this sparked a furious response for him.

Finally, it ended up where I forecasted it would: in court.

The League board tried to negotiate a deal with ITV Digital, but could not get one. So they sued and got absolutely nothing.

Well, when I say nothing, that's not strictly true: they got a massive legal bill.

But it does not end there. The next thing Heckle and Keckle – AKA Harris and Burns – did was to go and sign a four-year deal with BSkyB for £90 million, without the mandate from the clubs.

This meant a loss of millions for the clubs when they probably could have negotiated a deal with ITV Digital for some money, or got together with the Premier League, negotiated a bit more collectively and got proper money.

Not surprisingly, this new deal sparked a furious reaction. I labelled Burns and Harris morons, which was the headline on the back page of the *Sun*, and Theo said that he wouldn't allow them to run a kebab shop. But the deal was done, and each Division One club was now £5 million worse off.

Eventually, both Harris and Burns had no choice but to step down. They had been on the receiving end of much vitriol from many sources, especially from Theo Paphitis, but on his departure from the industry Harris chose to single me out for criticism. I was not overly concerned. I am sure the fact that Seymour Pierce, the investment bank Harris was chairman of that had Theo as a client, had nothing to do with me being singled out by him.

Ironically, the chief executive of ITV Digital was Brian Barwick, who was later appointed CEO of the FA. Only in football would someone who had presided over the potential demise of so many clubs be appointed to head up the game's governing body.

All Division One clubs now had a £5 million hole in their cash flows, and there were going to be casualties. Within months of the ITV Digital balloon bursting, five or six clubs went into administration and it was thought that there would be many more.

Palace could have been one of them, but they were fortunate enough to have a benefactor – me – who would pour money into their coffers.

I was now firmly entrenched in the football world and the media was plugged into me. I had been strident in my views, and I didn't care how people took the things that I said. Football was a business and should be run like one.

Yes, of course it was a public business, and what you said and did was in the public domain. But so what? That was a good thing in my opinion because after the Harris and Burns debacle the Football League was dramatically restructured and the boys' club mentality was changed. Commercial initiatives were introduced and people with sound business sense now headed up reform committees.

Football was all about money, and the second tier of English football, the Football League, had been dragged, kicking and screaming, into the twenty-first century.

8

TRIALS, TRIBULATIONS AND BLUEPRINTS

After a long, eventful and sometimes excruciating first season at Palace, I thought to myself it was time for a nice little break . . . not likely! 121, the buyer of The PocketPhone Shop, decided to launch a big fat claim against me for the princely sum of £6.5 million of the money they had paid for PPS. Outrageous! The new CEO had changed pivotal aspects of the way the company ran, creating a negative impact on the company's financial position, which reverberated in one direction . . . Mine. Contemplating the end of my first year at Palace, reflecting on the nigh on £20 million I had spent, and now there was the added prospect of a bloody big court case, I decided that for the foreseeable future, the streets of London were not paved with gold. I upped sticks and moved to Spain, not with a spotted handkerchief and a cat, but with six supercars, a brand-new boat and one right-hand man to a rather nice eight-bedroomed house in Marbella.

Once safely ensconced in my 'Marbella Palace', I decided it needed doing up, hoping that at least one Palace I owned at this time would be fitting of my new status in life, whatever that was. Funnily enough, I scrutinised every peseta (pre-euro days, accuracy an' all that), unlike the millions I spent on footballers without batting an eyelid. So home was now España, which became the base for many a decision.

No sooner had I applied my suntan lotion, put my black socks and sandals on – not! – and nearly sunk my boat, than football was back on top of my to-do list, the small matter of having no manager, no captain of the good ship Cash Drain Crystal Palace FC.

Managerial vacancies are well publicised and when one is up for grabs it's a bit like a line-up from the film *The Usual Suspects*. 'So come on down, Joe Kinnear, Mark McGhee, Peter Taylor, George Graham and Dave Bassett.'

Me being me, I immediately passed comment about the merits of Graham and Bassett. In my vast experience of just one year, I labelled them dinosaurs.

It prompted a call from Bassett. I had history with him, after parting company with Steve Coppell, and Bassett had gone into the press calling me some 'Billy Whizz' – whatever that meant! – for coming into football and sacking Coppell.

I wrote to Dave 'Harry' Bassett (perhaps Mike Bassett could have been better . . .) at the dizzy heights of Barnsley, where he was plying his trade as manager, saying I thought he would be better served minding his own business, and wished him 'success in his pursuit of accurate information'. I got my own letter sent back with 'Bollocks – H' written on the back.

So when Bassett had a go at me for the dinosaur comment I explained, 'By dinosaur I meant majestic beast.' He laughed it off, calling me a saucy bastard.

After turning my nose up at most applications, I interviewed Steve McMahon, ex-Liverpool player and Blackpool manager. I liked McMahon, but he was just missing something. Phil Smith, the agent who sold me Ruddock, approached me. For some reason that escapes me now, he still had credibility with me. He was representing Steve Bruce, the ex-Manchester United captain and former manager of numerous clubs.

Bruce was the manager of Huddersfield Town when we had played them in the third game of my first season and in my opinion he was a total disgrace. He had showed no interest in the game and his body language was awful, turning and scowling at his chairman Barry Rubery. After the game, over a drink in his board-room, I told Rubery the best thing he could do was to 'fire that disrespectful wanker'. Six weeks later, he did.

Having perhaps had a hand in getting Bruce dismissed, it was ironic that I had now been convinced by Smith to interview him. So Steve Bruce flew to Spain to meet with me at my house.

When interviewing someone, rather than the usual boring standard questions, I try to throw them off balance and get them to show their true selves.

'So, Steve, tell me something. I saw you last year when we played Huddersfield and I thought you were a disgrace. I told your chairman that if a wanker like you worked for me I would fire you! Explain to me why I should now think differently.'

Bruce's face went a bit ashen. He sucked in some air and then answered, 'I expected a difficult interview but bloody hell!'

He then went into his reasons for his bad attitude towards his chairman – it was all around broken promises and the sale of players when they were challenging for promotion. Bruce admitted his conduct was wrong and he knew it and had learned from that.

Steve Bruce was a very difficult man to dislike. He was very personable and exuded the inner strength of someone who had captained the biggest club in the world under the best manager in history, Sir Alex Ferguson.

He shared my ambition for promotion and felt we had a strong squad and with a few additions getting into the Premier League was very possible – he especially liked the 'Pest' Clinton Morrison. He spoke of standards and management style. By the end of our two-hour chat, he had sold himself to me. I made up my mind to offer him the job.

Around this time I bumped into Douglas Hall, vice-chairman of Newcastle United, the biggest club, well, in Newcastle, fresh from the notorious visit to a well-known knocking shop in Marbella with chairman Freddy Shepherd where they had infamously branded 'all girls in Newcastle dogs' and been caught in a sting operation by the *News of the World*. It turned out that Sir John Hall, Douglas's father, lived virtually next door to me; I was to form a good relationship with both Halls, taking advice from experienced and wily Sir John and well, getting drunk with Dougie, which he was indeed very good at.

They invited me to Gibraltar as Newcastle were over and there I met the late great Bobby Robson and took the opportunity to get his opinion on Steve Bruce, who himself by chance was a Geordie.Robson was positive although I am not sure he was 100 per cent au fait with Bruce's track record. As is often the case in football, coincidences occur and later that year we drew Newcastle in the FA Cup.

With my belief in loyalty, it was important that Steve Bruce got on with Stevie Kember and Terry Bullivant, as I had made keeping them on a condition of his employment. I flew them over so they could all meet. They got on famously, so to celebrate my new 'dream team' I took them out on my boat, much to Steve Bruce's horror as he hated boats and spent the afternoon green, and I almost lost my first-team coach, nearly drowning Bullivant on one of my jet skis.

We had dinner in the evening and a real feeling of optimism was shared, the excitement was evident and I felt at that dinner we really had something.

No expense was spared in preparing for the new season. The team trained in a fantastic training camp in Marbella, one soon used by Bayern Munich and Inter Milan. There was a different feel from the Alan Smith time, there was a feeling of togetherness within the squad, and I even joined in training! Bruce demanded absolute respect from the players and he got it too. He was organised and professional in everything he did, a throwback I suspect from his Manchester United days. I was impressed by the control he had over the team: he imposed a strict regime and certain senior highly paid players like David Hopkin, who didn't like it at all, toed the line, knowing exactly who was the boss.

During the pre-season, problems sparked up again with Jamie Pollock, who unfortunately had returned from Birmingham. There was a dispute over a £10,000 fee, which had been agreed if Birmingham kept him for more than a month.

Even though I had been on the conference call with Karren Brady and Trevor Francis when this had been agreed, it had been omitted from the loan document and Birmingham were refusing to pay it.

I liked Karren and respected her in many ways, but she could be a bit of a madam and in this instance she told a big, fat fib. I called David Sullivan, Birmingham's co-owner, giving him my word that this had been agreed.

He said 'tough', implying that I was a liar, and he wouldn't pay it.

This paved the way for years of bad feeling between Birmingham, its co-owners David Gold and David Sullivan and myself.

Pollock returned, having undergone an operation without prior permission from the club, as was his way. He was also a stone and a half heavier, but he refused point blank to do anything about it. I had no desire to start the new season with more confrontation but there was no way I was allowing this attitude. So to coin a phrase from *Cool Hand Luke*, 'What we've got here is failure to communicate.'

On the subject of dead weight, we had taken the opportunity to rid ourselves of Neil Ruddock. It was much easier to get rid of him than the autobiography he had released earlier in the year. Piles of unsold copies were sitting on our club shop shelves gathering dust!

So after consulting with my HR Director Kevin Watts on the best way to handle this 'problem', we put Pollock on notice in writing: he would be weighed every week and if he failed to weigh in at the required weight he would be given an official warning. Rather than take on board a reasonable request from the club, Jamie Pollock decided to do exactly as he pleased.

At the first week's weigh-in, his weight had gone up rather than down. We issued the first verbal warning. The second week his weight was up again, so we issued a second verbal warning and the third week there was no weight loss so he received a first and final written warning.

In the fourth week there was no weight improvement. Pollock was now heavier than the weight he had come back with, which had already been deemed unacceptable. So we did something that no other football club had done. We fired the player and removed him from our payroll.

Typically, despite the circumstances, the PFA jumped in to defend Pollock and a tribunal was convened at the Football League comprising the usual suspects of blazer wearers from the FA and

Football League. After a farcical hearing the panel ordered us to reinstate him and put him back on the payroll. This was typical football self-regulation so we lodged an appeal.

At the appeal hearing we took a leading QC as well as the club's physio, George Cooper. George was a lovely lad, quite young for a physio, but very competent. His problem was that he was a bit too concerned with being popular with the players, which can often be the case with physios. Even so, I liked him. He agreed with the club's stance and considered Pollock to be overweight.

In the hearing we argued we had followed the disciplinary code to the letter. This was contentious as far as football and certainly the PFA were concerned. It would set an unwelcome precedent to uphold our right to sack a player for repeated breaches of discipline. The panel didn't want to make a controversial decision and preferred to find a way round the problem.

George Cooper was put on the stand and explained all manner of technical jargon around weight, not really answering the questions that were being asked.

Eventually, one of the new appeal panel, Lawrie McMenemy, the ex-Southampton and England assistant manager, exploded, 'For God's sake, man, it's a simple question: is he fat or not?'

George bottled it, saying technically he was not fat, which was vastly different from the discussions we had had and clearly did not help. I rolled my eyes at him, disappointed that he seemed to prefer popularity with players than with his chairman, but it seemed that he had folded under pressure.

Eventually the panel agreed that we had the right to stipulate a player's weight, but perversely claimed we had issued one warning too few for him to be fired, which given I had an HR expert who had handled thousands of employees for me at PPS was not actually right.

So according to them we had the right to do what we had done but we hadn't done it the right way.

We had to take Pollock back in the knowledge that the panel had made it clear we were actually within our rights to stipulate that he be at a certain weight. The internal football channels had now been exhausted, and we were stuck with this absurd cowardly verdict.

So I made Pollock train with our new academy director, an ex-army instructor, who ran him and ran him until two weeks later he weighed in at an acceptable weight level. No sooner had he reached the required weight than he got signed off with stress and returned to his hometown in the north-east.

For this disappearing act I removed him from the payroll and waited for his return, which never came. Curious to see where this Scarlet Pimpernel of a player had disappeared to, I hired a private detective to find out what he was doing. The detective told me he had seen some funny goings-on, which, for legal reasons, I am reluctantly prohibited from telling you about. Eventually, Pollock did come back, driving all the way to the training ground in London and, with his newly strange behaviour, refused to come in, saying he couldn't face it. Pollock's agent phoned on his behalf and a deal was done to release him from his contract. Despite the aggravation it was a pity about Pollock, as in fact he was not a bad player, but I was paying him to leave and I had to write off the £750,000 I had paid Manchester City for his services.

This may seem harsh but this player was disruptive in the dressing room, disrespectful towards management and had no regard for the club. If he had been allowed to ignore our reasonable wishes it would have opened the doors even wider than they already were in the liberty-taking football culture.

*   *   *

No sooner had the Pollock issue been resolved than the season was upon us.

Our first game of the new Bruce era was away to Rotherham, who without doubt had the worst facilities in the league. The changing rooms were dire, with so little room the players had to change on the bus, and the boardroom was not much better, not that I had much to compare it to as I never went into many board-rooms.

Their chairman was about eighty years of age and hard of hearing. So when I arrived in their boardroom, cocky and full of myself, I tried to talk to him but he couldn't hear me.

I lit up a cigar and was told I couldn't smoke. 'No smoking!' he bellowed.

'That's OK, I have one, thank you.'

I asked him what business he was in and he said, 'Scrap.'

'Crap?' I said, trying to hide my laughter.

Another member of the Jordan fan club successfully signed up!

We ran out 3–2 winners after a very unimpressive first half where we fell behind twice.

After the match, Bruce decided he was unhappy with the goal-keeper Kolinko, so I went and bought Matt Clarke from Bradford for £1.25 million. We also took Steve Vickers on loan from Middlesbrough, joining the other new additions of Tony Popovic, the Australian international centre half, and Jovan Kirovski from Sporting Lisbon.

We had started off the season very well, winning our first three games. Then, after losing a couple of matches, we recorded seven straight victories, taking us to the top of the table.

The only disappointment was losing to bloody Millwall. It was the first time we had played them in a competitive game for years and I was anxious to redeem the humiliating 6–0 defeat in the pre-season friendly the previous year. A win would be a big deal for the Palace supporters, not to mention bragging rights with my mate Theo Paphitis.

Millwall fans had a habit of ripping the toilet seats out of other people's stadiums, so as a joke I removed the seat allocated for Theo and replaced it with a toilet for him to sit on during the game. Given his Greek origins I had all the guys in the boardroom dressed in togas and we had kebabs in the corner; my ignorance was pointed out to me by Paphitis: kebabs come from Cyprus and togas are Roman. My joke monumentally backfired as Millwall beat us 3–1. To add insult to injury my close personal friend banged the lid on the toilet seat relentlessly after every Millwall goal and had a whale of a time . . . Did I want chilli sauce with that?

After the game Steve was choked as he knew how much this match was likely to have meant to me and the fans and swore blind that as long as he was managing the club I would never witness another gutless performance like the one I had just seen, which turned out to be the case, given how long he stayed.

I really liked Steve Bruce, he was my kind of man. There were no excuses when things went badly and he was humble when things went well. He led by example and I thoroughly enjoyed his company.

One evening we went for dinner. Bryan Robson, the former England captain, joined us. He had recently parted company with Middlesbrough and was very bitter about the club's chairman Steve Gibson. Robson disappointed me, as ultimately he had lost his job for not doing well and he was extremely disparaging about a chairman who backed his managers to the hilt. I hoped that his outlook was not one my guy shared.

Press speculation was building around the future of Trevor Francis at Birmingham as they were not doing well and he was rumoured to be for the chop. The word on the street was that Bruce was their preferred replacement. The rumour mill, as often was the case, picked up momentum and soon he was odds-on favourite to replace Francis if and when he got the boot, which sure enough he did.

I was extremely disappointed with Bruce because he sat on the fence, despite me urging him to be more forthright in his allegiance to Palace. He would come out with sound bites such as 'I am Crystal Palace manager until someone tells me otherwise.' Not helpful.

Birmingham, in an insidious way, had kept up the whispering campaign in the media for some weeks before removing Francis. How did I know it was Birmingham? Let's just say all the press exclusives came from the *Midland Sports* reporters. It aggravated me. 'Piss off and find your own manager like I had to' was what I thought, and that soon spilled out of my trap in an outburst the media loved.

'Why would Steve Bruce go to Birmingham, what was the last thing they won? Err . . . nothing.'

'When were they last in the Premier League? Err . . . never.'

And my particular favourite: 'What's the best thing about Birmingham? The road out.'

I was not expecting any Christmas cards postmarked Birmingham.

Sure enough, via Karren Brady, Birmingham made a formal approach to me to speak to Bruce and, predictably, I gave them a resounding no. Madam seemed a little put out, but no was no.

Thinking it best, I spoke to Bruce about Birmingham's approach before somebody else told him. I also decided that, despite Steve being here for only three or four months, I was going to stave off those vultures at Birmingham by giving him a much-improved package. Let's call it a Brucey bonus.

Bruce was pleased and proceeded to tell me his heart and head were with me and he just wanted to tell his wife Janet about his new deal. So off I flew back to Spain, having spoken to the agent and agreed with him the terms of Bruce's new contract.

That was the last I heard from Bruce for two days and when we finally talked his attitude had changed completely.

By that time I had it on good information that the agent Barry Silkman, an ex-Palace player and well-known 'dancing partner' of David Sullivan, had been seen having a chat with Bruce at a reserve team game.

So my manager who had said 'my heart and head are with you, chairman' was now 'torn' because Birmingham were a big club and looked after him when he left Manchester United. I knew then he wanted to go.

I was pretty pissed off when I flew back from Spain for a midweek game. Since arriving at Palace Bruce had been looked after, supported, bought several new players and been offered a new contract. Before the match he tried to come and see me but I was busy. We lost 1–0 and failed to set a new club record of eight consecutive wins so at the end of the game I was in an even worse mood. I thought to myself that there was no way now that Bruce was going to come in and ask me if he can speak to Birmingham, but he bloody well did.

He said he owed it to his family to go and speak to Birmingham.

'What about what you owe me?' I asked.

Our great relationship was in tatters within minutes, especially when I told him in no uncertain terms that he couldn't talk to Birmingham.

He became offensive and said he hated it here.

'Two weeks ago you told me you loved it here,' I said.

'The hotels we stayed in were shit.'

'Steve, you chose the hotels you stayed in, not me.'

'The players hate you.'

'The players don't hate me, Steve.'

'You didn't back me in the transfer market.'

'I have bought every player you have asked me to, Steve.'

This conversation was going nowhere and there was no point in it continuing. I got up, shaking my head, and left him sitting there, stewing in his own nonsense. Later that evening, as I was driving back to the Grosvenor Hotel, which by this time was now my UK base camp, his perturbed agent Phil Smith phoned me, saying Bruce claimed I had sacked him. I advised Smith that was not at all the case and left him to mull over with his client what the next move should be.

The next day Bruce didn't show up for work and then all hell broke loose. The press had wind of it and I spoke to them, saying Bruce was going nowhere.

Two days passed with no contact and then he phoned me on the Friday. A very terse conversation ensued. In our last meeting he had said some insulting things to bait me, so now I was going to show him my teeth. He told me he was going to resign, but due to the fact he had signed a contract with a nine-month notice period, I enjoyed telling him the facts of life: he was in fact going nowhere.

Before employing Bruce, we had reviewed the standard manager's contract. Given I had gone through two of them, I knew that the problem with managers was that if you fired them you had to pay up their entire contract but if they wanted to leave they just walked out leaving you high and dry. It was totally inequitable so we had changed the standard form contract, inserting a notice period, and also added a specific clause about gardening leave. It was a new phrase to football but one that was common practice in most industries.

Bruce was now caught in the new clause we had introduced.

He said he was going to fax in his resignation, so I pointed him back to his contract with a degree of relish, telling him that perhaps he should talk to his new mates at Birmingham but, oh dear, he couldn't do that, could he? I hadn't given him permission.

Bruce then implied I was talking to him like a dog, and I replied that couldn't be true because a dog has loyalty and he had none.

Despite my anger at his actions I was saddened. In the few months we had been together I had believed we were really onto something.

I also realised there was no way back and enforcing the nine-month notice period was not overly viable. But I was not prepared to let Bruce just up and leave and allow Birmingham to disrupt my club and pay nothing for it, as well as probably coming back at a later stage to unsettle my back-room staff and playing squad with invitations to join them.

The football world was perplexed. They had never seen anything like this. Normally the manager would just go but here was a chairman talking about gardening leave and notice periods.

It pretty soon dawned on Bruce that I was entirely serious. He was in the unfortunate position of not being able to resign and join Birmingham as I was taking court action to enforce this notice period and had applied for an injunction. I think when he first heard the term 'gardening leave' he genuinely thought it was something to do with working in a garden! Segments of the media applauded this stance, as a first and long time in coming; even the copper-haired Adrian Durham from talkSPORT, the agent provocateur of football commentary, came round to my way of thinking after a debate on radio.

I put the dynamic duo of Kember and Bullivant in charge for the next game away to Walsall and left Bruce to contemplate his navel.

Oh dear, the suit
that fashion forgot.
My first impression of
the football club was
that it was a bit like a
Butlins holiday camp,
but I think I may have
taken it a little too far.

The time of ambition and drive –
the halcyon days building an empire
at The PocketPhone Shop.

Crystal Palace manager
number 1 (*left*): Steve Coppell.

Manager number 2: Alan Smith.

In the stand away to Blackburn Rovers,
the first league game of my ownership.
Little did I know what joys awaited.

Nearly relegated at Stockport County. I likened it to 90 minutes in the dentist's chair, much to my own dentist's chagrin.

Clinton Morrison celebrating with Dougie Freedman after surviving relegation at Stockport County. Freedman's goal was enough to secure our safety.

My dream team:
Bruce, Kember
and Bullivant who
started so brightly
but ended so
disappointingly.

Steve Bruce leaving the
High Court in London
after the club won a temporary
injunction preventing
Bruce from quitting the
club without serving nine
months notice.

Manager number 4:
Trevor Francis.

Manager number 5:
Steve Kember.

Manager
number 6:
Iain Dowie.

The dream achieved: Neil Shipperley (*above*) scores the £50 million pound goal in the 2004 play-off final against West Ham. Cue celebrations (*left*).

(*Facing page*) One of my favourite players, Andy Johnson, celebrates scoring in yet another win against the soon-to-be champions of Europe, Liverpool.

Winning promotion in 2004 meant that I had delivered on my promise to bring
Premier League football to Selhurst Park a year ahead of schedule.

Consoling Iain Dowie on the pitch at Charlton after being relegated from the Premier League. With what was to come later, perhaps my grip on his neck should have been slightly tighter.

I flew to Las Vegas with a group of friends including my old manager Alan Smith – who says you can't fire someone and still be friends! – to watch Lennox Lewis regain his heavyweight title against Hasim Rahman. I was a huge boxing fan and had seen many of Lewis's fights.

As if owning a football club was not enough of a gamble I had taken to spending a lot of time and money at the casino tables. There was a variety of antics, mostly involving places like the Crazy Horse. Those that have been there will know what I am talking about. As the saying goes what happens in Vegas stays in Vegas.

Meanwhile, whilst I was off enjoying life, Bruce was in limbo and, judging by the letter he wrote me, pleading me to let him go. I cruelly jibed at the time that I knew it was from him because of all the misspellings. This was a whole new world for him – he may have been the captain of Manchester United but this was my playing field.

Whilst I was away, Palace recorded a resounding 4–1 win over Crewe, keeping us in the top two and putting me in a very good mood. That night Lewis won the fight in convincing style.

We were returning on the Tuesday and I was going to go straight to a game in the evening as we were playing Gillingham away.

As we walked through LA airport, a stunning girl breezed past us, and we all remarked how beautiful she was.

When we got on the plane she was sitting opposite me in first class and I kept looking across at her.

She appeared to know one of the air hostesses, a girl called Cheryl, who as it turned out was the niece of the former Liverpool manager Roy Evans. I enquired about the girl across the cabin. Her name was Sarah, and she and Cheryl lived together in Thornton Heath, a stone's throw from Palace's ground.

I arranged with Cheryl that we would swap numbers and meet up later in the evening for drinks, and later that night a friend and I met the girls in the Grosvenor House Hotel at about 10.30 p.m.

Sarah and I hit it off and we all went out to the nightclub Elysium, joining her friends. All of a sudden Mandy Smith the model, Lady Victoria Hervey the socialite, Tara Palmer-Tomkinson and a host of other girls surrounded me.

Sarah and I soon started dating, yet at this point I still didn't know her last name. So I asked her. I had spent time trying to impress her with my ownership of a football club only for her to announce her surname was Bosnich. She was the soon-to-be-ex-wife of the former Manchester United and now Chelsea keeper Mark Bosnich.

The Bruce case finally came to court and to my delight we were given an injunction, putting Bruce in the very difficult position of having to serve out a nine-month notice period in his contract. I had created a precedent in football but the reality was a solution had to be found and lo and behold, within a day or so of the verdict, the Birmingham co-owner David Sullivan telephoned me and left a message on my voicemail.

I would have loved to have kept that voicemail message and played it to Bruce.

It went something like this: 'Simon, Dave Sullivan, well done for the verdict, brilliant stuff, you rode in like a champion, good for you. Look, I know we have expressed interest in Steve Bruce, but to be honest you want too much money and whilst the rest of the board want him, I don't really rate him and I'm not really that keen to have him. But I am just phoning because the others do. Anyway give me a call back if you want to.'

I called Sullivan back, left a voicemail and he phoned me straight away.

'So, David, you don't want Bruce then, judging by your voice-mail.'

'Well, Simon, I am not bothered really, but it's the others, you see, they want him, but you want too much money and that's not going to make it happen.'

'Dave, I haven't mentioned any money so you have no idea what I want. So I am not sure how you can say that. Your lot have never spoken about money because you wanted to nick him for nothing and now you can't. If you want to do a deal, let's do one. If not, let's leave it.'

Sullivan said, 'OK, how much do you want?'

'Three hundred thousand,' I said.

'Two hundred and fifty thousand—' he tried to respond.

'Not finished yet, David. Three hundred thousand, plus all my legal costs covered for the injunction, which are about thirty grand, and also I want you to cover more costs, as I am being sued for unfair dismissal because Steve sacked a female masseuse, saying that there was no place for women in football. I am sure your Karren will appreciate hearing that.'

Sullivan ignored my reference to Karren Brady, mulled it over for a minute and then agreed to meet my demands.

'I also want Bruce signing a confidentiality agreement so he keeps his mouth shut and does not make up stories to justify his actions. I also want hands-off agreements for a year regarding my staff and players, and he can't join you until after 11 December, when we play you.'

We agreed on these things and were just about to wind up the call when a thought popped into my head.

'David, sorry, one other thing. That £10,000 you knocked me for in the summer on Pollock? I'll have that as well.'

I could sense in his tone that Sullivan didn't like that, but we agreed and the Bruce chapter, as far as I was concerned, was over. It was a shame – Bruce had done a brilliant job while he was at Palace, and I believed he and I could have gone on to achieve big things had he stayed. I still believe that Steve Bruce is one of the country's best managers. We have since become firm friends and on numerous occasions he has apologised and we've both put it down to experience.

Since Bruce's departure, the team's form had slumped. We were rudderless and I needed another manager. In another one of life's ironies, at the bidding of the omnipotent Phil Smith, I interviewed Trevor Francis whose exit from Birmingham sparked the string of events that led to Bruce leaving Palace.

Trevor, as Bruce had before him, flew to meet me in Spain in mid-November 2001 and, as was my way, I threw in an opening question to get him off balance and see the real person.

'Trevor, I have always found you in management terms to be dull, boring, uninspiring and lacking in any real charisma and passion. Why would I want someone like that in charge of my football team?'

Trevor's response was extremely strident and full of passion, which, I remarked glibly at a later date, was the first and only time I saw that emotion from Trevor. He was on his feet and very demonstrative, assuring me that he was far from dull and desperate to succeed. He felt aggrieved with Birmingham and wanted an opportunity to prove a point. He felt that Palace would provide him with that opportunity.

I liked what I saw from Trevor and was also pleased to note that he was happy to work with Kember and Bullivant. There was that loyalty thing of mine again.

Later that evening in November as he left for the airport lightning struck a big tree in my garden. Perhaps I should have picked up on the omen.

I appointed Trevor and called my third managerial press conference in fifteen months. I was getting very adept at these press conferences. My message was simple: the reason why I had appointed Trevor Francis was to get promotion into the Premier League and my words ensured that the watching world was in no doubt about my expectations of Trevor or any other manager.

After a run of four straight defeats, Trevor took control of his first game against Kevin Keegan's Manchester City, one of the sides he himself had played for, the League's stand-out team. He was given a rousing reception by the fans and we produced a very good performance, winning 2–1.

Our next game was Birmingham City away. Trevor was looking forward to returning to his old stomping ground and I wanted to win the game to give Bruce and Birmingham the finger.

Following my derisory comments about Birmingham, the West Midlands police asked if I required a police escort. Typically I just laughed it off and said no. When I arrived at Birmingham I began to rue that decision, given the abuse levelled at me in the car park outside the ground. I went into the stadium quickly, as I wanted to go into the dressing room and wish the players luck.

To get to the dressing room I had to walk through the stadium and down the concourse in front of the Birmingham supporters. On the way there were howls of abuse but fortunately it was half empty. But on the way back it was full, and upon seeing me they surged forward, trying to get at me. Stewards dived in from everywhere to stop the surging fans getting over the barriers. I smirked over at the Birmingham fans, who then covered me in spit and punches were swung over stewards narrowly missing me.

Undeterred I took my seat unfazed by all of this and for ninety minutes all I heard was, 'Simon Jordan is a wanker, is a wanker.'

It made me laugh and I have to admit it is quite surreal listening to 20,000 strangers singing abuse at you.

Typically, rather than uphold their chairman's honour, the team put out a particularly inept performance and lost 1–0.

Despite my indifference to boardrooms, I went into Birmingham's and was greeted by David Sullivan, who after some small talk announced quite loudly that he had a question he had been meaning to ask me. 'Are you gay?'

Clearly Sullivan meant that as an insult. So I responded, 'Why? Do you fancy a crack at me?'

I laughed it off but was seething inside.

Within six months they had called me a liar, disrupted my football club by trying to poach my manager for nothing, and now for their own amusement were making comments designed to insult me.

Despite a brilliant start after Trevor came in, the campaign became an anti-climax.

There were no real highs. After Bruce departed, we fell down the league from being top to mid-table obscurity by the end of the season. I supported Trevor by buying Kit Symons and Danny Granville. As the season really started to tail off – and despite grave reservations – I spent £2.25 million on Ade Akinbiyi from Leicester to try to reignite it, but it was in vain.

Initially I had flatly refused to sign Akinbiyi for weeks and when I say flatly I do mean flatly. But Trevor kept on and on and got what he wanted.

Despite his quirks, I genuinely wanted Trevor to succeed, but I had a nagging doubt that he was going to struggle. He was stubborn in everything he did and even when he was clearly wrong he would be bloody-minded about it.

Trevor laboured through the year and the fans became a little disillusioned with him. There were disagreements between Kember, Bullivant and Francis. Things were not harmonious.

As well as being disappointed personally by the manner in which the team was performing I was genuinely disappointed for the fans. I was desperate to give them a team they could be proud of. The team's lacklustre performances were demoralising, especially when we played away, for people who had travelled the length and breadth of the country and spent fortunes supporting their team. I had earlier refunded fans in a particular match for an abhorrent display away to Barnsley, but clearly I couldn't keep on doing that.

I remember one game against Reading in particular. The team's performance had been abject and I stormed out of the ground in a fit of pique straight after the final whistle. For some reason I was driving myself that day, and as I hurtled out of the car park, I saw a Palace fan on crutches hobbling down the road. I had seen him at Selhurst Park as I often walked around the stadium before games, checking on the performances of my staff in different areas and speaking to the fans. He always sat in the section of the stadium reserved for disabled supporters.

I pulled over, buzzed the window down and asked the young man where he was going. He peered into the window of this shiny black Mercedes and was clearly gobsmacked to find that the enquiry came from his club's chairman. After he recovered his senses, he told me that he was going to the train station to travel back to London.

'Get in, let me give you a lift.'

I drove back to London, talking to this young man. His name was David Pinner, and he told me about how much he loved his football club and how he went to every game. He told me about his life and what he suffered from. The poignancy of this really hit me: here was a young man who struggled with serious afflictions, yet he got on with his life in such a positive way, and his football team meant so much to him. On the other hand, I had a group of young footballers who had everything, but who couldn't be bothered to lift a leg. At that moment I was so angry at the players – how dare they not represent this young man properly!

We arrived at London, where he was going to get a train back to Croydon. I drove us to my London home, the Grosvenor House Hotel. I pulled up on the forecourt, hailed David a taxi and made sure this young man got a black cab home. I gave him the money for his fare, as I felt it was the least I could do. Then I made a mental note to ensure we gave young David a parking bay as he had told me with glee he was getting his first disabled car that week.

I also made a note to myself to remind me to tell Trevor and the players of my feelings about how they let people like David down.

In our last few games of the season we were poor and one player stood out in his poorness: Clinton Morrison didn't lift a leg. My dear friends at Birmingham were suggesting again through the press that they would like to buy Morrison. I knew this was likely to be true as when at Palace Bruce had raved about the 'Pest', saying he thought he would be a £10 million player. I spoke with Karren Brady, suggesting I knew how much Bruce fancied the player and what he said his valuation was likely to be, but in the interests of keeping it real, I wanted £5 million for Morrison, subject to them being promoted. I was led to believe that would be acceptable. Of course, with all things Birmingham it turned out to be as clear as mud.

Morrison was of course aware of the interest and was being,

shall we say, careful with himself, so much so that in one game Trevor substituted him at half-time. Trevor recounted the story to me after the game. Apparently he had exploded at Morrison, who stood up and physically confronted Francis and the manager backed down. At that moment Trevor had the eyes of the dressing room on him but he couldn't deal with a little pest like Morrison. When Trevor told me this I was disappointed that he felt he could tell me this as if it merited some form of support from me, and I was gobsmacked that he had caused the confrontation and yet when it arrived had been unable to deal with it.

In hindsight, I believe that in a lot of the players' eyes Trevor had probably lost the dressing room. One of the things you have to appreciate about players is that they are very crafty and work things out very quickly. They know when things are not right and they know how to exploit that.

To make matters even worse, while Palace's season had faded, my dear friend Theo Paphitis's Millwall were in the play-offs against Birmingham and Steve Bruce to add insult to injury. The first leg at St Andrews had finished 0–0, making Millwall firm favourites to secure a place in the play-off final.

I went along to the second game with Charles Koppel, the Wimbledon chairman, to support Theo. It was the only time that I ever hoped Millwall would win, as it was the lesser of two evils as far as I was concerned. Birmingham scored in the last minute to win the semi-final through Steve Vickers, a player I had signed with Bruce at Palace on loan.

Theo was crestfallen and the Millwall fans were raging. The scenes inside the ground were frightening, but they were nothing to the scenes outside.

Millwall fans went on the rampage, throwing petrol bombs and setting police horses on fire; it was absolute carnage.

We waited for a while before leaving, but once the Millwall fans spotted me they jumped on the bonnet of the car and tried to smash in the windows to get to me. Fortunately my driver John put his foot down regardless of whether any of them would get injured in the process.

It was 2002 and World Cup year and the Beckhams threw their infamous party.

As it turned out, my now girlfriend Sarah was best mates with Victoria Beckham, so we were cordially invited to this white tie and diamond affair, the biggest on the social calendar and one I most certainly didn't want to go to.

I had no interest in David Beckham and the media obsession with him and his wife. As far as I was concerned, he was just a footballer. However, I had met his wife Victoria on a number of occasions and thought she was a very funny and pleasant girl. Sarah insisted we went to the party and eventually I agreed.

On the day of the event I was still pissing and moaning about going. The first person I bumped into was Chris Eubank, who I had no intention of talking to. Sarah went up to the house to see Victoria so I was milling around. We had to be driven from the meeting room to the marquee and I got to share a car with George Best and his young bride Alex, who I was to meet in two years' time in very different circumstances.

To be fair it was a fabulous event and full of very interesting people. My mood lifted when I looked at the seating plan and discovered I was sitting with the actor Ray Winstone. To my disbelief I was also on the same table as Steve Bruce, but fortunately he didn't show up.

I got on famously with Ray Winstone, who was a big West Ham fan. He was with his best mate Richard Maher, who had sold the

Beckhams the house that became known as Beckingham Palace. Both Ray and Richard were to become very good friends.

All of the England team were obviously there as well as Sven-Göran Eriksson and Nancy Dell'Olio.

The whole afternoon was spent getting very drunk and in the evening the auction came round, which was conducted by Graham Norton. I looked through the auction list for something I might like and saw a one-hour golf lesson with Nick Faldo and decided on that for my brother, as he was mad keen on golf.

Lot after lot came up and Ray Winstone spent £7,000 on a massive bottle of champagne signed by the whole Manchester United team.

When the golf lesson eventually came up I told Sarah to bid for it. I was bidding against Jamie Oliver and the DJ Goldie and I had now decided come what may I was going to have it. Within five minutes the bidding was up to £20,000 and Ray told me to leave it while Victoria Beckham looked over at Sarah as if to say, 'What are you doing?'

But I was going to have it, and eventually I did, with a winning bid of £37,500.

Well, it was for a good cause because the money raised went to a children's charity.

The rest of the evening passed in a drunken blur. I do remember talking in great length to Sean Bean about his beloved Sheffield United, which he had just invested money into – of course, 'invested' is football parlance for giving away or losing, as I told him with great aplomb.

I also had a conversation with Dwight Yorke, who knew Sarah very well. He was one of the best men at her wedding to Bosnich. Why was it, I asked Yorke, that when there were so many extremely wealthy footballers in the room not one of them had put their hand up once for anything during the auction? Yorke blathered about not having as much money as chairmen. As I got to know Dwight over the years I came to realise that was his stock in trade: blathering.

Ironically, despite my paying an extortionate amount for this golf day, my brother never had it. When my secretary contacted Faldo's secretary to arrange the lesson, he was extremely non-committal on dates. Over a period of about nine months she tried to arrange this day until in the end my patience snapped.

I wrote Faldo a letter telling him that if he didn't want to do something he shouldn't commit to it. I also told him I had paid the money and it had gone to a good cause, but as far as I was concerned fuck his one-hour golf lesson. Mind you, given his rapidly declining form he probably needed it more himself.

He wrote me some flaky letter back but I leaked the story to the press, who did a number on Faldo. Quite right for someone who, to my mind, had acted in a mean-spirited way.

As my second eventful season drew to a close I found myself again in reflective mood; I was beginning to come to the conclusion that football was not what I thought it was.

When I had PPS it was all about challenges and achievements and doing it together. In football, the exact opposite applied. It was an environment based upon liberties, lies and disrespect.

The very people who should be supporting you would often be working against you. I wanted to build this football club to be a unit that was all for one and one for all.

What I learned was that it was indeed 'all for one and then fuck all for me', and the chairman's role firstly was to put his hand in his pocket, then to be a shoulder to cry on when things were not going right. And when things were going well? Then a chairman was someone to be marginalised or even disrespected.

I appeared to spend most of my time in conflict with managers, other clubs, the authorities, players and agents. All of these factions seemed at one time or another to conspire to work against me.

But – and it was a big but – I had taken on a challenge. I was not one of these fair-weather owners. In the two years I had owned the club I had missed only one competitive match and in my entire tenure of nearly 500 competitive games I missed less than ten.

I took on every battle. I backed everybody and what I got in return was to be called Mr Chairman, not much of a trade-off really but that was football for you.

I was determined to get the club right and the way I wanted it. I had said I would get the club up and straight and in the Premier League in five years and I would damn well do it.

Birmingham eventually made an offer for Morrison in the summer of 2002. To my considerable disappointment, they had been promoted through the play-offs. Needless to say I was expecting the £5 million we had discussed earlier.

What I got was an offer of £2 million. The ITV Digital crisis was biting. As they left the Football League, Birmingham were seeking to take advantage of clubs with big holes in their cash flow.

I knew Bruce wanted Morrison, so I reminded Karren Brady she had agreed to pay a certain figure. She responded, 'Times have changed.' The Morrison deal went round and round in circles. But just as the pre-season started and the players returned to training we had got the offer up to £3.5 million. We also had factored in a player to come from them to sweeten the deal.

I spoke to Trevor about what players from Birmingham he might be interested in and he mentioned Martin Grainger and Curtis Woodhouse. As we were losing a forward, I mentioned Andrew Johnson, a young striker they had on their books. He was quick. I had seen him in the League Cup Final for Birmingham against

Liverpool and I thought he would do well for us in the Football League.

Trevor reluctantly agreed, with a parting shot saying that Johnson 'only goes one way', which I thought was amusing as the same had been said of Trevor when he was a player. If Johnson was half the footballer Trevor Francis had been, he would be some player and, given that Trevor was the first million-pound player, who knows? If we ever sold Johnson we might get nearly £10 million in today's market place!

Trevor has always liked it to be reported that he chose Andy Johnson, so there you go, Trev. With his glowing endorsement of Johnson it made me take him as part of the Morrison deal.

As it turned out I got a young man who went on to be a fabulous player for Palace. He restored your faith in players because he was such a decent young man who epitomised all the good things in sport. Hard work, decency, honesty and ability, oh yes, AJ was very special.

Unlike Ade Akinbiyi, or Akinbadbuy as he was now known.

He was injured and I sent him to America to the world's leading knee surgeon, Richard Steadman, as he had a major problem with his knee which was to keep him out for six months whilst I was paying him £16,000 a week.

For a change, during the summer of 2003 we added some new players to the squad. We brought in Curtis Fleming from Middlesbrough at right back, Danny Butterfield from Grimsby, Darren Powell from Brentford and Shaun Derry from Portsmouth. Shaun was to become one of my favourite players during my ownership of Palace. We also signed a goalkeeper from Lens, Cédric Berthelin, as well as adding Dele Adebola to our attacking options. We looked as if we had a nicely balanced squad and again the ambition was promotion to the Premier League.

Unfortunately, we lost David Hopkin. He was suffering from a very serious ankle injury and should never have passed a medical in the first place.

I had to write off the £1.5 million I had paid sixteen months ago and pay him over a million pounds to leave. Hopkin was intransigent: despite not being fit he wanted two years' money and I only got him to make a small concession. It was disappointing that a player the Palace fans considered a hero, who had made vast amounts of money from moves from Palace and back, would not be fair given the circumstances, but that's the modern-day footballer for you.

Our pre-season was OK, and despite my concerns about the Francis, Kember and Bullivant triumvirate I was optimistic approaching this season.

Our first game was away to Preston, which was always a difficult fixture. Invariably we came away with nothing. The game marked the introduction of two players who were to have big parts in shaping Palace's future.

Derry scored the winner and AJ went to hospital.

I was first at the hospital, followed by Trevor Francis after the game. Derry's agent, Phil Graham, who was supposed to be his players' biggest supporter, was nowhere to been seen, except hanging around Ricardo Fuller, who was just about to sign for Preston and represented his latest pay cheque.

In our second game of the season, something was to happen that would destroy our season, the players' regard for the manager and strip away the impatient Palace fans' last real vestiges of support for Trevor Francis.

We played Bradford, and despite us opening the scoring they equalised late in the game.

But Trevor did something inexplicable after they scored. He

'appeared to' turn around in the dugout and punch the reserve goalkeeper, the Latvian Alex Kolinko.

It was spotted by the fourth official and Trevor was sent to the stands.

No one knew what had happened as people had been watching the game but I had looked at the bench as I always did and saw Trevor punch the player.

He sat next to me in the stands and was raging, saying that he had slapped Kolinko because he was laughing when the opposition had scored.

This quite frankly was an astounding situation. No one had ever heard of a manager hitting a player in the dugout during the game.

The game finished 1–1 and very quickly it filtered through to me that the police wanted to interview Trevor.

I asked Dominic to go and stall them and went to intercept Trevor, in order to advise him what to say.

He was in the manager's office and was just about to go and see the police with his hand wrapped in a tea towel with ice inside it, like a boxer after a fight, to take the swelling down.

'Christ, Trevor, take the ice wrap off your hands, for God's sake. You go down there with that on and you're asking for trouble. You told me you slapped him; let's go with that,' I said. 'In fact, go and get changed and leave it to me. I will deal with the police.'

I explained to the police that Trevor had left the stadium and the club would deal with it. The two officers were not happy but as no one had brought any charges they had to go with it.

I phoned Trevor on the way home and told him not to talk to anyone until I had it under control.

The next day the usual protagonists came on justifying their existence. The PFA demanded a meeting and got a flat no because it was club business and I would deal with it. Brendan Batson, their deputy chief executive, threatened to come down anyway, so I advised him that if he did I would have him arrested for trespassing. I liked that threat. I had used it successfully on the player Fullerton and was more than happy to use it on the PFA.

I had had enough of the PFA, especially Batson, who as far as I was concerned was supercilious and arrogant in his treatment of me and who had got up my nose on more than one occasion.

Then we had to deal with Phil Graham, Kolinko's agent.

I called Dominic and Phil Alexander into the room so they could listen and put Graham on speakerphone.

'Phil. How can I help?'

'Well, Simon, it is more how I can help you.' He then proceeded to tell me that if I paid him a £50,000 fee, and paid up the player's wages for two years – around £500,000 – and gave him a free transfer, thus writing off the £650,000 I had paid for him, he thought he might be able to stop Kolinko pressing charges against Trevor Francis.

Suffice it to say that the call did not bear any fruit for this agent, and after I put the phone down, I expressed my opinions of agents such as Graham clearly, not using particularly eloquent or complimentary language.

What I did was go to the training ground on the Thursday after the Tuesday night game. I asked Trevor to come out of his office and then sent for Kolinko to come and join us.

I decided to walk them around the training ground, away from prying eyes and ears, to try and create a more relaxed atmosphere. This was the first time they had laid eyes on one another since the incident.

Trevor had time to reflect and was regretful, although it was clear that he was also concerned he could be put in the clink by Kolinko.

As we walked I talked, trying to inject some levity into the situation.

Kolinko was visibly upset and I advised him that what had gone on was wrong and Trevor knew it and deeply regretted it.

Trevor chipped in, pleading with Alex not to press charges and ruin his life.

Kolinko was in tears of rage remarking in his broken English that he would kill someone if they laid hands on him.

I had it! The solution! I told Trevor to put his hands behind his back and then told Alex to punch him so we could put this to bed.

All the blood drained out of Trevor's face. He was not quite believing what I had just suggested as he looked at this giant goalkeeper with mortal trepidation. Kolinko just shook his head remarking again in broken English that he was 'no happy, but I forget' and there it was, over and forgotten. And if you believe that you will believe anything!

The issue of Kolinko was put behind us on the surface, but clearly it had affected the team's morale as we only won one game out of the next ten and were seventeenth in the league. This was relegation form.

Our poor form in the League wasn't replicated in the League Cup, where we beat Plymouth 2–1, Cheltenham 7–0 and Coventry 3–0, and it appeared to give us some impetus again, very similar to the 2000 season.

We then beat our arch-rivals Brighton 5–0, which sent the Palace fans into euphoria and revived their faith in Trevor. Andy Johnson also set out his stall with a stunning hat trick, with another during the following game against Walsall as we registered four wins out of four.

But the financial climate was biting and the club was haemorrhaging money.

We had lost substantial amounts of money in the first two years, but these had been controlled losses as I had invested heavily into the playing squad and the academy, as well as the stadium and training ground.

But now attendances were down and we had lost £5 million from the ITV Digital deal. This resulted in significant cash calls on me. This was not to advance the club but to stand still.

I decided that we had to get control of our cost base and looked very closely at all areas of expenditure and cost. The investment in our academy proved to be bearing fruit. Where once it had been a disparate environment detached from the first team producing nothing but jugglers, it was now becoming what I had set out for it to be some two and a half years earlier: a disciplined, methodical, inspirational environment producing players that were now legitimate contenders for the first team. Gary Borrowdale, Ben Watson and Wayne Routledge were the first of a crop of players that over the next six years were to see Palace's academy revered as one of the best in the country.

And we fought relentlessly to keep the academy despite the Premier League wanting academies to be the preserve of their clubs only.

I spent a lot of energy in this area, as I saw it as the saving of my sanity, and worked the oracle to get a sixty by forty indoor surface on metropolitan open land. This required planning permission, which was perceived as impossible to get.

After two years of endless lobbying I got permissions for a temporary indoor surface. Then, after endless meetings and calls to action, we invested in an inflatable dome to fulfil the FA's ridiculous requirements, one of them being an indoor surface for training in 'inclement weather', i.e. rain.

The FA didn't like it and it is my belief that they were actively seeking to remove our academy licence and saw our innovative indoor facility as an opportunity to try and revoke it. Our academy licence had been under threat prior to my purchase of the club. We only had a temporary licence subject to adherence to the final FA requirements, a provision of the indoor environment. I had done it and the rules were silent on the structure and I advised the FA that failure to license us fully would result in the mother of all lawsuits. We got it and I suppose it was one of the few benefits of having a reputation for being forthright.

As I went through the operation, I saw we were carrying costs we didn't need, and by costs unfortunately I meant staff. I made a number of redundancies and the only area spared was the academy.

I laid off the reserve team manager, Dave Swindlehurst. While the reserves were doing well, we had more than enough personnel to cover that role without needing to employ a specific individual. But as a favour to Steve Kember, who was an old teammate of Swindlehurst's, I had second thoughts and told him I would bring him back in a different guise with more responsibilities. The one proviso was that he had to keep quiet about it. So what did the idiot do? He told the press he was going to be brought back, which resulted in me following through on my original plan to lay him off.

This was typical of a lot of football people. They had far too much free time on their hands and loved to talk. After money, one of the biggest commodities in football is gossip and they could not keep their mouths shut. By announcing that I was bringing him back it meant it compromised the validity of other redundancies I was being forced financially to make.

So I had no choice. I called him in and told him the news face to face. He reacted very angrily and got almost physical, shouting and screaming at me. He was a big man but sod this, he was in my office so he got it back with both barrels.

He told me I was not a proper Palace man, whatever that is, and that he was Palace through and through.

'Bullshit,' I replied. 'When Palace was in turmoil in 1980, you pissed off to Derby as soon as you could.'

Swindlehurst went muttering and spluttering and I continued to make the savings because I had to apply business sense to running a football club that was financially crippled without my money holding it up.

In December 2002 we played Millwall and for the first time since I bought Palace we beat them 1–0 at home.

I had endured two years of endless ribbing from Paphitis and didn't even get to gloat after the game because I had to attend a fortieth birthday party in Manchester.

The team's inconsistent form continued, then we drew Liverpool in the FA Cup and recorded a famous 2–0 victory in the replay at Anfield with ten men after drawing the first game at Selhurst Park.

I didn't go into Liverpool's scabby boardroom this time and when we scored our goals a few of our directors celebrated, prompting one of the stewards to come up to me and ask me to calm them down. Bad losers.

Trevor basked in the reflected glory of it and we went out a day or so later for dinner at Signor Sassi in Knightsbridge. It was around the corner from the Grosvenor, where I lived, and from Trevor's house which was on, believe it or not, Trevor Street, off Trevor Square.

For the first time in his fourteen-month tenure Trevor seemed happy and comfortable. We had become good friends and we had a ritual before every game: I would go and have breakfast at his, which Helen his wife would cook for us. We called it our pre-match meal.

On one of those Saturdays, Trevor produced his mobile phone, telling me with a grin to listen to his voicemail. The previous night Jim Smith, former Derby County and Newcastle manager and number two to Harry Redknapp at Portsmouth, had called Trevor, they had a chat and then the call finished. Unbeknownst to Jim, sometime later he sat on his phone and redialled the last number called, Trevor. What we got to listen to that morning was a somewhat inebriated Jim Smith having a rant with Harry Redknapp about one of their star players, Paul Merson. The content was pretty extreme – let's just say Smith was far from complimentary about Merson, particularly his attitude towards not travelling with the team to games and his non-appearance at training. What was additionally funny was that Harry could be heard agreeing and it was the exact opposite of what they were saying to the press regarding the player.

We drew Leeds United in the next round, which heralded the return to Palace of Terry Venables, now a hugely unpopular figure after the disastrous Goldberg era. We had a full house for the game and Venables was the centre of attention as the pantomime villain.

The game was a travesty and we lost 2–1.

Dermot Gallagher the referee failed to award a goal that was two yards over the line, which brought the FA down on my head after my outspoken remarks about his officiating. They eventually let me off with a warning. But we lost that game and the potential of a lucrative Cup run and Venables, some would say, got to rob Palace twice in less than four years.

After the Leeds loss we were now out of both Cup competitions and were twelfth in the league. I hoped that we would now push on up the league, but unfortunately the exact opposite happened.

Early in February there was another unfortunate incident with the goalkeeper Kolinko.

Trevor had been playing him despite the early season incident but he had recently lost his place in the side. He was due back in the team for an away game at Leicester and as I was leaving the Grosvenor Hotel to go to the match my phone rang. It was Alex Kolinko.

'Chairman, I no play.'

I was stunned and asked him where he was and he told me he was stood outside the dressing room.

I told him to get back in the dressing room. I was gobsmacked that a player was calling to inform me that he was effectively going on strike.

I reminded him that I had looked after him and he said, 'Chairman, you are a liar, no one looks after me besides my agent. I no play.'

I went out on the hotel forecourt and exploded at the player, reminding him he was talking to his chairman and that I had never lied to him. It made no difference: he wouldn't play and it was clear he was finished with Palace.

I fined him two weeks' wages. Initially the PFA tried to intervene but Mick McGuire, who was now the deputy chief executive, agreed with the club. He was no admirer of Kolinko's agent Phil Graham and we moved the player out on a free transfer after I had paid £650,000 for him, which was a shame as he was a good player, but the die had been cast at the beginning of the season.

Trevor had added Noel Whelan to his squad on loan from Middlesbrough. He came with a reasonably big salary and reputation. When I asked Trevor what he thought about Whelan he responded by saying he was very good-looking.

Quite what that had to do with football I didn't know.

I soon discovered the player agreed with Trevor in his assessment.

He cried off from an away game, saying both he and his wife

were sick. When I returned from the game I went out to the trendy St Martin's Lane Hotel in London's West End for the evening and who do I bump into? Noel Whelan, who was rather stunned to see his chairman out and about. So much for him being sick and so much for him staying on loan with Palace too.

Another striker, Ade Akinbadbuy, had been recuperating for six months after his extremely expensive operation in America. Like all players he was put on the rota for corporate appearances, except for some reason he believed he was exempt from such things.

We had recently signed a shirt sponsorship deal with the Lambeth Building Society, who were sponsoring our academy. They were opening a new branch and requested one of our senior players to attend the opening to cut a ribbon or something.

So we committed Badbuy to it. Two months earlier he was given a reminder, and again a month out, a week out and the day before.

On the day he never showed. I was straight on the phone to Trevor and I wanted it dealt with. I wanted the player disciplined and fined. Trevor agreed and he said he would deal with it. A day or so later Trevor phoned me and explained how the player had got upset when reprimanded, had rejected the fine and had asked the PFA to intervene. On top of that he had picked up a chair and thrown it at the window in Trevor's office.

I didn't understand why Trevor appeared to take such relish in telling me situations he had failed to deal with. He didn't seem to understand his inability to deal with these situations reflected on his control and management of the players.

I asked Trevor to get the player in his office later that afternoon for a meeting with me. When he arrived late and walked into Trevor's office, I immediately told him to wait outside until I was ready to see him.

I let him sweat for a while and then summoned him. I was outraged that a player thought he could do as he wished. As he attempted to sit down I asked him what he was doing. Akinbiyi was confused. I told him to stand up, as I hadn't asked him to sit.

'You cost me £2.25 million, sixteen grand a week, and haven't kicked a ball for six months. I sent you to the best knee specialist in the world, and this is how you repay me.'

I then got onto the chair-throwing incident and dared him to do it again in front of me.

After a relentless five-minute tirade from me he was very apologetic.

Trevor popped up now, having found the courage of my convictions and condemning the player's behaviour.

It was agreed that Akinbiyi would donate three weeks of his wages to charity and would advise the PFA that he no longer required their help. He would also write to the Lambeth Building Society's MD and apologise. Actually, I thought better of it: we wrote the letter and he signed it.

It was not long after this that I decided to put him out on loan to Stoke and eventually as part of cost-cutting I paid Akinbiyi some of his contract and let him go on a free transfer, writing off another £2.25 million in transfer fees.

This was proving to be a wonderful business. Fallouts and payouts were all I seemed to get out of football.

Against this backdrop of underlying turmoil in the football club I had other issues going on. I lost the court case with 121 over the £6.5 million warranty reclaim. This had been ongoing for two years. I had paid enormous legal fees and now had launched an appeal, which a short while later overturned the original verdict in my favour. That should have been the end of it but they took the case to arbitration which would take a year to be heard.

As the season wound down, amid the backdrop of disharmony and a growing lack of belief in Trevor, I wanted him to illustrate to me by means of a written blueprint how we were going to achieve my goal of promotion to the Premier League.

After eighteen or so months we were going nowhere. What I wanted was a clear illustration of what we were going to do and how we were going to achieve it. Yes, it was a business tool, but why should a business that requires a massive investment not have a clearly outlined plan? And how could its manager not understand how he was going to achieve its goal? Trevor greeted me with a look of bemusement when I told him what I wanted.

To be fair to him, he had a stab at it – and after I had read it, it was exactly what I wanted to do to him. In essence it said that more of the same was the order of the day.

I asked Trevor to do it again in a fractious meeting in the board-room and he refused. I lost my patience and walked out in frustration.

Sitting on the steps outside my office I thought that wasn't right for me, so the next morning I went to the training ground and fired Trevor.

I don't think he was surprised. I almost got the impression he was relieved when I told him. He just nodded, remarking it was his birthday the next day, and without thinking I said, 'Many happy returns, Trev!'

Trevor was a decent man and to this day remains a good friend. We had shared some good moments, notably beating Millwall at last, the old rivals Brighton and the Liverpool games, and some bad, especially being dragged along to *Madame Butterfly* at the Royal Albert Hall by our partners.

Crystal Palace was just not the right club for Trevor. Some places just don't fit with certain managers' faces and Palace and its supporters never really took to him.

When we parted I advised Trevor we would have to work out a settlement between us and not to get his agent involved.

Trevor ignored my advice and got his agent Leon Angel involved, a man I grew to dislike immensely.

I railed against agents and I more than anyone brought them into the public domain and made them and their activities public knowledge. But this guy was near the top of the pile as far as I was concerned and I refused to deal with him.

Six months and numerous conversations later we still hadn't agreed compensation. By now Trevor had grown fed up with Angel. He asked me if I could discuss the matter with his friend Nick Rogers, a man I had met on numerous occasions and respected. Within an hour or so Trevor had his settlement.

9

IT'S NOT ROCKET SCIENCE

I had a serious conundrum after repeatedly asking managers to take on Steve Kember and Terry Bullivant as part of their structure. Now Trevor Francis had left, Kember was banging down my door for the top job.

I felt duty bound to give him a shot as he had always been overlooked in favour of someone who invariably failed to deliver. This was a classic case of 'be careful what you wish for'.

Anyone looking for pearls of wisdom about recruiting managers from within should consider this. If players come out and say they like a certain coach and hope he gets a chance as manager the same players, by the very nature of their inadequate performances, will get him the sack sooner rather than later. As soon as an assistant manager or coach becomes the manager his relationship with the players radically changes. He is no longer their confidant or shoulder to cry on. He is the reason why they are not picked or don't get something they think they are entitled to and the football graveyard is full of them.

My next challenge for the approaching season was Wayne Routledge. Our young and highly rated starlet was making quite a name for himself. He had just returned from a pre-season tour with England under-19s to rave reviews from the critics. But I was more concerned by what was going on off the pitch, and right under the eyes of the FA. I had heard disturbing things about young players being tapped up by other players' parents on behalf of agents.

Wayne had made it into our first team at the tender age of seventeen. He was a product of my prized academy and someone I had watched come through the ranks since he was fourteen. I took a particular interest in Wayne's development and also got to know his mother Sheila well. She was a single parent, and I made sure that the family's needs were part of the equation in our handling of the player.

I gave him his first scholarship, his first pro contract and was instrumental in ensuring Trevor Francis gave him his first-team debut.

So imagine my utter disgust and fury when an agent called Paul Stretford phoned my secretary to advise her that I was to talk to him and no longer directly to the boy or his mother.

Stretford had got to Wayne whilst he was away with England. It was a disgrace that agents had access to young players while they were away on England duty and believe me, it was rife in the industry. This was another fine example of the FA, an organisation that was supposed to police football, who banged on about the crucial development of young players in the game but did bugger all to protect clubs against predatory agents. And people wondered why I had numerous altercations with them.

Stretford was just another of the agents that in my opinion operated when it suited them in a manner which ignored regulation. He became better known as the agent of another Wayne – Rooney – and in recent years his wrongful conduct got the attention it deserved with a substantial ban from the game.

20

In the instance of my Wayne, I refused to deal with Stretford, banned him from the training ground and the stadium and attempted to talk some sense into the ungrateful player and his mother. But despite my best efforts, it was ultimately a battle I was to lose.

During my time in football I worked tirelessly to reduce agents' influence and expose them in their true light. It still bemuses me why the only people in football who pay nothing yet earn out of it are agents.

Football clubs pay League levies on gate receipts and transfer fees. Players pay membership fees to the PFA, broadcasters pay to broadcast and fans pay to watch.

And agents? They pay nothing. I believed there should be a levy put on agents' fees that goes back into the football family, albeit a very dysfunctional one.

To my mind, on the whole most agents were little better than skin traders and it was incumbent on the football authorities to control this unnecessary evil that, in my view, served no greater good.

The Football League started to introduce regulations where clubs had to declare if an agent had been involved in a deal in a bid to eliminate the threat of agents getting paid by both the buying and selling clubs. Putting out strong guidelines was perhaps in no small way down to me regaling the media with my views on agents at every opportunity.

Back to the season in hand. The cash flow forecast for 2003–04 predictably did not make good reading for me. It showed I needed to put £9.5 million into the club just to stand still. This didn't influence my decision to appoint Kember, but it did get me focused on stopping paying both big transfer fees and big wages for players.

Portsmouth had been promoted the previous season without paying big transfer fees and I figured that if we got it right we could replicate that.

I reshaped the management structure and brought in a new finance director to try and enhance the financial side of the business.

I also needed someone to assume control of the club on a day-to-day basis as I was based in Spain, fighting court cases and looking at other business projects.

The decision was between my brother Dominic and Phil Alexander, chief executive in title as a result of his fortuitous rise during administration. He was not a CEO in outlook or deliverability; he was a sales director.

So I decided to make Dominic vice-chairman so Phil didn't lose face by being stripped of his title.

I didn't appoint my brother out of nepotism but because he was the best person for the job. Dominic paid attention to detail and over the three years he had been at Palace had changed large aspects of the on-the-ground operation, eliminating all manner of abuse and upping standards across the business.

But Alexander and Dominic's relationship was far from harmonious. Dominic had scant tolerance for Alexander's lack-of-detail approach and Alexander resented reporting to him.

There were numerous explosive confrontations as Alexander resisted controls being put on him. I could see Alexander's strong points, even if Dominic couldn't. I wanted him focused on generating income and having grown tired of the arduous task of dealing with agents I put Phil in charge of transfers and sales, working to guidelines set by me.

Soon we saw the departure of Wimbledon from Selhurst Park and ultimately from football.

They went into administration in June 2003 and then controversially re-emerged as the MK Dons.

I was sad to see Charles Koppel, the Wimbledon chairman, a personal friend and close ally against all football bullshit, suffer such awful abuse from his own supporters.

The Wimbledon fans expected to get promoted or have success on crowds of 4,000 or less. Who was supposed to pay for that? The death threats and verbal abuse Charles suffered because he was proposing to move them to Milton Keynes to make them viable was unforgivable.

Wimbledon's unfortunate demise had an unexpected benefit for us. At Kember's request we took Neil Shipperley, a former Palace striker, on a free transfer from the administrators in lieu of charges they had to pay us for being a tenant.

One of the summer's biggest announcements in football was the news that a certain Roman Abramovich had bought Chelsea and was to unleash spending power the like of which football had never witnessed before.

We had arranged a pre-season game against them before his arrival and therefore were the first English team to play the newly assembled Abramovich-fuelled Chelsea.

Trevor Birch, the chief executive of Chelsea who had been instrumental in bringing Abramovich in, allowed us to keep the entire gate receipts rather than the customary 50/50 split, which was a rare act of generosity in football.

In and around the time I was appointing Steve Kember, I received a phone call from Tony Adams, the ex-Arsenal and England captain, who wanted to become Palace's new manager. It was a very strange phone call, as Tony seemed to have developed a very slow and deliberate way of speaking.

His delivery was very pronounced, littered with long words and parables of wisdom. It was not the Tony Adams I had met before but a new one, a highly educated philosopher of football, an Arsène Wenger protégé.

After I had removed the Friedrich Nietzsche book from his mouth and told him he had the square root of fuck all of a chance of managing at this level at this stage, the real Tony Adams emerged with a mouthful of expletives.

We then spoke in an honest fashion about football and I told him I was happy to give him a shot as Kember's number two, learning his trade and then taking over in a few years.

That wasn't good enough for our Tony. He was going to get a job in the Premier League or First Division.

I told him there was no way that would happen and eventually I believe he landed at League Two Wycombe Wanderers and I am pretty sure he was not an unqualified success there!

The pre-season came and went and there was a feeling of accord amongst players and management. The campaign had started with promise. We won our first three games and sat on top of the league. Everything looked rosy in the garden but along came the dog to piss on the roses.

Firstly Matt Clarke, our goalkeeper, was forced to retire, which was very sad for the lad and extremely costly for us. I had spent £1.25 million on him two years earlier and only got thirty-eight games from him. Fortunately he had an insurance policy to compensate him whereas we got nothing.

So we signed Thomas Myhre on loan from Sunderland, which proved to be very ironic, given what occurred at the end of the season.

I liked Kember and I wanted him to be successful. But everything was a joke for Steve and he had never really been under pressure. Stepping into the breach a couple of times and steadying the ship was vastly different from running it.

All of a sudden and inexplicably the wheels just came off.

We failed to record a win in seven games, taking only two points and dropping to twentieth in the table.

I tried to get Kember going but he was his usual happy-go-lucky self. It was clear that happy-go-lucky meant comfortable for players and it was not working.

The media vultures were circling overhead and the results kept on getting worse until we reached 1 November and played Wigan away in a televised game.

There I witnessed the worst performance of a Palace team for some time. I was a few minutes late and we were already 1–0 down.

As I got to my seat a woman steward shouted 'tie' at me and stopped me. As usual I was not wearing one. I said no thanks and she literally grabbed me and pushed one in my hands with the strict instruction to wear it.

I sat down next to Bullivant, watching us go down 2–0 after just thirty minutes. But what disturbed me most was the dire performance and complete lack of commitment from the players. So putting on a bleeding tie was the last thing on my mind.

Looking at Bullivant I asked what the hell was going on and his shrinking violet reaction told me he and Kember were lost.

Theo Paphitis phoned me and told me the TV cameras were on me every five minutes and I looked like I wanted to murder someone. Bullivant, probably, if I could have got away with it.

At half-time I went inside, forgetting the tie, and over came Nora bleeding Batty stewardess, who grabbed me and refused to let me in until I put the bloody tie on. I could hardly have a scuffle with her. By the size of her she would have probably beaten me up anyway. Northern charm at its finest!

The second half got even worse and we conceded a further three goals to lose 5–0.

Dave Whelan, the Wigan chairman, had made disparaging remarks about me a couple of years earlier when Steve Bruce left them to join Palace, so I avoided going in the boardroom. As the game finished I went to leave, passing Whelan, who stuck his hand out. When I shook it he said to me: 'You must be very embarrassed, your team are pretty crap.'

I never forgot that. As I was learning all too frequently, in football your words often come back to haunt you. And they did for Whelan.

After this humiliating performance I felt I had nowhere to go and on the Monday, after maintaining radio silence for the weekend, I fired Steve Kember and Terry Bullivant.

After firing them I sauntered into the dressing room at the training ground, told Kit Symons what had happened and asked him to step in as a player-coach. He was very apprehensive and didn't jump at the opportunity as I thought he would. Later on in the day he telephoned me in a far more positive mood and said he wanted the opportunity as long as he could bring in his own assistant manager, Stuart Gray, the former Southampton boss.

Clearly since we had spoken in the morning someone had spoken to Kit and urged him to take the opportunity.

I left him with the thought that I was grateful for him stepping in and that I was going to look for a manager but at this moment in time his hat was in the ring if he wanted it to be.

* * *

My relationship with Sarah Bosnich came to an end in November 2003, as I had no desire to settle down. That added to my good temper.

By now I had been a multi-millionaire for over three years. Instantaneous and significant wealth is something you have to learn to be comfortable with. It's one thing being the owner of a business worth £75 million, another thing entirely when you have that worth sat in your own bank account.

You do change, but others around you change much more. People I had grown up with and known for years now treated me completely differently.

Everywhere you go people open doors for you and pretty soon you buy into all of that. Everything is first class and all of a sudden you stop checking bills because it doesn't matter.

I had a £2.5 million penthouse in Chelsea, a £6 million villa in Marbella, a permanent suite at the Grosvenor House Hotel on Park Lane and a boat worth £2.5 million.

I flew everywhere by private jet, had fifteen luxurious cars, a wardrobe with over a hundred tailor-made suits and a full-time chauffeur.

I spent money as if it were going out of fashion, because I could, and because I was earning £40,000 in interest a week.

That said, owning a football club was making a big dent in my fortune. I was focused on achieving what I wanted with Palace but I also wanted other outlets for business. I had set up the magazine *Octane*, tried to buy the TV production company Planet Rapido and looked at all manner of other investments.

And all this time I lived a life of decadence. Whatever I wanted, I bought.

What I'm trying to get at here was that it wasn't about being rich or flash. Not quite.

What I had was irreverence towards money. It was the end product of success and was not the thing that motivated me. Having money was fantastic but if you were not careful it took away desire and hunger and replaced it with ego and falseness.

With a smoke-and-mirrors business like football you could become detached from the things that made you successful and then believe the things you read about yourself in papers and magazines and on TV.

All of a sudden you could become a caricature of yourself.

After a few years of vitriol between myself and Ron Noades, the former owner of Palace and – in my opinion – the undeserving owner of Selhurst Park, I tried to come to a deal to buy the stadium. Noades was open to sell, the only problem was he wanted double what it was worth, £12 million. Over lunch I tried to reach some form of agreement. As one American president said: 'We do not negotiate with terrorists.' I should have taken this advice, I felt like I was dealing with one. Of course I'm joking, but Noades would not budge.

I offered £9 million, then £10 million, which was already massively higher than the £6.4 million valuation, but he would not move. I endured lunch with this tiresome man trying to find a deal whilst listening to his opinions of how I should run the football club. Eventually I said I would give him £10 million, plus a further £3 million if/when we got promoted to the Premier League, thus a million more than he wanted. The response was no and, as a final insult, he said I would never get Palace promoted. That was the last conversation I was to have with that man.

Whilst Kit was setting up for his new role I was searching for my sixth manager.

Tony Finnegan, an agent and friend of Ian Wright's, suggested Stan Ternent, the Burnley manager.

I asked Wrighty about Stan and he was glowing about him as he had played for him under Coppell in 1990 when Ternent was first-team coach.

Ternent was a tough northerner whose management style was no nonsense, forthright and upfront. No, let's not dress it up, he was aggressive and he stood no nonsense from players. The more I thought about it the more I liked the idea.

The press were doing the usual uninformed speculation about who the next manager would be, running all kinds of names.

The one they kept harping on about was Peter Taylor, from Hull City. He was a former Palace player and had previously shown interest when we had the vacancy in the summer after Trevor had gone. I never fancied Taylor, considering him to be a coach not a manager. With press speculation being rife, I decided to phone Adam Pearson, the Hull chairman, and let him know I had no interest in Taylor, so one Saturday I phoned Pearson and left a message on his voicemail, asking him to call me back. Unfortunately, he got the wrong end of the stick and called me, raging on my voicemail that I was phoning him about his manager on match day. I phoned him back and left a very curt message. Eventually we cleared up the misunderstanding, but three years later there was to be no such misunderstanding around Taylor.

I met Stan Ternent in my suite at the Grosvenor with his agent and his assistant manager Sam Ellis. He was very cocky and it felt like he wanted to talk down to me a little, as he was much older and more experienced in football. Like most people he had precon-ceived notions of me. I mentioned I considered him to be a strong independent man who had 'bollocks' and was not intimidated by anyone and made his own decisions and stood by them. So why then, I asked, did he need his hand held by his agent and assistant manager to speak to little old me, who was on my own? He clearly had enjoyed listening to me praise him, but the last bit caught him on the hop and after being thrown, he came back guns blazing and I liked him.

Meanwhile, Kit had taken his first two games and got noteworthy draws but I was still in the frame of mind to shake things up. I was fed up with players taking the piss and underperforming and constantly having to sack managers and pay them off.

So I decided to offer Ternent the job and phoned Finnegan and said I was prepared to offer him the same salary as Trevor Francis, £320,000 a year, and once agreed I would approach Burnley.

Barely an hour had passed and Finnegan was back on the phone.

'Stan says bollocks, it's not enough money.'

At first I thought he was joking but quickly it became apparent he was not. That pissed me off as Ternent had specifically told me it was not about money, it was about opportunity, and he believed Palace offered him that.

Suddenly it was all about money. I had offered him top dollar, but he still wanted more. So I pulled out and said to Finnegan, 'If it's all about money let's just leave it.'

I barely had time to put the phone down when Ternent came on the line.

'Chairman, you are making a big fucking mistake. I know more about football than you will ever know. This is a huge opportunity you are missing out on. You're going to regret this.'

He sounded like he was half-cut.

'OK, Stan, interesting way to resign from a job you haven't got, but let's leave it, shall we?' and I put the phone down.

I had quite fancied having him, but he had just turned out to be a bit of a clown.

But it was to get worse. I was going to meet Theo Paphitis at Millwall's ground to go out for dinner and on the way there Ternent left me a series of messages, each one worse than the last. When I got to Millwall I played them from my voicemail to Theo, who was incredulous and we all burst out laughing.

Clearly Ternent was drinking, the last message, left in a broad Lancashire accent, was 'Chairman, I am fooking great and you are fooking shit. I have got a fooking Bentley and a fooking Mercedes. You have made a big mistake. You haven't got the bollocks to answer my calls so fook your job.'

I phoned him back. He didn't answer so I left a message. 'Stan, thanks for your insightful commentary. The next time you apply for a job you might want to stay out of the pub whilst talking to your potential new chairman. Anyway, well done. Enjoy your next port and lemon, you buffoon.'

I also interviewed Neil Warnock at that time and had grown to like him a lot. We had a little bit of handbags in my first year when Neil had floated a mischievous rumour that we were selling Clinton Morrison and taking Marcus Bent in exchange, and giving them a million on top, a rumour that was designed to unsettle young Morrison and had annoyed me.

He had all the characteristics I wanted and we had become friends during my early tenure at Palace. He came to London and I interviewed him in my penthouse flat on Chelsea Bridge. We got on very well and he liked our squad but decided he wanted to try and finish what he had started at his beloved Sheffield United. We kept in touch over the years and were to have our time later.

Kit had got the team into some semblance of order with three draws and a win in his first four games.

But I was still looking to bring in a manager. I decided to bring

Terry Bullivant back into the fold as a special football adviser to me with the brief to go and find me a manager. Terry knew me very well and knew what I wanted and expected. We were inundated with applicants and Bullivant was interviewing around the country.

Two people phoned me direct who I didn't want to see, Steve Cotterill and Iain Dowie. Cotterill just annoyed me because he was so persistent and I am sorry to admit that I couldn't take his West Country accent seriously.

Dowie left me his résumé on my voicemail and I thought people who do that are convincing themselves, rather than me, of their capabilities.

Kit hit the buffers a little, losing three games in a row. At a social function I made an observation about how poorly Dougie Freedman was playing and perhaps Kit should consider dropping him. It was an observation, not an order.

But later that evening he was quite off with me, saying he was not going to be told who to pick.

Phil Alexander told me that he had overheard the assistant Stuart Gray saying you can't have a chairman telling you what to do and Kit had listened to this bad, out-of-context advice and acted upon it. In that moment Kit Symons ruled himself out of any serious consideration for the job, not because he took exception to my advice but because he took an antiquated attitude towards an owner's ability to make comments.

Bullivant was interviewing numerous candidates and bringing back dossiers on each applicant. After three weeks of interviews we had a number of candidates but Bullivant was absolutely adamant that the stand-out person was Iain Dowie and despite my reservations I agreed to see him.

Dowie apparently had a degree in rocket science and interviewed well for a football manager. He was professional, articulate and prepared. He had done his homework and had hunger and desire; he also had produced a report on the club, one at the time I thought was very impressive and unique. The ability to write such a report helped him get the job with me, but was to prove very unhelpful to him later on in a very different environment.

It didn't take me long to decide that he was right for the job. He was on his way out of Oldham as they were struggling in administration so he was free and clear to join Palace.

When it came to the terms I only offered him a short-term contract of eighteen months. I didn't want to get caught out with another substantial pay-out to a manager who failed to deliver.

I also set down a salary much lower than Messrs Bruce and Francis had enjoyed.

Iain wanted to discuss his salary and I refused to negotiate. My offer was take it or leave it. Dowie was taken aback by this but agreed. This impressed me, as he was backing himself on what he had said, which few managers do. I now believe that in actual fact he harboured resentment towards the offer, which would manifest itself at a later stage.

We were scheduled to play Reading away live on Sky TV on Saturday evening. I finalised the deal with Dowie on the Wednesday and decided not to announce the appointment until the following Monday. After weighing it up, I also decided to tell Kit after the Reading game.

My primary concern was that we needed to get a result at Reading. The papers were speculating that Dowie had the job so when I arrived at the Reading ground the busy Phil Alexander had spoken to Kit, who was aware of the rumours and was very down.

Alexander suggested that I should speak to Kit before the match, and I made a decision against my gut feeling, one that attracted infamy.

I went to see Symons and suggested we had a chat. Given the dressing room was busy we had to go outside as there was nowhere else to go. No one was in the tunnel area so I decided to have a conversation with Kit at the bottom of the step below the line of the pitch, and out of eye and earshot – or so I thought.

To this day people like Chris Kamara who covered the game for Sky maintain they heard the conversation. I accept they may have been unbeknownst to me able to see as the cameras were below the line of the pitch. But there was no way they could have heard what was said; otherwise their condemnation of my actions wouldn't have been so definitive.

The Symons conversation went like this:

'Clearly I can't legislate for rumours and press speculation but I have made a decision and I will be bringing in Iain Dowie.'

Kit was not surprised but was disappointed. 'Fucking hell, chairman, that's great. I thought you were going to tell me and give me the courtesy, I am fucking well owed that.'

I interrupted him. 'Hold on, Kit, I gave you an opportunity to gain some invaluable experience, experience you can't buy and it will probably be good for you in the future.

'I said that I would tell you when I had made a decision and only on Wednesday did I agree with Dowie and only yesterday did I tie up his contract.

'So the first opportunity I would have had to have told you was last night and up until walking in the stadium it was my intention to tell you at the first practical moment, which would have been after the game.'

Kit snapped. 'That's fucking great, chairman. I get you out of the cart and you show me no respect.'

'You got me out of the cart? Let's not forget, Kit, you were one of the fucking players that put me in the cart, as you put it, in the first place.

'I gave you an opportunity and am grateful for your help. I have made a decision to go with Dowie.'

Kit started to protest a little more but I stopped him in mid-sentence as I could sense he was going to say something that would be very damaging for him.

'Kit, do yourself a favour. Let's leave it there and not say anything else, because you never know what may happen next.'

I walked away, as I had earmarked Kit Symons to be Dowie's number two, and Kit calling me all kind of names would have made it difficult for me to make that appointment.

On getting back to the boardroom I saw that Chris Kamara and his Sky colleagues were replaying the footage that had been shot without my knowledge. I was coming in for some very heavy criticism, which would continue the next morning on *Goals on Sunday*, the programme hosted by Chris Kamara, with one of the guests, Chris Coleman, a Welsh teammate and close friend of Kit Symons, going on about how out of order I was.

We beat Reading emphatically 3–0, and at the end of the match Dowie phoned me and jokingly said did I still want him to come in on Monday.

Dowie did come in on Monday and Kit Symons did become his number two, thus starting another era with another manager. Iain Dowie was given the same remit as those who preceded him: promotion to the Premier League.

Despite being nineteenth in the league, in the press conference announcing Dowie's appointment I said I still felt promotion wasn't beyond us. It caused a degree of mirth amongst the journalists and the first questions were to Dowie about unrealistic expectations and pressure.

Dowie performed admirably in this press conference, upright, forthright, full of confidence, knew his challenge and was up for it.

I was heartened as his words were exactly what I wanted to hear from my new leader and if his actions matched the words there was cause for renewed optimism.

Dowie's first game, as chance would have it, was home to Millwall, a year to the month since the last time we had played my old mate Paphitis's rotten old rabble and beaten them.

Dowie was given a hero's reception by the fans, but we proceeded to lose 1–0 and I found Theo had plenty of time to hang around in my boardroom relishing the victory to my ear and bar cost.

Not only that but Paphitis and I had a bet on the result. The forfeit for the losing chairman was to wear the opposing team's mascot's costume in the return fixture. So now I had to wear Millwall's Zampa the Lion's get-up and run around the New Den. Of course this was a fact my close personal friend kept to himself by referring to it in his programme notes week after week leading up to the fixture.

I had made a bet and was fully prepared to honour it, but a few weeks before the game he offered me a get out of jail card. If I matched what the Millwall fans raised for a testicular cancer charity – their long-serving centre forward Neil Harris had recently suffered from it – I wouldn't have to wear the outfit. 'No thanks,' I replied, 'a bet's a bet.' Theo then explained the real reason for his kind face-saving gesture: they had reliable information that certain segments of their charming fan base were really looking forward to my appearance as Zampa, so much so they intended to bring washing-up bottles filled with petrol to squirt at me before setting me on fire, so it was a little bit more like a death sentence. Needless to say I took up Theo's offer. Their normally tight-fisted fans raised over £5,000, which I matched. So I sent our mascot 'Pete the Eagle' to present a big cheque on the pitch before one of their games, not that that stopped the ever-charming Millwall fans giving me barrel loads of abuse when we played them next.

In December 2003, as well as installing another new manager at Palace to achieve my dream of getting into the Premier League, I made the first inroads into fulfilling another one.

For a while now I had a vision of re-forming the iconic band The Specials, my favourite group.

After doing months of research I had arranged to meet my hero Terry Hall, the former lead singer of The Specials and Fun Boy Three, with his manager at the Grosvenor House Hotel.

I had tracked Terry down via Alan McGee, the founder of Creation Records, who looked after Oasis.

He put me on to Steve Blackwell, Terry's manager. Steve was an Aston Villa fan and coincidentally we had just played them in the cup at Villa Park, where I had met 'Deadly' Doug Ellis, the Villa chairman, who I took a great liking to. He was a character, he even let me smoke my cigar in his boardroom, with the words, 'You have broken every other rule in football, you may as well break another.' So this gave myself and Steve something to talk about.

We spent two hours talking. This was a band that had barely spoken for nearly twenty-four years. Terry and I became firm friends, as we remain today. He knew that I had this massive passion and said to me, 'We need someone like you to pull us together.'

In the early part of 2004 I left no stone unturned to re-form this band. Everybody told me it was impossible to get them back together. I met some of the Madness boys who told me no way.

I got every band member's phone number and set about calling them. I tracked Jerry Dammers down and arranged to meet him.

Jerry was the founder member of The Specials, and also the founder of Two-Tone, the label. He was also a bloody nutcase. I met him in the Grosvenor. He was a hero of mine, a musical genius who by now reminded me of something from Middle Earth, all long beard and no teeth.

Jerry was very strange and very contradictory.

In one breath he stated categorically that The Specials would never re-form and in the next he was curious to understand what I might pay.

I left my first meeting with Jerry none the wiser but all the more determined.

I worked with Steve Blackwell to put together a financial plan to show the members of the band what could be available to them should they re-form.

I eventually made contact with all of them. Some were very pleased to hear from me and others, like John Bradbury, were downright rude.

I did an interview with the *Evening Standard*, announcing my passion for the band and how I wanted to re-form them, which created a lot of interest. The headline read 'Too Much Too Young', the title of one of the band's most famous songs and a sly wink at my age as a football club owner.

Bit by bit things started to take shape. I had a vision of putting The Specials on at Selhurst Park and I tried to buy their back catalogue. I also put a formal contract in front of Jerry Dammers offering £1 million if the band re-formed.

*   *   *

I put The Specials and that dream to the back of my mind for a bit and got on with more pressing matters. Iain Dowie brought one member of staff with him, John Harbin, the fitness coach. He was a middle-aged Australian and more than just a fitness coach he was Iain's confidant and, in some instances, mentor.

Harbin was a fantastic man with a rugby background. He had no interest in the nonsense of football and footballers. He just went about the business of changing players' mind-sets.

He was absolutely vital to Dowie. Without Harbin there would have been no success, he was that important.

Dowie walked out in his second game away to Ipswich Town like a man who had a sense of his own destiny. Ipswich were fourth in the league and going well. I watched him, chest pumped out, striding down the side of the pitch. Palace were outstanding, winning 3–1 and looking like a side that was on the up.

In the next four and a half months I was to see the team I financed finally fulfil my expectations. The only problem was under Dowie I found the whole experience an anti-climax. He was very difficult to get on with. It was as if he was in a competition with me.

His father was a trade union leader, which came as no surprise to me.

He always went looking for an argument or was rude and disrespectful on the telephone.

Whenever that telephone conversation resulted in me suggesting he should come to see me, a completely different person would turn up, apologetic and contrite. I suspected that was the calming influence of John Harbin.

After all the campaigning for Dowie by Terry Bullivant, his reward from Dowie was to be completely marginalised and left out in the cold to such an extent that Terry decided it was best he leave Palace. There you are, football at its finest: loyalty and respect non-existent.

During the January transfer window Dowie made two signings: Mark Hudson, a centre back on loan from Fulham, and Mikele Leigertwood on a permanent deal from Wimbledon. We also took Birmingham's reserve goalkeeper Nico Vaesen on a three-month loan and this time the opportunistic sods got really lucky . . .

Despite the growing dislike I was developing for Iain I still gave him my luxurious penthouse on Chelsea Bridge to live in.

I wanted to try and get along with him but in the end I just thought it wasn't worth it and left him to get on with his job.

What was not open to debate was the effect he was having on the team. In his first ten games he took twenty-two points, title-winning form in any league.

We had jumped from nineteenth to ninth, two points off a play-off spot, spearheaded by the unbelievable goal scoring of Andy Johnson. There were some fabulous performances: 6–3 at home to Stoke, 5–1 away to Watford and 3–0 away to Neil Warnock's Sheffield United.

That particular performance really meant something, not because Neil had turned us down, but because Sheffield United were a benchmark team for me. They had an indomitable spirit, but we took them to pieces and totally destroyed their resolve to the point that Sheffield virtually gave up, which was something I had never seen from a Warnock team.

At that moment I believed we could actually go and get promoted. I had said it for nigh on four years and now I could sense it coming to pass.

Football was now show business, the players were the rock stars of the noughties. Highly paid and very high profile, they had gone from being solely on the back page of the papers to being front-page news. Most teams had their fair share of celebrity supporters and Palace had theirs: Bill Wyman, Bill Nighy, Ronnie Corbett, Timothy Spall, Jo Brand, Neil Morrissey, Eddie Izzard, Nigel Harman to name a few. One that sticks out in my memory was a Hollywood superstar, who telephoned me out of the blue to attend a game.

I was sitting in Spain, minding my own business, when my mobile phone rang and this softly spoken Irish voice came on the line telling me who it was and asking if he could come to the game on Saturday against Norwich and would it be OK if he brought his son. Not believing who it was, I passed him off to my secretary to get some tickets and promptly put it down as a bit of a crank call and forgot all about it.

So imagine my surprise when I walked into my boardroom on Saturday and was greeted by the lead actor in *Schindler's List* and the new *Star Wars* film. Liam Neeson was a big Palace fan. His best friend lived in Stockwell, a fellow actor who had supported Palace, and had introduced a young Liam to the club when he moved to London from Ireland. He was a charming man, who described it as an honour to be in the boardroom, looking at all the pots and pans in our trophy cupboard, I tried to reconcile in my mind who had the honour here as standing in front of me was one of the world's best actors.

There was a more disturbing side to footballers' fame when in late 2003, staying in my London home the Grosvenor House Hotel, I walked into the famous red bar for my customary gin and tonic and saw a group of footballers in the bar. They saw me too and promptly made themselves scarce, probably realising I was likely to know their club's chairman. That was the last I saw of them until the next morning, when one of the doormen from the Grosvenor told me about a controversial set of allegations surrounding some footballers about a sexual act that had come to be known as 'roasting'. Apparently this term had been coined by certain players.

So imagine my horror when the only person named in an article written by the *Sun* regarding these serious and somewhat distasteful allegations was myself, reporting that I had been seen in the bar when the players were there. Quite why I was mentioned I don't know, but it was later brought to my attention that certain players who were there believed that I had talked to the press, which I most certainly had not, as I had no knowledge or interest in what those players got up to. Later on, when we tried to sign Carlton Cole on loan from Chelsea when we went up to the Premier League, he wouldn't sign for us, apparently because the chairman had 'grassed them up'.

During this period of games we played Stan Ternent's Burnley and I made a point of being around the dressing room area as Ternent had said some inflammatory things to me on the phone and via other people. So I made sure I was there for him to say the same to my face.

When he emerged from the dressing room, I said: 'Nice to see you sober, Stan.'

He went for me and the stewards had to get in front of him as he tried to swing a punch at me.

I just laughed. To be fair on him, several months later after we got promoted I got a letter from Stan, saying I had got it right and apologising for his behaviour. And with that I changed my mind about Stan Ternent and whenever I saw him at games from then on we always got on well.

As the team was going into the ascendency my relations with the media reached an all-time low. For four years I had been very open and accessible but I felt that in the last year certain factions had gone from taking a professional perspective to personal attacks.

Some of the drivel that was written about me was just unnecessary, especially that written by the local and London press.

I had gone out of my way over the years to give these guys the best access, as I believed it was good form to give preference to them, and they repaid me by being snide, commenting more on my appearance and my personal life than on the performance of my team.

In the end I tired of this. The London *Evening Standard* was the main culprit. I had enough and banned them, remarking at the time that if they wanted to write crap about my club and me then they could do it from outside the ground and not whilst they were sitting in my stadium eating my biscuits.

I also decided that I would withdraw from talking to all forms of the media as I thought Sky had said some crappy things as well, always highlighting the negative and never praising the positive. I thought I would let the team do the talking, which was quite good timing, given we were doing so well.

Rather than the *Evening Standard* sports editor calling me to see what was wrong, he had the arrogance to phone the MD of our shirt sponsor, Churchill Insurance, saying that I had banned them from covering games and suggested that they were losing coverage and should reduce the money they spent with the club.

When I found out who the editor was I phoned him and asked him what he thought he was doing. He told me that his paper made our football club and helped the team succeed and win games.

'Are you bloody mad? You report events, you don't influence them.'

He actually believed what he was saying. I mean, people say I know about arrogance but this guy's behaviour was off the charts. Rather than calm things down he made things ten times worse.

Now I was incandescent and continued the ban, only relenting towards the end of the season. But I decided never to speak to that paper again and I never did. Whatever they wrote in the future concerning me never had one direct quote from me.

By the way, the editor was a guy called Simon Greenberg who became the communications director of football at Chelsea Football Club. After departing Stamford Bridge he then became part of England's 'successful' bid team to stage the 2018 World Cup.

The next four games saw us hit a blip, taking just four points and dropping down to twelfth and nine points off the play-offs.

I went to see Millwall play Sunderland in the FA Cup semi-final at Old Trafford to support Theo Paphitis and his rabble, now managed by Dennis Wise – or Napoleon, as we called him.

Dennis had come to speak to me at Palace after leaving Leicester in, shall we say, less than auspicious circumstances.

I met him with Trevor Francis and it looked as if we were going to take him when Trevor had a dramatic change of heart and Dennis went and joined Millwall.

Sometime later I bumped into Wise and he claimed Trevor had called him and said he wanted to sign him but the chairman – i.e., me – had blocked the deal. Strange that, as I had done no such thing. This was just another case of Francis not wanting to deliver bad news, I suspect.

Talking of Leicester, around this time, Leicester City under Micky Adams were having a mid-season break in La Manga, Spain, when some of their players got themselves into a serious situation and several of them were arrested and held over alleged sexual offences. Phil Smith, the agent, phoned me. One of his players Paul Dickov was amongst them and Phil wanted some help. He knew I lived in Spain and fortunately for him and Paul, it turned out my lawyer was related to the district judge in the province they were arrested in. Phil explained it was a case of mistaken identity: the girls involved were prostitutes and the footballers had been set up.

The Spanish authorities were not planning to release them until they were arraigned, which could take some time. I reached out through my lawyers and got these players released from prison and allowed to return to the UK, where the matter was resolved. I liked Paul Dickov as a player and trusted what Phil Smith had told me, which was later borne out to be true, but getting them out of Spain was very important for justice to be served. Dickov's wife Jan phoned me and thanked me, as did the player himself. Later, when I signed Paul, he never quite did it for me, despite promising me he would as he owed me a huge favour. But as is so often the case with players: they never pay their dues.

I watched Millwall reach the FA Cup Final and, as thrilled as I was for Theo, our loss of form at a critical point in the season left me thinking that I might be denied my day in the sun.

I underestimated Dowie's resilience as we won six and drew one out of our next seven games, beating two teams, West Ham and Sunderland, who were to appear in our immediate future.

In one of those seven games I jokingly prayed for Andrew Johnson not to score a goal, as by this time his prolific goal scoring during this season had put him on £7,500 a goal.

He scored a hat trick against Crewe, giving him a £22,500 goal bonus for one game, and when we got a penalty I was actually screaming for someone else to take it. It was a bit silly, really, as winning that game was critical for our play-off ambitions. He took the penalty, and scored.

Our last game was away to Coventry. If we won we were in the play-offs; if we lost and Wigan won, we were not. Unbelievably, Coventry tore us to pieces and we were 2–0 down in the first half – and it could have been five.

In the second half we were slightly better but still lost. By then news had filtered through that Wigan were winning 1–0. Just as we thought we were out, Brian Deane headed an equaliser for West Ham in the dying minutes, thus putting Wigan out and us in the play-offs. It was a goal that was to prove fateful for West Ham, and one I had to listen about from Brian Deane every summer I bumped into him in Marbella from then on.

Personally, I couldn't have been happier for Wigan and Whelan. After all – fancy losing a play-off spot to a crap team!

Behind the scenes, I had been working for some six months with Investec, a big financial company, on a deal to restructure Palace.

I had agreed a deal in principle for £15 million, which would help the hugely under-pressure finances of Palace and me personally, given pursuit of my ambition was very costly and we had forecasted losing £9.5 million this year alone.

Having run the club for four years with significant personal investment – from rebuilding the playing squad and the academy to buying the training ground to improving the stadium – this deal was the light at the end of the bleak tunnel we had been traipsing through since the collapse of ITV Digital.

As well as all this I was still pushing on The Specials front and had now spoken to all the members of the band. Pretty much five out of the original seven were on side with the idea of re-forming, although I suspect there was still a degree of scepticism amongst them.

I spent a lot of time with Terry and Steve Blackwell. Terry was concerned that nobody wanted to see them and they had long since been forgotten. I told him in no uncertain terms how wrong he was.

Jerry, though, was still very resistant so when I was invited to do *Soccer A.M.* with Tim Lovejoy, who I knew to be a huge Specials fan, I took Terry along with me to talk about them and make it public knowledge that there was a will within certain members of the group.

I took Terry with me by helicopter to the FA Cup Final, as he was a huge Manchester United fan. Manchester United ran out 3–0 winners but I was disappointed for Theo. I felt that this Cup Final was as much about his achievement as a chairman, taking Millwall from the brink of the abyss to a new stadium, play-offs for the Premier League and now an FA Cup Final, and he never really got the recognition he deserved. No wonder Theo became so disillusioned in the end and got out.

We had drawn Sunderland in the play-offs by virtue of the fact we had finished sixth and they had finished third.

The excitement leading up to the game was enormous and we sold out very quickly.

I was not nervous going into the game as I believed I had solved the financial problems, and the play-offs and potential promotion to the Premier League were all upsides for me.

The only thing that had infuriated me was that Birmingham got to do it to me again: they said they wouldn't extend Nico Vaesen, the goalkeeper we had on loan from them, unless we paid them £50,000 if we won the play-off semi-final and a further £200,000 if we got promoted to the Premier League.

Talk about victims of our own success. I had no real choice, so through gritted teeth I agreed to the legitimised blackmail.

On the evening of the game I called my directors into my office, wanting to have a drink with them as this had been a very difficult season. We had all worked hard on a number of financial and logistical initiatives and were on the cusp of something really special.

As we were having this drink together my phone rang. Lisa my PA put through the MD of Investec. He was phoning from the States, seemingly unaware of his timing, to tell me that the £15-million deal we had agreed – the deal I had considered of significant importance for the club – was off.

I couldn't believe it. Without letting on that something had troubled me, I asked the directors to excuse me for a minute.

I tried to establish the reason why, but the MD could only apologise. The deal had fallen through minutes before the biggest game in my four years of ownership of the club.

I had spent six months working on this deal and had exhausted all other avenues for finance. Outside the Premier League the only game in town had been Investec and now that was gone.

For some reason despite this dire news I was philosophical. I literally sighed and thought, 'Let's hope we win tonight.'

I always stood at home games and this habit never changed during all my years of ownership. I was very reactionary, and when something I didn't like happened in the game I would disappear down the stairs and out of the view of the crowd to express my frustrations. Poor Stephanie, the boardroom hostess, would be greeted with me coming into the boardroom effing and jeffing.

As I was waiting for the teams to come out, Alan Smith, my first manager, walked past me to take his seat and said, 'I bet you are shitting yourself.'

'Nice,' I thought.

It was a great game in which we ran out 3–2 winners. After we had gone behind, as was the norm for the season, Andrew Johnson scored, taking his total to thirty-two goals for the season and somewhere in the region of £150,000 in goal bonuses alone.

We had played Sunderland a few times over the last few years and their chairman Bob Murray and board of directors were not the friendliest and most welcoming people.

When they had been in the Premier League and drawn us in the Cup they had been downright inhospitable and rude.

After an exciting match the fans had invaded the pitch and, in front of the section containing the Sunderland fans, taunted them with their celebrations. Immediately, Dominic and I went out and physically got the 200 or so exuberant fans off the pitch. I'm not sure how many other chairmen would have gone onto a pitch to send off overzealous fans.

It didn't stop my old pals the FA fining the club £15,000. These arbitrary fines annoyed me intensely and when we appealed they simply upheld the original decision and then, to add insult to injury made the fine bigger!

The second leg was on the Monday in Sunderland.

This was a massive moment in my ownership, yet I was still very relaxed.

But at half-time we were 2–0 down after dominating the match and seemingly on our way out. Yet for some reason I still had a serene feeling of calm.

In the second half we plugged away but Julian Gray got sent off, thus reducing us to ten men, and with barely a minute left to play we were dead and buried.

Or so I thought.

From a corner and with the inevitable whistling from the Sunderland fans to put intimidating pressure on the referee to blow the final whistle, substitute Darren Powell headed home.

The goal should never have stood as Neil Shipperley committed virtual GBH on their goalkeeper.

Extra time came and went and we now faced a penalty shootout.

Yet despite the magnitude of this moment I remained composed.

Before the penalties were taken I snuck out for a cigarette with my brother and just sort of sighed with a 'what will be, will be' shrug.

I sat there in the Stadium of Light, watching the penalty shoot-out, which could literally change the immediate direction of my future and finances.

The order escapes me as far as penalties were concerned but it turned out that on three separate occasions we had a penalty to score that would enable us to win.

I watched the players in the centre circle and I remember young Wayne Routledge at seventeen being sent up to take a penalty, thinking how could players much older and more experienced than him put him under so much pressure.

Of course when he did, he missed. Eventually Michael Hughes, probably the most experienced player on the pitch, walked up from the centre circle like a man heading towards the gallows.

That walk seemed like a lifetime before he stepped up and scored and put Palace into the play-off final, the 'richest game in the world'.

I remember celebrating and also trying to be magnanimous with the Sunderland directors.

My phone went red-hot and I answered call after call, then I got one from Freddy Shepherd, the Newcastle United chairman, who couldn't stop laughing.

When he did he wanted me to pass the phone to the Sunderland chairman Bob Murray, which of course I would not do. Well, I might have if Murray had been at the game, such was the rivalry in the north-east.

As far as Shepherd was concerned I had made his year and if we were out in Newcastle our money was no good.

For the play-off final we drew the smaller end of the Millennium

Stadium with an allocation of 34,000, which sold out in six days.

We booked the Vale of Glamorgan Hotel in Cardiff. This was the lucky hotel and no one who had stayed there had lost since the play-offs had been staged in Cardiff since 2000.

Our opponents, West Ham United, had missed a trick there, but as the twelve days leading up to the monumental game went past it appeared they were relaxed about most things. The vibe coming from their end was that they believed that the final was a foregone conclusion.

I flew to Spain, preferring to be out of the way of the media scrum leading up to the play-off final, staying in Spain until Friday 28 May, the day before the game.

On the Thursday night before the final we had a corporate event.

It was a sporting dinner, hosting 500 Palace fans who came to dine and be entertained by a variety of entertainers and after-dinner speakers.

This year the compères for the after-dinner speeches were Alan Brazil and Mike Parry, the hosts of the talkSPORT radio station.

As the play-off final was only two days away there would have been extreme optimism in the room, so what followed was doubly outrageous.

Onstage, Parry and Brazil unleashed a tirade of abuse about Crystal Palace and ridiculed the club's chances of beating West Ham in the play-off final.

Understandably the audience became quite agitated and restless. Dominic was overseeing the event and was listening to these two idiots – who were being paid by the club – stand up and be derogatory. He was concerned that the audience were getting inflamed but it didn't stop Parry and Brazil, who singled me out for some special attention.

Eventually Dominic got security to remove them from the stage fearing a riot was about to break out. They were shepherded out of the marquee and into the boardroom.

Dominic phoned me in Spain, told me what was going on and said that he had removed them from the stage before things got very ugly.

I was relaxed about it, probably because I was detached from it. I told Dom not to lose his head, and to try and control the situation. Once in the boardroom, rather than the situation being defused, Parry appeared to want to inflame it all the more. Dominic asked them what right they had to be so abusive. Why would they come into our place of business and insult the club, its supporters and its owner?

He was greeted with the response, 'Fetch us a drink, son.' Dominic called them a cab and had them removed.

I have never found out why they chose to behave this way, I had had no real dealings with either one of them. Perhaps it was a case of people forming opinions of you without even having met you, which is often the way in football. Unfortunately they chose not to leave it there, and on their radio show the next day they broadcasted the fact that my brother and some other goons working for me had manhandled them out of a corporate event for no reason.

Meanwhile, I was travelling back to England from Spain. It was the day before the game.

I had friends flying from all over the world to watch this game and my mood was still very good, despite the previous evening's events.

As I boarded the flight I decided to pick up a bunch of the morning's papers. I was looking through them in the airport lounge when I turned to an article written by a journalist called John Cross from the *Daily Mirror*.

It was a full-page spread titled something like 'Palace Players in Bonus Crisis'. The article described how on the eve of the play-off final the Crystal Palace team were in disarray as the owner – i.e. me – had refused to pay the players their well-earned bonuses. As a result, the club was in apparent turmoil and some players were refusing to play.

This was all news to me. It was a piece of malicious reporting on the part of a journalist who I had had run-ins with before. Irrespective of whether the article was wrong or right – and believe me, it was wrong – the timing of it on the Friday before the play-off final was designed to destabilise the club before this game.

Now I was agitated. A pair of buffoons taking the piss out of the club was one thing, but it was something entirely different when a national newspaper decided to print an article full of untruths and misrepresentations. I hadn't spoken to the media for the best part of six months and on the eve of this game I had this.

I was on the phone to my lawyers instructing them to draw up a writ, which I served on the paper as soon as I landed in the UK. The upshot was the paper had to print, of course at a later stage, a retraction and pay substantial damages. I did waive my rights to compensation and an apology if the paper sacked John Cross, the journalist who wrote the poisonous article. They declined my generous offer.

The next morning I borrowed Mohamed Al Fayed's helicopter, which was emblazoned with the Harrods livery, and flew with an ensemble of mates to Cardiff. We landed in the hotel grounds in the full glare of the world's media but I still had no interest in talking to them whatsoever.

From the hotel we travelled to the game, a fifteen-minute journey by minivan. The driver couldn't get us close to the stadium as we had left it late so he dropped us as near as he could. But he had dropped us off at the wrong side of the stadium.

This was the side where the West Ham supporters were situated and we were required to walk right through them to get to our entrance.

It didn't really bother me and off I set with my gang behind me. I got about hundred yards before I was hauled back by my friends, who decided this was a very bad idea. Indeed, as the volume of abuse began to rise once I was spotted, Theo Paphitis pulled me back and said, 'Be sensible, let's walk round.'

Reluctantly I agreed. I assumed his motivations were solely for my well-being but later he told me he was actually in fear of his life. There was only one person West Ham fans hated more than me on that day and that was the chairman of Millwall Football Club.

It was a beautiful day, momentarily ruined when I came into corporate hospitality and there, resplendent in a Crystal Palace tie, was former chairman Ron Noades. I believe he came to this game so that if Palace lost, he could wallow in my demise.

It was a sweltering day and I was wearing a suit that by now could probably have walked itself out to the directors' box. As it had become my lucky suit and I had worn it to every game since the end of January I dared not go to the match without it.

I had developed superstitions and couldn't help it. Before every game John my driver had to play Elton John's 'Are you ready for love' as that bloody song had been played on this winning streak.

The game ebbed and flowed. There were nigh on 80,000 fans and the magnitude of the occasion and what it meant to every single person there couldn't be overestimated.

I remained outwardly unfazed in my held-together-by-dry-cleaning Ozwald Boateng suit and my ever-present sunglasses.

Both sides had good chances to open the scoring but at half-time in the world's richest game the score was 0–0 with all to play for.

The second half flew by, until the sixty-second minute when we scored and went 1–0 up.

Bedlam broke out in the directors' box in our section. All my executives and I were up, punching the air.

As the moment calmed I looked across at my counterparts at West Ham in their section and I thought that if I were in their shoes, I would be saying to myself, 'Knock yourselves out celebrating, you fuckers, there is still thirty minutes to go.'

So I made sure that I cut the celebration as short as possible. In this as in every game, I kicked every ball, disputed every refereeing decision that didn't go our way, and did it at full volume.

Time exploded and space contracted. The clock crawled as we entered the last ten minutes of the game.

Paphitis leaned across and told me with ten minutes to go that it was worth £5 million a minute. After what seemed an hour there were five minutes to go and he leaned across and said, 'That's worth £10 million a minute.'

And every long minute that ticked past he did the arithmetic.

I looked at my dear friend with two minutes to go and said: 'Yes, mate, I fucking well know it's worth £25 million a minute.'

Then injury time finally came and went, the referee signalled the end of the game, and Crystal Palace owned by Simon Jordan – yes, the club I owned – had won and were now headed for the Premier League, the biggest, richest league in the world of football, taking our place amongst the elite where in my mind we already belonged.

I was remarkably calm, feeling the four years of battles with everyone and everything had taken their toll. Not talking to the media for six months, my strained relationship with Dowie, the insults from the two buffoons and the newspaper article on the Friday before the game had added to my mood of disenfranchisement. I never enjoyed that moment the way I should have.

As I sat there, Theo told me to get down onto the pitch and celebrate and applaud the fans. I didn't want to but he made me see sense. So I went downstairs to the dressing room area to go out through the tunnel and onto the pitch.

As I went to walk out, Nick Craig, the in-house legal eagle for the Football League, stopped me.

'Sorry, Simon, you can't go out there until the trophy has been presented.'

'For crying out loud, Nick, this is the moment I have waited for.'

'Sorry, Simon, it's Football League rules.'

I turned to flounce off, but then a thought dawned on me and I turned back to Nick Craig and said, 'Football League rules, OK then, that's fine. But I am not in the Football League any more. I am in the Premier League so get out of the way.'

I walked past him out onto the pitch to 35,000 screaming Palace fans.

There are moments in life you are lucky to be part of. Yes, this was the achievement of Iain Dowie and his coaching staff and the players, but it was because of me they were here to achieve it.

Standing in the centre circle, my phone going into meltdown, I spoke to Ian Wright, who was screaming down the phone, 'You did it, Sim!'

I walked around the stadium waving, taking in the euphoria and elation of the crowd, an amazing outpouring of optimism and good feeling.

So this was what owning a football club was all about!

I walked down the tunnel with Dominic after being on the pitch for about twenty-five minutes.

I remember a Sky camera following me and I just looked at it and gave it a shit-eating grin. That grin was for all the people who had been against me.

Sky wanted to do an interview but I ignored them, preferring to kick a ball in the warm-up area with my brother.

We sat around for an hour or so in the hospitality lounge and Nick Craig came in to remark, 'Here is one Football League rule you won't mind.'

As we were now a Premier League club, I had to resign from the Football League.

After an hour or so I walked out of the Millennium Stadium with my mates and looked at the empty street. No one had the number of the driver to pick us up so we decided to walk across the road to a local pub. It was heaving inside with Palace fans, and as I walked in the roof came off.

It was the best fifteen minutes I could have spent with the people who make a football club, the fans. Once the driver arrived we made our way back to the Vale of Glamorgan for a big knees-up.

As the celebrations broke out, Debbie, Iain Dowie's wife, had only this to say to me: 'That's going to cost you.'

Charming and unnecessary. She was, of course, referring to the new contract her husband would invariably be demanding and I suspect was a throwback to the non-negotiable contract I gave Dowie six months previously.

When the party was in full swing Phil Alexander suggested I say a few words and as I went to take the microphone Dowie grabbed it and gave a speech. I didn't think it was his place to do it, but I let him, only to be further disappointed when he made references to myself as 'not being so bad all in all' and generally was a little unnecessarily sarcastic about our relationship.

The next day we flew back in the helicopter. As we passed over

212

London and Stamford Bridge Theo Paphitis pointed it out and I gave it a cursory glance, remarking, 'Yeah, I will see it next season,' which was greeted with a flurry of abuse from Paphitis. Also at that time Theo announced that he believed that Palace would be in the Premier League for three seasons: autumn, winter and spring – very funny!

I read the papers, which were adorned by Palace's achievement on the back pages and numerous pictures of me. *The Times* even had a headline: 'Golden Boy Does It Again'. It wasn't the way I would ever describe myself.

Arriving back in town I felt very melancholic. Paul Smith, a friend of mine, was a journalist and the chief football writer for the *Sunday Mirror*. He had come to know me well over the years and he wanted to do a big article on me. He knew I was disillusioned with football and although I was pleased with the achievement I was not ecstatic.

I did the interview and then left all my friends on the Sunday afternoon at the Grosvenor House Hotel celebrating and getting extremely drunk.

The piece was published saying that, having achieved my dream of getting Palace to the Premier League, I had spent much more than I had anticipated, had had more confrontations than I expected, and hadn't overly enjoyed the ride. There was a feeling of everything going on around me when really it was going on *because* of me. And that sense was only going to escalate as the big league beckoned. Maybe it was time for me to sell up.

Shortly afterwards Iain Dowie phoned and there ensued a conversation that was probably one of the strangest between an owner and a manager who had just worked the oracle, won the richest game in football and got promoted to the Premier League. Probably, with hindsight, I should have kept my views to myself.

He was off on holiday to Dubai and had unilaterally decided that there would be no open-top bus to mark our achievement. But wasn't that my call?

Prior to speaking to Dowie, I had thought about the last six months and what he had achieved, and it had been a phenomenal achievement. But it had taken place against a backdrop of constant belligerence and arguments between us. He was difficult enough to deal with in the First Division, God knows what he was going to be like in the rarefied world of the Premier League. His wife's rude and unnecessary comment about his contract no doubt reflected his attitude, and his somewhat snide speech at the post-match celebrations reverberated around my mind. I briefly contemplated firing Dowie. It would have been an unprecedented move to remove the manager of a team promoted to the Premier League before even playing a game; it was a step too far, even for me.

Add in the troubles I had with the media, the two buffoons at the sporting dinner, the disruptive newspaper article on the eve of the play-off final – all this made me feel unhappy at a time when I should have been full of pride and happiness. I couldn't help but think that it was such a shame. And with this mind-set I answered the phone to Dowie.

I told him what was on my mind, omitting the firing bit, and said that I didn't enjoy working with him.

This stopped him in his tracks for a moment. To be fair on him he said, 'Simon, that can't be right. We have to fix that. We are going into the Premier League, and this is your club and we need to be together.'

This brief moment of harmony was replaced very quickly with a list of players he wanted, players out of contract, and, of course, his new contract.

Dowie and I reached an accord, a sort of agreement to get along with each other, and this was supported by me bringing his brother Bob into the fold.

Bob had been doing a lot of work with Iain over the last six months, scouting and match reporting, and I got on quite well with him, so I brought him in as an intermediary to work between myself and Iain as a director of football.

To this day I remain undecided whether that was a good move or one of my stupidest ever.

The dust had hardly settled before I was inundated with every conceivable demand from players, managers and coaches, and that was before you even got into the realms of buying new players.

The benefits of getting into the Premier League were for everyone else but the owner.

Managers, coaches and players all had sizeable bonuses for the promotion. I think we paid circa £3 million in such bonuses. We paid millions out to other clubs who had promotion clauses on players we had bought from them.

Then, of course, the existing playing squad had salary increases for the Premier League and there were players on the last year of their contracts that we had to renew at the manager's request, which again was not insignificant.

Then we had the contracts of the management. This was Dowie's moment. He had taken the salary I had told him he would get when he had been offered the job six months earlier; now the boot was on the other foot. He got a 500 per cent pay rise on top of a half million bonus for achieving promotion.

In what seemed like hours since the final whistle, the best part of £7 million had been added to the cost base and that was even before you started to buy for the Premier League.

*   *   *

I had placed a bet with the bookies at the beginning of the season on Palace to get promoted, which I was not really allowed to do. So I had got John my driver to place it. I had bet £2,000 on promotion and got a betting slip showing odds of 33–1. I had won £66,000 from the bookies, or so I thought.

When John went to collect my winnings the bookmakers said this was never odds they would have given.

'Pardon?' was my response, so I sent John back with a flea in his ear to get the bloody winnings.

I was in a bit of an awkward position as I couldn't go myself and put them in the picture surrounding their 'not a legitimate' bet bullshit.

In the end they paid out but only on the basis that it was 33–1 each way rather than straight on, and given there were four teams in the play-offs they paid out at 8–1.

Not a lot I could do really as I was not supposed to bet on my own team so those bastard bookmakers legged me right over.

This was symptomatic of my bittersweet experiences in football. Sometimes even when you won you lost.

10

WELCOME TO THE BIG TIME

After my tempered reaction to promotion to the Premier League I adjusted my attitude; after all, this was what I had set out to achieve. This was why I had bought a football club and now we were there, amongst the purported big boys. We had reached the promised land of football and I was now the youngest ever owner of a Premier League football club.

Unfortunately my jar of honey was topped up with vinegar. Literally less than a week after promotion 121 succeeded in claiming back in excess of £4.5 million off me. My lawyers heralded this as a victory as the original claim was for £6.5 million. They appeared to forget that I had paid them £1 million in fees to save a further million.

Following the conversation with Dowie after the play-off final win I made a conscious decision to improve our relationship. I formalised his brother Bob's role with the club. I respected Bob's football knowledge and as his background was in commerce, he knew about the business side of things.

I made him director of football, and he was to become a conduit between Iain and myself. His first task was to look at player recruitment for the ensuing Premier League season. This was much harder than first anticipated; our scouting network was not really geared up for acquiring players for top-flight football. On the whole players required for the Premier League were of a different calibre than some we had previously bought.

We needed a team capable of competing in the Premier League, which brought about its own set of challenges.

In order to assemble a squad we had to first overcome the fact that a newly promoted team were the bookies' favourites for relegation. As players spent a large amount of time in their shops it was a task to convince them to join a 'doomed' enterprise, according to the 'experts'.

If you managed to hook a Premier League player, the next challenge was to convince them that if they were in fact part of a relegated team their wages would then be reduced, which of course met with complete resistance.

And while we obviously weren't competing with Chelsea, Manchester United and Arsenal for players we were competing with two other promoted sides and five or six established Premier League teams with bigger budgets, who were not only competing for players with us but ultimately for a place of safety in the league. Whilst gaining promotion through the play-offs was the ultimate high it gave all our rivals a four-week head start on us.

Invariably English players were overpriced, for no other reason than their nationality, as ludicrous as it sounds. And the eagerness, or perhaps desperation, of promoted teams to build a squad that met the expectations of the fans as well as your own ambitions frequently forced you into the European market, which is where we found ourselves. In my view, being forced into the European market because of price rather than ability to some extent reflects the current state of English football. Perhaps it is why we continue to have an overinflated opinion of our players and an underwhelming level of achievement

If our scouting network in England was challenged imagine our lack of expertise in a European market! But needs must.

As I was contemplating this I was invited to attend the annual summer AGM of the Premier League. The Premier League's communications director Phil French reached out via my friend the journalist Paul Smith, requesting a meeting with the chief executive Richard Scudamore, who was apparently intent on telling me how to conduct myself in the Premier League.

Suffice it to say I took an exception to such a summons as I had no desire to be told how to behave.

No sooner had I 'politely' declined this request for an off-the-record chat, I accepted the invitation to attend the annual Premier League summer summit.

I attended this two-day meeting for precisely two hours! Reflecting on the worthless meetings I had attended in the Football League whilst driving up towards Leicestershire, I decided that I'd get in, show my face, and depart as quickly as I could.

At the meeting of all the great and good of English football were my old pals David Dein of Arsenal, David Gold of Birmingham and such luminaries as Rick Parry of Liverpool, Peter Kenyon of Chelsea, David Gill of Manchester United and my old Geordie mate Freddy Shepherd the Newcastle chairman.

In the first meeting the newly promoted clubs, West Brom, Norwich and ourselves, were officially welcomed to the Premier League. Then there was a series of discussions surrounding developments with overseas rights and my particular favourite, rule changes!

All this was followed by a particular set of affairs I suspect explained Scudamore's attempt to muzzle me prior to the AGM.

Part of Scudamore's annual pay package included a ridiculous bonus for negotiating a new TV deal, which was surely a significant reason for him being there in the first place.

After he was asked to leave the room, David Gill, the chief executive of Manchester United and head of the Premier League's remuneration committee, announced that Scudamore should receive a £1 million bonus, which actually is peanuts compared to the £3 million bonuses he gets now.

I raised my hand and was given the floor. 'How bloody much?'

There was an audible intake of breath. David Gill gathered himself together and then said, 'Firstly, welcome to the Premier League, Simon, and secondly: nicely phrased first question.'

He went on to explain that Scudamore had negotiated the biggest Sky deal in Premier League history and considered this bonus appropriate.

I was forced to accept this, despite adding for the record that I considered achieving such things was what he was paid for and my grandmother could have negotiated a good deal with Sky in light of how desperate they were to retain the rights. I was promptly kicked under the table by Freddy Shepherd to pipe down, which I did muttering and grumbling under my breath a bit like Dick Dastardly's sidekick Muttley.

As the meeting wound down I decided that I wanted to get back into London. I departed, neglecting to appear in the annual photograph. I left Phil Alexander, who loved being in front of the camera, to sit in for me.

Soon after the Premier League meeting, with Dowie number one basking in Dubai and earning money for coaching rather than selecting players and Dowie number two trying to identify transfer targets, I decided to take a break from this febrile activity.

I flew home to Spain taking a group of close friends to my house for some rest and recreation and also to go to Portugal to watch England v France in Euro 2004. Amongst my group was Ray Winstone the actor. He had starred in a film, *Sexy Beast*, where in one scene he jumps onto a lilo and stays on it. This feat eluded the rest of the gang and we spent days wagering who could land and stay on a lilo in the pool, so Raymond, who conveniently neglected to tell everyone about his prior skills, unsurprisingly cleaned up.

When we tired of lazing by the pool and raucous nights in Puerto Banus, we took a private Learjet to Lisbon. When we landed my phone rang and it was my old pal Ian Wright, who we promptly arranged to meet. Upon arriving in the town centre we embarked on a drinking spree with England fans.

Mixing with fans from all over the country and drinking with them was not something Premier League chairmen did, but I was at heart a football supporter and that resonated with them. The fans loved Ray Winstone, who got very merry and rather raucous as well as 'rabidly patriotic'; ironic given Raymond was to be a 'goodwill ambassador' for England during the 2006 World Cup.

The game resulted in the French getting a lucky win and after a hot day and a disappointing result we wanted to get out of Lisbon as quickly as possible. As we departed the stadium we bumped into the Bolton chairman Phil Gartside and his manager Sam Allardyce.

I always liked Phil and Big Sam. But Gartside couldn't resist having a dig. 'Bottling it are we, Jordan? Want to get out before you play with the big boys?'

It was in reference to the article Smithy had written after we secured promotion and where I had admitted I was contemplating selling the club. (Coincidentally on that subject I did receive an approach from Colonel Gaddafi and his son, one I didn't particularly take too seriously, just as well, I suppose!)

My response to Gartside was: 'Piss off Phil. When you have put as much money as I have in a football club you can speak and by the way who in their right mind considers Bolton big boys?'

It was playful banter with an edge, which I took in good heart, but Ray took exception on my behalf and was all for 'beating up' Gartside, which wouldn't have stood me in good stead at the next Premier League meeting!

As we raced to the airport to get out of Lisbon we were advised there were four- to five-hour delays as all private jets wanted to leave at the same time. But my clever little secretary Lisa had changed planes and we were flying back in a turboprop aircraft, which looked like something out of *Indiana Jones* but was not subject to the same air traffic control. So we walked straight into a hangar, jumped on a plane and took off, waving at people like Noel Gallagher who were sat in the lounge and facing enormous delays. Within an hour we were back in Spain drinking at the bar in Puerto Banus.

Back at Crystal Palace we set about the serious business of establishing the exact financial landscape of the Premier League and buying players.

Putting aside all the media hype about how much promotion is worth, the main beneficiaries of this significant increase in money are very rarely the owners.

It's not a complaint; it's a statement of fact.

There is a huge misconception about the benefit that money from promotion brings.

The total amount of nigh on guaranteed money for promotion to the Premier League at the time was circa £19.5 million. Of course this dwarfed the money in the Football League but then so did the costs you were about to incur.

The guaranteed money you received was broken down like this:

in August you received your first instalment of £10.1 million, which was then followed by nine monthly payments of around £500,000, and two TV-related payments for featured games, one for £2.6 million in January and one for £2.1 million in June. Additionally you received £500K for each league place that you achieved at the end of the season, i.e. £500K for twentieth, £10 million for top, so what we had guaranteed was £20 million if we finished bottom and hopefully upwards of £21.5 million if we finished outside of the bottom three and avoided relegation, which of course was our devout intention!

I had already accounted for the first £7 million. This included bonuses and contractually obligated pay rises, new management contracts and payments to other clubs from whom we had signed players that had promotion bonuses written into their contracts.

I then sanctioned the recommended strengthening of the squad by Bob and Iain Dowie. We brought in twelve new players leading up to the start of our Premier League campaign as well as retaining 95 per cent of the existing playing squad and in doing so spent £6 million on transfer fees and increased the wages by a further £7.2 million.

So all in all with the original £7 million it added up to £20.2 million plus the best part of £500K in agent fees, which thus accounted for all the Sky monies and more. That was before the dramatically increased costs you encountered including the five-star hotels the team had to stay in and travelling by air.

See what I mean about little benefit for the owner? But of course I did have the 'priceless' kudos of owning a Premier League club.

The players we bought were from far and wide, from Budapest and Quito in Ecuador to as near as Southampton. The list of clubs we purchased players from had some exotic-sounding names: Inter Milan, Hertha Berlin, AEK Athens, Borusia Monchengladbach and Colchester United!

I gave Iain and Bob a free hand in decision-making, merely becoming involved in the financials. The only exception was the Inter Milan deal, which was set up by myself, via Phil Smith the agent and Roberto Bettega from Milan. Bob went out and completed the deal and we signed two highly rated players, Gonzalo Sorondo, a Uruguayan international, and the previously proclaimed Italian wonder kid Nicola Ventola, who had recovered from a serious injury and was now fully fit and raring to go – or so we thought!

The only deal I had serious concerns about was the Ecuadorian captain Ivan Kaviedes, who had been sent over on spec by an agent. It is universally accepted that you don't buy players from watching a DVD as you are hardly sent a video of bad performances and watching them in training is no substitute for watching them in competitive action. Despite my concerns Iain and Bob pressured me to pay a £600,000 fee for this player and I acquiesced.

Now I realise in Ecuador they were used to coups, but very quickly it was established this was not one for Crystal Palace. Within four months Iain had decided Kaviedes was not good enough and wanted to release him. I had to pay up a significant proportion of his contract and waste the £600,000 we had paid for him. Given he was so bad it was surprising to see him turn up as one of the star players of the 2006 World Cup, playing against none other than England's Golden Generation.

One player that we desperately tried to sign was Tim Cahill from Millwall. I knew the player well from watching him frequently and had agreed a fee with the club of £1.5 million, and offered the player three times what he was currently earning. Cahill came to the training ground to meet Iain, while I had the dubious pleasure of engaging with his agent Paul Martin from SFX.

Martin was an argumentative, cocky, flash agent, all Burberry and man bags, and the type I really loved! He told me exactly what he would accept for his client, which bore little resemblance to my offer. Despite an hour trying to find a middle ground I agreed to his terms.

Then came the ludicrous demand for an agent's fee of £150,000 for an hour's worth of arguments. He expected me to pay for a deal that was considerably more expensive than I had wanted and hadn't given me a single concession. What I really wanted to give him was a punch on the nose, not a bag of money.

The deal stalled and the atmosphere became very testy. Martin suggested I ask Theo Paphitis, the Milwall chairman, to pick up some of his fee. I phoned Theo in amusement, already knowing the likely outcome, and held the phone from my ear as he screamed obscenities down it, questioning the parentage of this agent.

The deal fell through against a backdrop of recriminations in the press led by my outrage at agents and their demands. Everton had been looking at Cahill for some time and stepped in and bought him. In my view I think we were being used to flush out Everton and Cahill was destined to go there anyway.

To add to my feeling of indignation I had two internal matters to deal with.

I had enjoyed a good relationship with Julian Gray, the first player I had bought back in 2000 from Arsenal. However, in the middle of 2003 he told me he was signing with the agent Paul Stretford, and since then had become truculent and difficult to deal with. We shipped him out on loan to Cardiff at the beginning of the promotion season. Kit Symons had brought him back in his stint as caretaker manager and Julian had been an integral part of the promoted team. But he had developed a disrespectful attitude towards the club. When his contract had expired he refused – or more to the point his agent did – all our offers.

Rules for players' contracts established under the Bosman ruling meant any player aged twenty-four or under at the end of their contract couldn't just walk out as a free agent. Clubs retained compensation rights. We ended up in a tribunal which would evaluate his worth to us if he joined another club.

It was a terse affair. Gray was petulant and rude and did the Clinton Morrison trick of kissing his teeth, which didn't go down well with me. The tribunal did not fail to disappoint me setting a ridiculously low fee. We had acquired Julian for £500,000 four years earlier and he had been a first-team regular with 125 games, part of a promotion side and highly rated.

The tribunal awarded us £300,000 and where did he go? Birmingham City.

The other matter was our young starlet Wayne Routledge, who had one year left on his contract. We offered him a new one, fearing we were very likely to suffer another ludicrous tribunal decision but primarily because we rated him highly. Our reward for my care and development of this player and his family was to be told he would not be signing anything by none other than my favourite agent Paul Stretford.

Worse than that, at 7 p.m. on transfer deadline day Tottenham chairman Daniel Levy offered the paltry sum of £1 million to buy this England under-21 star. An emphatic no was my response but this dragged on through the night with Levy offering ridiculously small increases, spending more money on his phone bill than he was upping his offer for Routledge.

At 11 p.m. and after the fiftieth time of saying no to Levy's insulting offers he moved the fee to the princely sum of £1.25 million. I then said that even if I wanted to do this deal, which I didn't, it could not be done as I didn't know where the player was, and terms to be agreed with the player and medicals would never get done in time.

I need not have worried on Spurs account as my loyal, respectful player and his delightful agent were in a hotel 500 yards around the corner from White Hart Lane. I was given the distinct impression everything had already been done so with that new and treacherous information to hand, I concluded my conversation, told Levy where to go and asked Bob Dowie to advise Wayne Routledge to be in training the following morning.

The first game of the season was upon us. We were playing away to Norwich City, a team that had been promoted with us from the First Division. There was a feeling of anticipation as we expected to secure all three points on our first outing. I was also looking forward to seeing how the newly assembled group of players would acquit themselves.

Arriving at the home of Norwich City I encountered a new Carrow Road, one that had Premier League gold dust sprinkled all over it. The place was alive: a sea of yellow Norwich shirts with a splattering of the new white away kit of my team in amongst them. You could feel the buzz of expectation in and around the ground.

I went into the boardroom to see my dear friend Delia Smith, the owner of Norwich. I was taken aback by the crowd in there, not to mention the large number of good-looking women, which was a vast departure from the boardrooms I had visited in the previous four years, which had often been like working men's clubs with Bernard Manning more likely to be in there than Linda Evangelista. Suffice it to say this ensured my attendance in boardrooms going forward was likely to be much more regular!

The atmosphere in the ground was electric, the game moderately exciting and it ended in a 1–1 draw to ensure we registered our first Premier League point. Andrew Johnson resumed where he had left off last season with our goal and of course a goal bonus, and I certainly liked the look of our new £1 million Hungarian national striker Sandor Torghelle, although I was to be in the minority on that one as this 'must have' player was soon deemed not good enough, and Dowie had no qualms about throwing away the £1 million I had spent on him!

Prior to the season I had a number of discussions with Iain Dowie about how we would approach the campaign. The idea being we would have a go from the first whistle and show no fear. Unfortunately in the five games that followed the exact opposite applied.

Our first home game at a packed, very excited Selhurst Park was against Everton. On a beautiful August day with the stadium swathed in glorious summer sun, the only thing hotter than the weather was the temperature of the fans' enthusiasm. We opened the scoring through Mark Hudson and AJ should have increased the lead but was denied by the thickness of the post. It proved to be a costly miss as Everton went on to equalise in the first half and scored two further goals in the second to beat us 3–1.

Three days later we faced our second successive home game, against the mighty Chelsea managed by the much-lauded José Mourinho in only his second game in English football and attended by Sven-Göran Eriksson, fresh from being outed in the press for having talks with Chelsea about their manager's job, and their multi-billionaire Russian owner Roman Abramovich and his heavy-weight security guards.

A huge myth existed around Abramovich's apparent lack of understanding of English. And that was absolute rubbish. Before getting promoted I had gone to St James' Park to watch Newcastle play a Chelsea side at the time managed by Claudio Ranieri. After the game I went into the boardroom and chatted with Sir John Hall, Freddy Shepherd and Douglas Hall.

In the corner about five feet away, was Roman Abramovich talking to his American chairman Bruce Buck in English. This fact eluded Freddy and Douglas as they proceeded to insult Abramovich with their opinions of everything from his dress sense to their perception of his 'Russian potato-peeling origins'.

I stood there with this almighty grin across my face. When they had run out of insults I delighted in informing them that Abramovich understood and spoke English. Most people with a modicum of decorum would have just shut their traps!

Not my Geordie pals, who carried on amusing themselves with another set of derogatory comments.

That said I had tried to engage Bruce Buck in conversation prior to the north-east abuse of Abramovich. Buck just answered everything I said with monosyllabic disdain, so I stopped in mid-sentence, looked him straight in the face and remarked, 'You're a pleasant fellow aren't you!' and turned on my heel and walked away from him.

Thus I was more than happy to condone Freddy and Douglas when they got bored with abusing Abramovich and started on Buck.

And people wondered why Freddy and Douglas frequently got into trouble!

Back to Selhurst Park. Abramovich spent most of the evening chatting to Eriksson – in English of course! Two gorillas that looked like they were going to shoot anyone who even dared to look in his direction flanked him.

Talking of murder, that's exactly what Chelsea did to Palace on the pitch. Despite only being beaten 2–0, we were never really in the game and Chelsea barely got out of second gear. What disappointed me was we were now in the Premier League and I for one was not overawed in any way so I didn't expect my manager or players to be, which appeared the case.

Our bad run continued, losing to both Middlesbrough and Portsmouth. We contributed to our downfall in each game by gifting an own goal to the opposition, as well as particularly inept performances by our new goalkeeper Julian Speroni.

The Portsmouth game resulted in a harsh assessment of Palace by the pundit Alan Hansen on *Match of the Day*. Not content with nicknaming our goalkeeper Speroni, 'Spilloni', the former Liverpool defender claimed that Palace were the worst side to ever grace the Premier League and had absolutely no chance of survival. His commentary was a bit over the top – had he not watched Mick McCarthy's Sunderland side of 2003 get nineteen points, the lowest ever!

Was this the same Alan Hansen who claimed you don't win silverware with kids? Not eight months after he regaled the world with that particular nugget Manchester United proceeded to do just that. Short of taking it personally and hoping Dowie was pinning up the reports in the dressing room for the players to see, we got on with the business of trying to win games and in the process making this ex-Scottish international, who knew a fair bit, in that respect, about playing in the worst teams, eat his words.

But still we continued to lose. AJ scored his third goal in six matches, but two strikes from Nicolas Anelka for Man City left us waiting to pick up our first points at home and rooted to the bottom of the Premier League.

The bad run came to an end with a 1–1 draw away to Aston Villa, one which we should have really won. At last we were off and running, following that draw with a 2–0 victory at home over Fulham. After the win Dowie dampened my spirits by publicly airing his views on me, saying that the club, i.e. me, hadn't supported him in the transfer market. He had waited for a win so he didn't look as if he was whining and normal service resumed between us with Bob in the middle.

We were back to our losing ways in the next game away, to Bolton, where I popped in to see my old mate Phil Gartside the Bolton chairman to let him know that in fact I hadn't 'bottled it' and we were here for three points. Of course the fact that we lost gave Gartside the opportunity to tell me perhaps I should have done!

The disappointment of losing to Bolton was made up for by trouncing fellow promoted West Brom 3–0 at home, with yet again AJ scoring, this time twice. At half-time I spoke to Jeremy Peace the West Brom chairman, who was having well-publicised difficulties with his manager Gary Megson. I remarked to Peace, 'How lucky we are to work for Megson and Dowie.' That sarcasm brought a smile to his face.

On 27 October, after ten league games and now out of the bottom three, we took on local rivals Charlton Athletic in the Carling Cup. This game was to be the start of some significant hostilities, which rumbled through this season and into the future. There was of course bad blood between the supporters as it was a London derby and also, when Charlton had fallen on hard times, they had been tenants at Selhurst Park and the Palace fans had never let them forget it.

I was told that Charlton had aspirations to win this particular cup tournament, so it was no surprise to me when they put out a full-strength side. What was a surprise was that we put out a virtual second-string side, making eight changes from the team that beat West Bromwich a few days earlier. Even so, we completely outplayed Charlton and won the game.

Before the game an incident had occurred that I was unaware of as I was late. When the teams were read out over the tannoy the announcer called us Crystal PalARSE, childish really, but my ever-busy chief executive Phil Alexander made an unnecessary complaint.

I walked out at Millwall every time we played there to the Smokie song 'Livin' next door to Alice', which the Millwall fans in unison had adapted to 'Livin' next door to Palace, Palace who the fuck are Palace'. I found this amusing, so I would have hardly been bothered by a silly announcement. But Alexander had complained and the silly sod announcer got fired and guess who got the blame for it!

I hadn't seen a great deal of my mates at Birmingham since their promotion in 2001, but I was seeing them at St Andrews the following Saturday.

During the week I was interviewed by Ian Payne of Sky. We spoke about the game and he tried to get some derogatory comments from me, given our past, but I abstained. Even when he quoted some slightly caustic comments about me by David Gold, the joint Birmingham chairman, I just countered with 'Empty vessels make the most noise.'

Upon arriving at Birmingham it was like the three years had never elapsed and I was greeted with a deluge of abuse from their fans/ morons. By now the relationship with Steve Bruce had improved, and on walking into the stadium, despite the insults being hurled at me left and right, I received a big hug from Janet Bruce, Steve's wife, and a big sloppy kiss from Karren Brady. I was not sure what was worse: the kiss or the abuse from the Birmingham fans.

Birmingham's co-owner David Sullivan, resplendent in his trademark Cossack outfit but looking like a little Russian doll, greeted me. He remarked on the fact that Andrew Johnson was gaining a reputation for getting penalties, as he had been awarded four so far this season. Sullivan said, 'I know what you boys are like. I hope we are not going to have any dodgy decisions today with all those bloody penalties you get.'

My mouth got the better of me. 'Have you seen yourself, David?

The only dodgy decision here today is the one you made, putting on that get-up. Are you doing the half-time entertainment, and is Karren the dancing bear?'

We won, my honour was upheld. Andrew Johnson scored and no, it was not a penalty! I still had to listen to the endless chants from the poet laureate-like Birmingham supporters of 'Simon Jordan is a wanker, is a wanker,' but this time I got to do it with a big grin on my face – no need to go in their boardroom this time!

This win was made more pleasing as I had bumped into Dwight Yorke in the Sanderson Bar in London the previous night, who by now was plying his trade on the bench at Birmingham. I had a £2,000 bet with Yorke that we would win.

The fact that a player was in a London hotel bar the night before a game probably explains where Yorke's career was at that time. Anyway, returning from the Midlands that night I went again to the Sanderson bar for a drink with friends and in strolled Yorke. I reminded him that he had a bet to pay, which he proceeded to welch on, saying he would send me a Dwight Yorke cheque that I could pin on my wall as some kind of souvenir! I suggested he kept it and invested it in his wardrobe; judging by what he was wearing, he was the footballer that fashion forgot.

After the delight of finally getting one over Birmingham our next four games were relatively easy encounters – Arsenal at home, Manchester United in the Carling Cup, then Liverpool away and finally Newcastle at home. Judging by some of our recent performances I considered we had two hopes of getting nine points out of the three league games: Bob Hope and No Hope, and unfortunately for us Bob was dead!

Arsenal arrived at Selhurst Park two weeks after their incredible forty-nine-match unbeaten run came to an end at Manchester United.

David Dein, the Arsenal vice-chairman, came into the boardroom and reminded me in his inimitable way of what a fantastic favour he'd done me in selling me Julian Gray and how he had played an integral part in getting the club promoted the previous season.

Dein remarked: 'I'm looking forward to seeing Julian play tonight and to see how he has progressed since leaving Arsenal.'

I replied: 'If that's the case why aren't you at the Liverpool game tonight, David?'

Dein looked at me somewhat perplexed until I informed him that Gray had walked out on Palace, joined Birmingham and left us at the mercy of a rotten tribunal.

Arsenal out-strengthened us in every department, but on a heady late afternoon in November and after a difficult first half, despite falling behind we battered Arsenal and soon equalised. We should have won the match in the last minute when the Greek international winger Vassilis Lakis missed an absolute sitter!

Dowie captured the imagination of all and sundry including the press, *Soccer AM* and Alan Hansen, with his infamous 'bounce-backability' line.

Talking of Hansen, he now had a sea change of view, claiming Palace were now worthy of their place in the Premier League and would more than likely stay up.

Thankfully for Hansen he is not on a prediction-related bonus for the BBC.

Next up was Manchester United in the Carling Cup at Old Trafford.

Naturally I looked forward to the game but I wasn't overawed or impressed by the opposition. It was just another game I wanted my team to win.

I wish I could say the same for everyone else at Palace. When I arrived at United it was as if someone had picked up our entire boardroom and dropped it in the VIP area. To a certain extent I could understand why everyone wanted to go but it didn't reflect my outlook and I was slightly embarrassed.

I had a similar attitude whenever Palace scored. My celebrations were very tempered and never over-elaborate: I always assumed we would score and felt over-celebrating was a sign of weakness. In the battle of the directors' box, over-elaborate celebrations merely made your opponents feel more important than they actually were.

After I politely declined an invitation into United's boardroom from Sir Bobby Charlton, Phil Alexander didn't need to be asked twice to take my place and predictably swooned over it like he stumbled across Aladdin's Cave.

Needless to say on a scale of one to ten the result wasn't important. We lost 2–0 but league points were far more important than historic scalps in the Carling Cup.

Around this time I had started to date Alex, George Best's ex-wife, and we both promptly turned up at Liverpool for our next league game.

It was bedlam. Having avoided entering Liverpool's unfriendly boardroom, we took to our seats and were confronted by a mass of photographers, snapping pictures of myself and Alex.

At the start of the season I had taken on Max Clifford to handle my PR and one of the objectives was to protect me against press intrusion in my private life. The reason for employing Max seemed logical. I felt there would be significant interest in my professional and private life especially as I was young and outspoken. As a single man in London I felt it was appropriate for someone to manage that.

Max had immense power in the tabloid market, so in a way it was like taking out an insurance policy. I was to use it on a number of occasions on behalf of some of my errant employees who got themselves in various scrapes with the media and needed my help and that of Max to spare their blushes.

Around this time an article was written by one of the tabloid newspapers which showed the irresponsible and potentially damaging effects of bad and inaccurate journalism. This particular article was about the rifeness of cocaine, raucous behaviour and sexual impropriety by Premier League players. Some of it was true, but they illustrated the article with a picture of Andrew Johnson falling out of a taxi.

This young man was the most committed footballer I had ever met. He barely drank, certainly did not do drugs, was in a good relationship and was now an England player. The picture was taken as he was chased down the road by paparazzi and he fell into a cab not out of one. Andrew was horrified and so was I; there was no mention of him in their article except this bloody picture which made him guilty by association. I sued them on Andrew's behalf. We got a retraction and an apology, also a significant amount for damages, which Andrew and myself gave to a children's hospice that Max Clifford had introduced me to. So at least some good came out of it.

The following home game against Newcastle was a real eye opener for me. It wasn't so much the 2–0 defeat that concerned me but the manner in which we lost the game that set alarm bells ringing. The scoreline flattered us. A team with no real expectations of accomplishing anything significant had comprehensively outplayed us. It was embarrassing and it dawned on me that we had a real fight on our hands to survive at this level.

Worse was to follow when Max Clifford set up an interview for me with the *Sunday Times*. It proved to be the most controversial I had done to date and would be published the day of the London derby against Charlton.

I was asked very leading questions and gave strident views in response. When I read the article that Sunday morning I regretted the way my views had been crafted into what was an explosive article. I appeared to be disparaging about major clubs, aspects of football and other chairmen, when in fact I had been extreme in my views, but had balanced them out. The balancing parts were conveniently left out and the acticle didn't reflect the true nature of what I said.

I was asked whether I had a reputation for not getting on with other chairmen and my throwaway response was: 'It's fair to say I think a lot of football club chairmen are tossers but I suspect they may well think the same thing about me.'

Of course the piece only reported the controversial first half of my answer and not the balance in the second. And perhaps I should have used a better word than 'tossers'.

Given my attitude of not feeling privileged to be in the Premier League I was asked a pointed question. Was I an admirer and respecter of the traditions and achievements of the leading clubs?

My response was that I was not a great respecter of traditions and values and felt there was a lot of bullshit in football. And a lot of bullshit in and around clubs like Manchester United and Arsenal.

What I also went on to say, which again didn't appear in the article, was that the achievements of these clubs were to be respected but they included certain factions that were full of self-serving bullshit.

The fallout, aside from unwanted back-page headlines, criticism on TV and radio stations, was that I got a phone call from Freddy Shepherd at Newcastle to say 'Hello, just one of the tossers here.' I acknowledged the fact I had earned that jibe.

It's one thing being strident but another thing allowing yourself stupidly to be taken out of context.

In the article I had launched an extreme tirade against agents, which was the only part of the piece I had no regrets about!

I had done many articles prior to this where I had been strident in my views but in this case my views had been taken out of context and they had crossed the line. I felt I had to get in front of this, so driving towards the ground I called Sky and asked them to allow me time to address the issues in the article, which they agreed to begrudgingly, given that I had hardly given them any time in the last twelve months.

After the damage limitation with Sky I went up to the boardroom and bumped into Richard Murray, the chairman of Charlton, and assured him that in no way the comments I had reportedly made were directed at him.

Murray smiled and said: 'I understand, we all get misquoted.'

It's funny how that attitude changed some five months later.

Anyway, to top off an unproductive day, we lost against Charlton, conceding a last-minute goal, which was becoming a regular feature of our season.

No sooner had the repercussions from the article died down than I had to travel to Manchester United, where I faced some disapproving looks and a few disparaging comments from certain directors of theirs.

I'd done the article and addressed it so if people wanted to go on about it I didn't really care. It was done and I'd drawn a line under it. I was far more concerned about the team's slide down into the relegation zone than the opinions of the Manchester United officials. I suppose the fact we got thrashed 5–2 would have been viewed as retribution.

Between the Manchester United game and the opening of the transfer window we dipped in and out of the bottom three with ever helpful reminders from the press that any team in the bottom three at Christmas always got relegated.

Around this time my old school Purley Boys had asked me to

come and address the pupils as they considered me to be one of – if not the most – successful ex-pupils.

Ironic, seeing they had expelled me!

Initially I said I was reluctant to do it, so jokingly they black-mailed me and threatened to release my old school report to the press. That was it: I had no choice, I had to do it.

I took along Andy Johnson for the star factor as he was now an England player. I gave a speech to the young students, who were sitting where I had sat twenty years earlier. Afterwards I got to listen to some of my old teachers who were still at the school and some who had loathed me claimed that they always knew I would be a success. Oh, really?!

On the field, results were poor and following the 1–0 home defeat against Portsmouth on Boxing Day we dropped into the bottom three. A credible point at Spurs briefly took us out on goal differ-ence but on the opening day of 2005 we lost 3–1 at Fulham and slipped straight back into the relegation zone.

The opening of the transfer window was a timely reminder of what managers seek to excel at: trying to spend your money.

I made significant funds available to Iain Dowie, who identified two targets, Michael Carrick at West Ham, and Dean Ashton at Crewe. West Ham accepted my offer of £3.5 million for Carrick, but he refused to even speak to Dowie and ignored his calls.

We offered Crewe £2.75 million for Dean Ashton. Norwich were also in the market for the striker so I called them and said, 'Let's agree the same fee to prevent a Dutch auction and let the player decide between us.' So what do they do? Offer £3 million and promptly sign him. Was I naïve? Perhaps. I was later to find out that Dario Gradi, the Crewe manager, had a dislike of me and was probably instrumental in the player not coming to Palace.

As the Dowie brothers had identified no other targets, the window closed without any new additions to the squad. For my trouble I got to read in the papers another public broadside from Dowie, claiming I hadn't supported him financially in the transfer market. He conveniently forgot a private discussion we had when he admitted his brother Bob had failed to do his homework in the market. Or that we had done our best to get the only two players he wanted and he was in fact comfortable going forward and believed, like me, we would stay up regardless.

Irrespective of failing to acquire players, in the last game of January we crushed Tottenham 3–0 at home and were three points clear of the relegation zone.

February brought a further four points and by the close of the month we were four clear of relegation. The Valentine's Day Massacre at Arsenal, where we lost 5–1, was rather humiliating but my spirits were lifted two days before the end of the month when we got to administer more pain on my mates at Birmingham. Andrew Johnson, who I had taken for nothing and been a make-weight in the Clinton Morrison deal, scored both goals. According to the pundits we were the team most likely to stay up this season.

So as we approached the last quarter of the season in reasonable fettle, it never really occurred to me that we would get relegated. I had fleeting thoughts that we might but I banished them from my head as soon as they popped in. Not from a state of denial but, as Nietzsche said: if you look into the abyss the abyss looks back at you. I wanted to look into the sun and being in the Premier League was Vitamin D in abundance.

My relationship with Dowie remained difficult but despite a few fractious moments where he had spoken out of turn in the media, or just been plain difficult, we had an accord of sorts. Maybe it was due to his brother Bob acting as a conduit between us, maybe it was because I had learned to tolerate Iain, or maybe Iain and I attached so much importance to staying in the Premier League that it overrode our personal differences.

Iain believed we would stay up. He believed in himself and the team. I found his positive outlook and leadership uplifting and appreciated his determination.

In March we only had two games. Relatively 'easy' fixtures against Manchester United, who were second, at home and the leaders Chelsea away.

Selhurst Park was buzzing for the visit of Manchester United. It was the first time we had played them at home since April 1998, on the cusp of the doomed Mark Goldberg takeover. That team was managed by Attilio Lombardo and got smashed to pieces 3–0. I watched the game that night from the Holmesdale stand. But this was a different Palace now, a supercharged one led by Iain Dowie that matched Manchester blow for blow and came out with a 0–0 draw against one of the finest teams in the world.

Talking of the finest teams, we played Chelsea next on a bright March afternoon. A group of friends and I walked down the New King's Road. It never concerned me what rival fans may or may not do. But it was fun, as I think the Chelsea fans were somewhat stunned to see me. We stopped off for a drink in one of the pubs and by that time the Chelsea fans had gained their voice and the abuse followed. It was all in good spirit though, as they knew I was a London lad like them and 'had done good'. Unfortunately, the result was predictable, a comprehensive defeat, although we did go in at half-time 1–1. We might have stood a better chance if our goalkeeper could have caught more than a cold that afternoon. We ended up losing 4–1 and our defence was as conspicuous in its absence as Roman Abramovich was in the directors' box.

Around this time something sinister happened in my personal

life. As I had given Ms Best a straight red card, I was often out in the high-octane London nightlife. In March 2005 I met a girl with whom I had a brief interlude. She has subsequently stalked me for six years, despite being arrested, put in prison, put on community service and given several restraining orders.

I tried to make light of it, saying what self-respecting single multi-millionaire does not have his own stalker? But having your family threatened, having hundreds of texts and phone calls a day for months on end, having lewd photographs sent to your hotel, stores phoning you up to pay for things she had ordered with your details, as well as strangers calling you up and abusing you whilst drunk with her, was not fun.

Back to football. After a great performance against Manchester United and a good effort at Chelsea, the next four matches were a disappointment as we took only one point in a draw at home to fellow strugglers Norwich.

In the other three games we were abject, losing to Middlesbrough 1–0 at home, failing to turn up at Goodison Park as Everton trounced us 4–0 and then a dire performance against Blackburn away on a cold April night, losing 1–0 when Mikele Leigertwood gave away an unnecessary free kick on the right of our eighteen-yard box, something he was to repeat very soon with devastating consequences.

After losing to Blackburn, I actually felt for the first time that we were going to get relegated. Before these games we were two points clear of the relegation zone and after them we were second to bottom, two points from safety. I saw the bright lights of the Premier League recede into the distance. Yes, I was not grateful to be there, and no, I was no respecter of protocol nor had I been brainwashed by some of the Premier League nonsense but I didn't want to go back to the Football League.

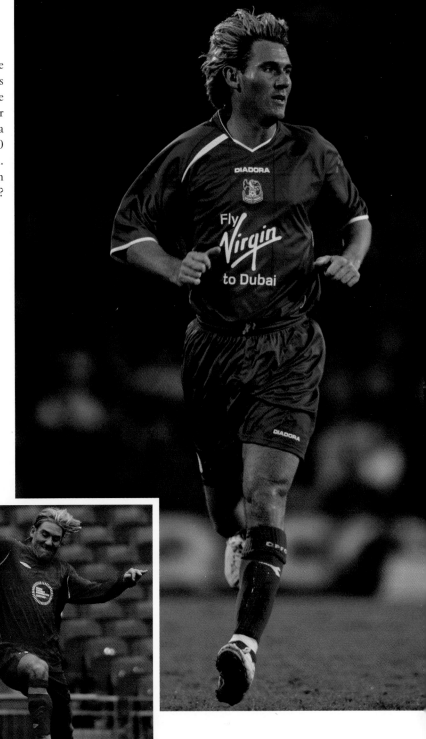

Playing in the Geoff Thomas testimonial game against a Manchester United XI in a reprise of the 1990 FA Cup final. Who says Chairmen can't play football?

Playing in the first game at the new Wembley, and scoring the second ever goal at the stadium.

Outside of the FA tribunal where I was found guilty of a ludicrous charge of improper conduct and given a gagging order, I was my usual reticent self with the press.

Flanked by my brother Dominic and Phil Alexander at the first leg of the 2006 play-off semi-final against Watford. My feeling of impending doom surrounding the game is being realised in front of me. We went on to lose 0–3. Bob Dowie is sat on my left, within earshot of my opinions.

Both myself and Iain Dowie arriving – not together, I hasten to add – in court for the landmark case where Dowie was found guilty of fraudulent misrepresentation.

Manager Number 7: Peter Taylor.

My close personal friend
Theo Paphitis with me as
guest of honour (not!) at a
PFA Gala Dinner (*left*).

With Lynval Golding of The Specials (*right*) at my
40th birthday party. Helping to reform The Specials
was one of my proudest achievements.

In the stands (*below*) with former England manager
Steve McClaren, Spurs chairman Daniel Levy and
my 'pal' Paul Kemsley, then vice-chairman of Spurs.

On the red carpet with Nick Moran, director of my film *Telstar*

With Nick, Carl Barat, JJ Feild and Pam Ferris at the World Premiere of *Telstar*.

Sat in my award-winning restaurant, The Club Bar and Dining in Soho.

Manager number 8:
Neil Warnock.
The headline was 'a
marriage made in hell'.
My best appointment
turned out to be my
last appointment.

The 2008 play-off push. Victor Moses, one of the
stars from my treasured academy celebrates scoring
against Burnley. He would later go on to be sold
for peanuts by the administrator.

John Bostock, revered as the best footballer
of his age in Europe. It was a disappointment
when he chose to go to Spurs.

Watching the 5–0 win against Burnley that clinches our position in the play-offs.

2008 play-off semi-final vs. Bristol City. The loss of this game resulted
in me taking decisions that had far-reaching consequences.

If you own a football club and if you have any real ambition, the Premier League is the only place to be. If you have been there as a player, manager, supporter and owner you don't want to be anywhere else.

After Blackburn, it dawned on me that this dream might be coming to an end.

I wasn't about to display my feelings, but I felt flat. Surprisingly, Iain Dowie picked up on it and lifted my spirits as he was so determined and so resolute.

And lo and behold, after four nondescript performances, at home we beat Liverpool, who were soon to be crowned European champions.

It was an incredible result and reignited my belief that we were going to stay up. We were back out of the relegation zone. During my ownership we played Liverpool seven times, only losing twice – not bad for a 'smaller' club!

The season came down to the last three games and it was a straight fight between us, Norwich, Southampton and West Brom, who were bottom and had been completely written off.

We played Newcastle and gained a credible point in a relatively boring 0–0 draw at St James' Park. I had to physically restrain Bob Dowie during the game because the pressure had clearly got to him. If he wasn't biting his nails he was up and out of his seat like some jack-in-the-box. As for Newcastle, a team that destroyed us earlier in the season, they were abstract and that's being kind.

Our final home game was against fellow strugglers Southampton, now managed by Harry Redknapp, who had defected from their fiercest of rivals Portsmouth. Portsmouth, ironically, were to play a pivotal role in our destiny.

The game was a feisty affair. We took the lead, they pegged us back. Two players were sent off, Sorrando for Palace and Peter Crouch for Southampton.

Then at long last we saw Nicola Ventola, our wonder kid. He had been injured all season and like something out of Roy of the Rovers he scored with his first touch to put us 2–1 ahead. The fortune I had paid this kid to never see sight of him till that moment was finally worth every penny.

Then, as was our way that season, disaster conspired to bring us down to earth with an almighty bump.

Amidst deafening whistles from the Palace supporters, desperate to see the game come to an end which would have sparked wild celebrations and was likely to have secured our place in the Premier League, we conceded a goal in the third minute of stoppage time.

Unfortunately it was the fault of young Ventola, who went from hero to zero, failing to control a ball thrown to him by our keeper, who should actually have booted it out of the ground himself. The ball came straight back into our box and Danny Higginbotham scored to hand Southampton a Premier League lifeline.

We now had one game left to save ourselves. West Brom were bottom and playing Portsmouth and it only dawned on me later why this game had such a major impact on our future in top-flight football. I had it on very reliable information that with Portsmouth safe, their legion of supporters demanded that they didn't lift a leg against West Brom to ensure Southampton went down. Unbearable pressure was put on the Portsmouth players and, while this was a major conspiracy theory and can never be substantiated, it was no help to us.

Southampton were home to Manchester United; Norwich, who were a point clear of the relegation zone and favourites to stay up, were away to Fulham, who, judging by recent performances were already on the beach; and we had the small matter of a London derby away to Charlton. As the Sunday approached the tension was building as literally all teams could save themselves, which I suppose made for compelling viewing.

Iain Dowie spoke to Chris Coleman, the Fulham manager, who assured him they would do their job and it was up to us to do ours. As old teammates you would expect nothing less. Iain took the players to Champneys for a day to ease the pressure and I flew up to the north on the Saturday to attend the massive annual charity ball hosted by John Caudwell, the billionaire owner of Phones4u, where I was to spend nearly £100,000 on auction items for a children's charity. The next day I was to give up a lot more money.

The Sunday morning arrived and with a slight hangover I jumped in my helicopter and flew to London for what was to be an eventful and controversial day. I landed in Battersea and with a friend drove my lucky Aston Martin over to Greenwich, only to get stuck in traffic. I arrived late again, annoying myself intensely as this was the most important game of my ownership to date.

Upon entering the Valley, the home of Charlton, I donned my lucky suit, the one I had worn to death last year, and walked into a boiling cauldron of an atmosphere. It was a full house and despite having nothing to play for both the Charlton fans and their team were massively up for the match, determined to send their fierce rivals down.

The game was played at a frenetic pace. Charlton went ahead and at half-time we were 1–0 down. Norwich were getting beaten 2–0 but still safe and both West Brom and Southampton were drawing. So it was pretty much as you were.

The last forty-five minutes of the 2004–05 season were both controversial and heart-breaking for some of us in Premier League history.

Fifteen minutes into the second half all had changed. Poor Norwich were now losing 3–0 and on the way to an incredible 6–0 defeat, despite being in the box seat at the start of the day. Southampton were losing 2–1 and on their way to relegation. West Brom had scored and incredibly were out of the bottom three.

And what of us?

The atmosphere in the stadium was electric; the intensity of the Charlton fans was incredible. I think both our players and management were surprised at how committed Charlton were to this game.

I remember Andrew Johnson telling me afterwards that at half-time he had spoken to Bryan Hughes, an old teammate of his, and asked why Charlton were playing like their lives depended on it. Apparently the directive from up high was this game had to be won!

Dowie brought on the fans' hero Dougie Freedman and within a minute he had levelled and it was now game on. Incredibly Dougie did it again and won us a penalty, which Andrew Johnson, against a backdrop of abuse from the Charlton fans, dispatched. With twenty minutes to go we were safe.

It was irrelevant what happened elsewhere and for thirteen minutes we dared to dream. Had Dowie worked the oracle again? Had Dougie Freedman popped up as the hero once more?

In the eighty-third minute, absolute disaster struck. Mikele Leigertwood gave away the same free kick needlessly as we had against Blackburn. Our goalkeeper came out like Superman, or in this case Cooperman, missed the cross and a Charlton player headed the equaliser.

With West Brom winning, the other two losing, incredibly they were staying up. We had seven minutes to try and save ourselves and when Charlton scored every conceivable emotion went through my head. Try as we might we never found that third goal.

The final whistle blew amongst celebrations from the Charlton fans, rejoicing deliriously in our demise as if they had won the Champions League. We had been relegated. Despite beating Liverpool, Spurs and Aston Villa, despite drawing with Manchester and Arsenal, despite doing the double over Birmingham and being unbeaten in our last four games, we were heading straight back to the Football League.

As I went to leave, I walked up the stairs past the jeering Charlton fans and was stopped by their chairman, Richard Murray, with whom I had enjoyed a friendly relationship. 'Enjoy the Championship, tosser!' he chortled, a reference to the *Sunday Times* article earlier that season. That was the start of open hostilities between the two clubs that were to have far-reaching consequences.

I started to walk away, stopped and turned back. I couldn't believe what he had said to me at a time of such desperate disappointment.

I confronted Murray, asking how he could say such a thing at such a time. Murray just grinned maniacally, and remarked that I had been rude by being late for the game and rude by not attending lunch.

'What?' I stammered incredulously.

His reason for being so insulting was I hadn't attended lunch, which I never did and always had my secretary politely decline.

He went on to mention the *Sunday Times* article, which I thought we had laid to rest on the day it came out, and then incredibly he asked me if I wanted to have a fight. 'Fight?' I said incredulously, 'I am a chairman of a football club, as are you. Besides, you are an old man.'

I left Murray smirking happy in his nonsense, reminding him: 'What goes around comes around.'

I went down to the pitch to console the players. One thing Murray's absurd outburst had done was dispel any feeling I might have about feeling sorry for myself and replace it with a galvanised spirit of 'We must get back.'

I actually gave Dowie a hug as, despite the fact we had got relegated and done it to ourselves by conceding late goals in the two critical games against Southampton and Charlton, he and the players had given their all.

In a downcast and despondent dressing room I spoke to the players, saying that I was proud of their efforts. We had come up short, but what did not kill us would make us stronger. I asked them if they liked this feeling, which of course they didn't, and suggested they remember it and take it on to the pitch against the first opposition next season.

And that was that: the lights went down. Or not quite. As I walked out of the stadium, still being jeered by Charlton fans and the disappointment now beginning to resonate, I bumped into Wayne Routledge's mother, who cheerfully announced I wouldn't be seeing Wayne next year as he was off. Charming!

One last thing to do. I phoned Jeremy Peace, the West Brom chairman, who was obviously in mid-celebration, and congratulated him. It was a hard phone call to make, but who said I was not magnanimous in defeat?

11

DOWN WITH A BUMP

Through the summer of 2005 I reflected long and hard about being relegated from the Premier League after just one season. We were the architects of our own demise. The Premier League campaign had flown by. It seemed as soon as we were playing our first game away to Norwich with optimism, exuberance and expectation that it was all over.

I was coming to the unwelcome realisation that I was unlikely to get what I really wanted – Palace to be a major force in top-flight football – and I couldn't indefinitely fund an impossible dream.

Palace had been christened the team of the eighties, not merely through their performance on the pitch, but also because of the size of the crowds. I remember sitting with my dad as a twelve-year-old in 1979 watching them beat Ipswich 4–1 to go to the top of the First Division, which would now be the Premier League, in front of over 40,000 fans. The club had an average of nigh on 37,000 supporters then, but six years later, after Noades had bought them and sold all their assets, barely 6,000 people were watching them.

Over twenty years the lack of investment and the sale of all its best assets to fund the football club and, in my view, its owner, saw the club spurn massive opportunities and eventually work its way backwards from being a team talked about as a potential 'Man United of the South' to being a club that just had potential.

Like a lot of 'potential' big clubs Palace had a core fan base. In our case, this was around 10,000 season ticket holders. When you looked at clubs like Norwich, Sheffield Wednesday and Leeds, who were not performing as well as us, they had double the amount of season ticket holders. This realisation put things into perspective. Despite the size of our catchment area we would never really have the kind of club that was the bedrock of the community. Chelsea, Liverpool and Manchester United shirts were worn in Croydon's high street. Damn sure Palace shirts were not worn in Liverpool or Manchester!

One of the ways, besides continual success, which marked a team as a Premier League club, was to build a brand-new stadium, but regardless of what I was prepared to do it was always going to be difficult given we were based in London, where land is at a premium and councils not overly interested in helping. Redevelopment was unfeasible given that Noades would not sell the stadium for a realistic price. The numerous obstacles surrounding Selhurst Park meant it was highly unlikely I could turn it from a 26,000 capacity all-seater stadium to a 35–40,000 capacity purpose-built stadium that could also house all the requisite facilities for 'secondary spend' opportunities. Thus the income streams were never really going to improve to the point where we could compete at the top end of football.

Despite all of this and a nagging feeling that I might have had my day in the sun, I decided I couldn't leave the club or sell it as it was.

When we got promoted I had felt I owed it to myself to stay

and now we were relegated I felt I had a moral obligation and a determination to right the injustices of the relegation by standing up and being committed, which is probably what I should have been literally!

At this time it probably became a bit more of a labour rather than a labour of love but I didn't want to leave tarnished by relegation on my watch. Also, this was Palace's centenary year, which was a big deal for the club and its fans, and I had the hope of getting back to the Premier League as a landmark for our hundredth year in existence.

With this in mind I gave Iain Dowie unwavering support in order to take us back to the Premier League at the first opportunity.

During the previous season I became very friendly with the actor Nick Moran, he of *Lock, Stock and Two Smoking Barrels* fame. We met over drinks at the Grosvenor in Easter 2005 and by June he had me funding and producing the West End stage version of a major award-nominated play he had written named *Telstar*. This involvement led me to my next relationship, with Meg Mathews, who was a guest at the opening party of the play and someone of whom I became extremely fond.

During the summer it was the fortieth birthday of my best friend Mark Ryan, the MD of Phones4u. His wife to be and I organised a week's partying in my house in Spain to celebrate this landmark occasion and the impending arrival of their first child and my goddaughter, Grace.

It consisted of a fabulous week of about twenty people staying at my house and twenty others in local hotels. I hired a film crew to film a documentary-style diary of the week as we ate in restaurants, went to nightclubs, raced cars on a day up in the mountains of Ronda, sailed my boat around the Med, had a fireworks display in my garden and generally had a bloody good time. Mark had all his family there and Meg joined us on a wonderful week which culminated in a dinner party held at the swish Mansion House club, which was part owned by my friends the Dalli Brothers, where we drank and ate our way through £25,000 worth of food and wine.

With a summer of distractions behind me I returned to the business of football.

In liaison with the Dowie brothers we had some decisions to make and some enforced on us. But the end result was further investment from me.

Over the summer certain players had gone by the very nature of the deals we signed them under, or by their lack of desire to play outside the Premier League. Joonas Kolkka left on a free transfer, Vassilis Lakis returned to AEK Athens, Nicola Ventola returned to Inter Milan and Gonzalo Sorondo took the charming step of signing for Charlton, of all people.

Talking of the Italian giants Inter Milan, they were scheduled to play in a prestigious pre-season friendly. But in July 2005 terrorist bombs went off in London, killing innocent people and causing widespread panic amongst the nation. Milan immediately cancelled their trip, which was totally unacceptable as far as I was concerned. Letting terrorists win on whatever level was condoning their barbaric behaviour.

So I had a rant on television and in the papers calling them cowards and asserting that like the Italian tank operators in the Second World War all they knew was reverse gear. The media picked it up with glee and the politicians got involved, with Tessa Jowell, the Minister of Sport at the time, and Mayor Ken Livingstone roundly condemning Milan's action. The end result? Internazionale came and won 2–0 in a damp squib of a poorly attended encounter, managed by a certain Roberto Mancini who now plies his trade at mega-rich Manchester City.

Coming to the business end of the pre-season, in terms of the squad I gave Dowie huge support and bought a variety of players to confirm that I was going to give the club more than a fighting chance to use his now famous bouncebackability phrase to full effect.

I spent £5.1 million, a significant sum, on new players. I signed centre back Darren Ward from Millwall for £1.25 million, Jobi McAnuff from Cardiff for £750,000 and Jon Macken from Manchester City for £1.1 million. Clinton Morrison came back from Birmingham for £2 million, and Marco Reich from Derby. Added to this was a raft of players who were still paid Premier League wages despite relegation. But my *pièce de résistance* was yet to come with mounting speculation that Andrew Johnson had played his last game for Palace.

Wayne Routledge's departure to Tottenham Hotspur, although not entirely unexpected, was a huge disappointment to me. His mother's timing in informing me he was leaving after we had been relegated from the Premier League was impeccable and now she made good on that threat or more to the point his God-awful agent, Paul Stretford, did. We had compensation rights, as the young England star was under twenty-four. But rather than go to the banana republic of a flawed tribunal system, we negotiated the best deal we could and settled for £1.25 million from Daniel 'Dick Turpin' Levy, the Spurs chairman.

Watching a young man of immense potential and part of my prized youth system disappear to Spurs did not sit comfortably with me.

I made one last attempt to talk him out of it. 'You can be a really proper player, Wayne, stay here and learn your trade and then you will get all the things that good players deserve.

'But if you lack confidence and believe you will never be a top player, go to Spurs, take the money and sit in their reserves.'

He went under the great guidance of his agent, who as far as I was concerned would receive a damn sight more money by engineering a move rather than a contract renewal, even though this might not necessarily be in the best interests of the player.

Routledge played the princely total of five games for Spurs before being shipped out to any Premier League or Championship club that could afford his new wages and altogether played fifty-three times in four and a half years. What a waste of talent. He will carve out a respectable career, but I believe he could have amounted to so much more.

The dust had barely settled when almost instantaneously I became embroiled in war with another agent who tried to manipulate a situation to his own advantage.

Andrew Johnson, our talismanic England striker and the highest English goal scorer in our Premier League season, was told by his agent he had been given the mandate by Palace to sell him and that he wouldn't play for England again in World Cup year if he stayed at the club.

The agent concerned was the divisive Leon Angel who I had previous issues with over the termination of Trevor Francis's contract in 2003. I decided this time to more than remove him from the equation; the tonic required for this particular ailment was total discredit.

Angel had the audacity to call a meeting with my management team of Dowie & Dowie. This was arranged behind my back, as if Angel thought he could go to my training ground to do a deal without my knowledge.

So I made it my business to turn up at this meeting, sitting in my training-ground lounge as Angel turned up with Andrew Johnson. It's fair to say he was not overly thrilled to find me waiting for him. From the first word that left my mouth he was left in no doubt of my views on the situation.

He was told he did not and would never have a mandate to sell any of my players, let alone my star player. Angel tried to get up on his high horse so as to look better in Johnson's eyes but I pulled no punches. I told him that in my view he was a disgrace of an agent whose only interest in the player was money. I pointed out that he had been AJ's agent for six months, and in that time he had done the square root of nothing for the player. Not even a boot deal, as Bob Dowie had secured that. On and on I went while Angel – who in my vivid imagination reminded me of Davros, the creator of the Daleks in *Doctor Who* – sat in silence and eventually slunk off the training ground.

This was all done in front of the player and although it made him feel extremely uncomfortable it was necessary so everybody knew where they stood.

After Angel left he went to the press stating that he was acting in the player's best interest, that Johnson wanted to move and that he had been given an exclusive mandate to sell him.

I used the media to try and exterminate Davros and stop this nonsense of agents acting like flesh traders, popping up whenever they thought they could initiate a move which would get them paid money, irrespective of what was best for the player and the club. I accused him of everything from trespassing to larceny and being the arch-enemy of the Doctor. I even went as far as to say I would rather support Millwall than allow Johnson to leave on my watch, that's how seriously I viewed it!

Angel threatened to sue me as I made my views on him very

clear in every medium. I practically pleaded with him in print to sue me and reported him to everyone from FIFA, the FA, football and the Warren Commission. The upshot was I met Andrew on his own, told him he was staying, promptly gave him a new contract with a financial reward for his achievements, which he was well due. This shut up the agent and the rest of the football world, who had said to a man that Andrew Johnson was never going to stay, as he signed a new four-year deal with the club!

We did of course have offers for AJ, notably from Everton, who bid something like £7 million, to which I enquired as to whether their chairman Bill Kenwright was offering to buy one of Andrew Johnson's trainers. And my old mates at Birmingham popped up with some imaginary offer, announcing to the press that they had made a £6.5 million bid. They must have sent it by a blind carrier pigeon, as I never received it. I'm not sure what the purpose of this announcement was as it made them look stupid. There was no bid and if there had been they would have been buying back a player they gave away for nothing and originally thought wasn't good enough to play for them.

With this matter now dealt with I had sent out a statement of intent that I was committed to Palace getting straight back up. Everybody invariably sold their best players when they went down and I didn't. I kept them and added a further five players. We now had a strike force of some £15 million-plus and a squad that was the strongest in the league by a country mile.

On top of the players, Dowie wanted a new assistant, deeming Kit Symons not good enough, despite Kit being in situ when we had got promoted from this division. We shuffled him sideways into coaching and managing the reserves and brought in as assistant manager Neil MacDonald, formerly Sam Allardyce's number two at Bolton, with the remit to specifically work on our defensive unit!

With all the above in mind I said quite innocently that in my view if this manager and team performed as I knew they could, there was no reason why we could not win the league. This was roundly condemned by certain factions of the football mafia as putting undue pressure on the manager. In my view it was a state-ment of fact. Why should I not say in a qualified way what I thought, so the fans understood where their club owner stood? And why should Dowie not be under pressure to succeed when he had the tools, for God's sake.

Suffice it to say he took exception to it! And some of his 'mates' in the media conveniently aired their views in the papers on his behalf.

But pretty soon I was to have the pen as I had just been offered a prominent column in the *Observer* and I was going to enjoy correcting certain perspectives. My first column was fittingly entitled: 'Why agents should be neutered'!

The season started with this expensively assembled squad full of expectation, and with Dowie's bouncebackability ringing in their ears.

Our first game was at home to newly promoted Luton Town. I hoped that my last words to the players in the away dressing room at Charlton about taking their feeling of dejection out on the opposition was prevalent in their minds. But we duly lost to a team widely tipped for relegation!

We followed that up with another defeat to a Wolves side that had been in the doldrums for some time. So after two games we were bottom of the league and there wasn't a whiff of bounce-backability. In fact, it took us till the middle of October, some two and a half months into the season, before troubling the top six and as far as winning the league or getting automatic promotion, we never got anywhere near the top two for the whole season.

Finally we recorded our first win of the season at home to Plymouth. After that win and a few further decent performances we looked as if we were building a head of steam when disaster struck. We lost Andrew Johnson in the seventh game of the campaign away to Reading, a knee injury caused by his own bravery challenging a full back trying to clear a ball, which was bloody sod's law as I fought so damn hard to keep him. We lost him for a third of the season. Somehow football appeared to have cruel twists even when you tried to do the right thing.

By now I was in full flow with my fortnightly *Observer* columns. I had possible subjects provided by the paper but was encouraged to create my own subject matter. I wrote about agents, players, referees, clubs and the joke that is our English FA amongst other subjects. Throughout the seventeen articles I produced the FA was a regular feature as the way they operated and continue to operate is, in my view, a national embarrassment.

The columns were the first time an owner/chairman had lifted the lid on the world of football and shown it for what it really was: a murky world at times, full of self-interest. The column also opened the game up to the people who it belonged to: the fans. I tackled big issues like Sepp Blatter, technology, stadium standing, agents, players, FIFA, UEFA, G14 Clubs, racism, other chairmen and, of course, the FA.

The FA was our governing body; we were the country that gave the world football, yet it was a sham of self-interest, with chief executives appointed who in my view were not capable of the job and more focused on the perks of the title rather than the task at hand. Just look at this gallery of 'unusual suspects' charged with running our national game.

Adam Crozier, young and innovative, who left the FA in vast debt and then went off to spend millions rebranding the Post Office to Consignia, only for it to be changed back to the Post Office.

The amorous Mark Palios, who disappeared in the scandal of who was bonking the FA secretary Faria Alam most: the CEO or the England manager.

After heading up ITV Digital, a business that nearly ruined a huge part of English football, Brian Barwick got his reward by getting the FA's top job and presided over the debacle of the phenomenal escalating costs of building the new Wembley and the embarrassing attempted and ultimate appointment of England managers.

And let us not forget Lord Triesman, who talked a great game and in talking opened his mouth in the most unfortunate way and was forced to resign over his allegations that certain countries were trying to bribe referees, which no doubt helped enormously in collecting votes for our bid to secure the 2018 World Cup.

In my columns I exposed the nonsense of people who made anonymous decisions in quango committees, as well as the blazer and tie brigade who latched onto FA councillorships as a means to keeping their free England tickets and travel. I named and shamed them, much to their dismay and horror.

I enjoyed writing the columns and I most certainly liked wielding the pen. I worked with great guys at the *Observer* who researched and qualified some of my more outrageous allegations. I had no idea at the time that these articles were to be so popular; people stopped me in the street and raved about them.

Ian Wooldridge, the revered and much missed sports writer, dedicated a column to suggesting I should be brought in to run the FA! I am sure that went down like a lead enema in Soho Square. He also went on to to say he was going to potentially nominate me as sports writer of the year. I knew the articles must have been OK as even Iain Dowie begrudgingly admitted they were good!

What these columns also did was to demonstrate something to certain parts of the football world: that I was a man of substance and understood the game. This in some way transported me from a perceived rebellious innovator and troublemaker to someone with valid and forward-thinking views who was not frightened to air them for the advancement of our national game.

Of course, writing without care of consequence and showing situations and people for what they were would inevitably land me in trouble. This came with my fourth article entitled 'Call Time on Blatter's Village Idiots'.

The article was about refereeing standards. Sepp Blatter, the president of FIFA, refused to bring in technology, and like all good writers I used an example: the refereeing performance of the official of the recent Palace v Reading game. The FA charged me with 'improper conduct', making me sound like some kind of pervert. So not only did I lose my star player in the Reading game, the FA was now charging me for having an opinion about it. Talk about double whammy, although the thought of being charged was about as troublesome to me as a cloud on a sunny day.

I was summoned to Soho Square, but as I had written about my impending FA disciplinary hearing and its location in my *Observer* columns, they changed the venue to a secret location for a 'transparent' hearing. It was not secret for long, as I immediately informed Sky Sports news.

Apparently, when you are charged by the FA they ask for your total net football wage in order to establish how much they should fine you. I advised the panel of the £32 million I had invested in the last five years, which worked out at minus £127,000 a week, and told them that I was more than happy to receive a rebate.

The hearing was a farce. They had only two options, both with serious consequences for them: do not discipline me and perhaps set a precedent; do and open a can of worms with me and be unable to control what I may or may not say and do. They decided on a halfway house solution: a fine of £10,000 suspended for twelve months, dependent on me not saying anything derogatory. With this they sent me on my way suitably admonished!

The gag lasted all of three minutes as I walked out and did a live piece to Sky on the hearing's doorstep, declaring it a kangaroo court comprised of ill-informed, self-important buffoons who had no idea of what was right and proper and that any fine would be paid in one-pound coins delivered in a wheelbarrow to Soho Square. No fine followed!

On top of that I wrote in my next column all about the hearing, under the title of 'So who is Barry Bright?', the chairman (or, in my mind, chairbuffoon) of that hearing. I described the whole event in detail and yet they still refused to implement the fine. I continued to bait them in my next six articles. The fine stayed, but they never enforced it, despite me ignoring every aspect of the gagging order.

On the field the season started as a disappointment and peaked and troughed much like my relationship with the manager. Halfway through we were seventh in the league, some twenty-seven points off top and eighteen points off second, so automatic promotion was out of the question. Our best-case scenario was the play-offs. We were where we were, so we had to make the best of it, and make sure we made the play-offs in the highest possible position.

The season was full of anomalies. We would thrash a respectable Coventry side 4–1 away and the very next game lose 1–0 to our arch-rivals, bottom-of-the-league Brighton, in front of a disbelieving and packed home crowd, then in the following game beat the mighty Liverpool again in the League Cup 2–1. The only consistency we had was inconsistency.

Throughout the season the uneasy truce with Iain Dowie was always at the fore. He was back to his belligerent argumentative best, always looking to be contrary and clever wherever he could and, disappointingly, Bob had got a little caught up in the world of football to the detriment of the commercial side of the business.

Dominic was running the club day to day and I wanted him to exert control over the commercial activities and I would liaise with the football management. Perversely, this involved more contact for Dominic with the football side. Certain commercial activities included the football operation which led to Dominic having to tolerate nonsense from Bob and Iain about budgetary controls.

Budgets were agreed for all aspects of the club, from medical supplies to travel and accommodation. The football operation budget was drawn up by Bob and Iain and approved by me, and then systematically ignored by them, which caused conflict with Dominic as he sought to ensure they controlled their agreed costs.

By the end of March, after beating Watford for the second time in the season, with five games to go we were fifth, and pretty much secure in the play-offs. My expectations were we would push on to get as high up that mini play-off league as possible. But what we did was to win only one of our last five games of the season, producing arguably our worst run of the campaign, taking five points out of the last five games and finishing sixth.

In between the rigours of the campaign Geoff Thomas, the former Palace captain, who had fought so bravely back from the ravages of leukaemia, had a testimonial game. It was to be a re-enactment of the 1990 Cup Final between Palace and Manchester

United, a game that arguably kept Alex Ferguson in the Manchester United job as they narrowly beat Palace to give Ferguson his first trophy after nearly four years in charge.

Somehow or another I got roped into playing. As with all football chairmen it was presumed I knew nothing about football and most certainly couldn't play! So in front of 15,000 fans I came on as a substitute and I will leave it to the local press to describe my performance.

'Well, he's certainly got bottle, hasn't he? Playing alongside the Palace 1990 FA Cup Final heroes is one thing but doing it in white boots sporting highlighted blond hair was potentially a recipe for public humiliation. But to be fair to the Palace chairman he pulled it off just because he turned out to be quite good.'

As I watched the last five League games I witnessed a team coasting into the end-of-season play-offs. In our last game of the League campaign we lost 1–0 away to Sheffield United with a particularly tepid display and I took this opportunity to remark to Bob Dowie that I had grave concerns.

The fact we drew Watford in the play-offs seemed to instil even more complacency as it was universally greeted by players and management as a great draw, one we would walk through, given we had beaten them twice already during the season.

I did not share this view. I struggled to see how a team that laboured through their last five games in poor form was going to get itself up a level. I felt Watford, having finished third and been beaten twice by us, had probably learnt more from those losses than we had from the wins. Again I voiced that to Iain and Bob, who took exception to my sentiments of concern and caution.

As the play-offs approached my pals at Birmingham City in the

Premier League were embroiled in a relegation battle that they were ultimately to lose. At the time their co-owner David Gold announced in an interview: 'If there was a God then no way would Crystal Palace get promoted and Birmingham get relegated.'

Now I thought at the time that was particularly uncalled for and it really hurt my feelings! It had slipped my mind that I had written a big article recently in the *Observer* about owners of clubs, mentioning Birmingham and David Gold specifically, which had clearly provoked his untimely outburst. I had said that if I had to read another article about an East End boy made good I would impale myself on one of the dildos he sold.

The play-offs were greeted with their usual media frenzy and the first leg was at home. Strangely given the magnitude of the game and the fact it was a virtual London derby it was not a complete sell-out. Only 22,000 fans turned up. Perhaps they knew something.

After an even and uninspiring first half we fell apart in the second and were 2–0 down after sixty-five minutes. My worst fears had been confirmed and when Watford scored their third goal in the eighty-fifth minute, I looked across the directors' box to where Bob Dowie sat and said: 'I told you so.'

I had sensed what was going to happen. I hoped my gut feeling would be wrong, but I was proved to be right in the worst possible way. We now faced the never-achieved task of overturning a first leg loss in the second game and winning by four clear goals.

After the manner of the defeat morale in and around the club was very low and despite the feelings I had voiced prior and during the game I still felt it was important to maintain a positive outlook.

If they could score three then so could we. I knew this was a bloody long shot but a leader has to lead even in the face of adversity. Iain was still bullish despite the heavy defeat but as football clubs are like sieves with information it emanated quickly that certain players had completely given up the ghost.

It was a non-event of a game. It is difficult to put into words how one feels watching an opportunity slip away like that. Can you imagine going on *Deal Or No Deal* and you have two boxes left. One has £50 million and the other has 50p. And one of the conditions is that someone else chooses the box – and they pick the 50p. That is what it is like losing in the play-offs. You could of course lose in the play-off final, which would be pretty bad, but losing in the manner we did was far worse for me. Some teams go out all guns blazing, whereas we just failed to turn up.

The game ended in a 0–0 draw and we never even looked like scoring. The only example of any passion was when a brawl broke out on the touchline because Aidy Boothroyd, the Watford manager at the time, refused to return the ball after it went out of play. I thought at the time, 'Typical. We can manage to be brave off the pitch but not on it.'

To add insult to injury the FA saw fit to fine us for it.

I congratulated the Watford board and left, not really wanting to be around the place whilst they were rejoicing at our expense. Unfortunately for me I got stuck in the damn Watford car park, as we were unable to get out, and was subjected to twenty minutes of joyous home fans giving me barrel loads of abuse. I have to say it takes remarkable restraint not to get an Uzi out when you are gutted and celebrating fans are taking the piss out of you. There is no such thing as football fans showing humility in winning, they just stick it to you.

And that was that. The lights went down for another season, a year almost to the day of relegation from the Premier League at the hands of Charlton. Another juddering disappointment, a year wasted, an opportunity spurned and we were looking forward to another twelve months trawling round the second tier of English football.

I can bear most things but I hate waste and this was a wasted opportunity.

I never spoke to Iain before the game or straight afterwards, but that was how he appeared to want it. He was a law unto himself and as long as he was successful I tolerated it. He never wanted comradeship, he didn't have an 'all for one and one for all' mentality. He wanted to do things in a certain way.

Dowie could manage down but had no ability to manage up and that was to prove his undoing, and, I have since heard, was his undoing with future employers.

After a couple of days I returned to Spain and, seeing as my manager had made no effort to contact me, called Dowie on the way to the airport and left a voicemail message.

It could be concluded from the events I have described that I would be in an unhappy mood, but once I have adjusted to something and then accepted it, which on the whole I do pretty quickly, I become philosophical about things and this was how I approached the phone call with Dowie.

Of course I was disappointed but to some extent it was over. Like any normal employer I wanted to know what had gone wrong and why. That proved to be fatal – how dare I ask such invasive questions!

The conversation that was to have far-reaching consequences for us both started at about 8 p.m. as I sat in my garden in Spain. After a brief exchange I had the audacity to ask him why he hadn't called me after the game. That was the high point in the conversation.

Very quickly the conversation turned into a pissing competition, which I allowed myself to be dragged into. Dowie seemed intent on baiting me and achieved his aim. After listening to him tell me he didn't want to discuss our failure in the play-offs as it was over, he promptly moved on to tell me that if I had supported him in the Premier League we would have stayed up and how I had created pressure and unrealistic expectations on the team at the beginning of the season.

I have to admit that for about three minutes I thoroughly lost my temper. Clearly I am no shrinking violet and I let him have full-on my feelings about what he had just said and the way he had acted.

No punches were pulled on either side and I make no apologies for what I said. I told him that whether he liked it or not he worked for me, not the other way round, and he should learn his place. For two and a half years I had given him the benefit of the doubt and I was tired of this constant, divisive, disrespectful crap from him.

The storm eventually passed and we both regained our composure. The conversation moved on to more constructive matters about the following season. We agreed that it was likely Andrew Johnson would now go as I had promised him that if we didn't get promoted, he could leave. Dowie asked if he would get the funds and I said it was likely he would get a significant percentage of them for reinvestment.

Then, like a bolt out of the blue, he told me he was considering leaving Palace so he could return up north to be with his family, who had shown no wish to relocate during his two-and-a-half-year tenure at the club.

I am rarely speechless. We had moved on from the row, spent twenty minutes talking about the new season, he had asked for more money for players and more backing and got them. Then, as if I was talking to a different person entirely, he told me he wanted to leave the club. I was flabbergasted, and said if he wanted to leave to go and work up north and be near his family then that changed everything.

Dowie went on to say that he would stay until a job came up. I said, 'How can that work? I can't allow you to buy players knowing you want to leave. That's absurd!' and terminated the call.

Within half an hour Bob was on the phone. He wanted to act as mediator but I saw little point. I told him as I had told his brother that I had things to think about.

After digesting the Dowie call I came to the conclusion that if he wanted to go he could. He had failed in my eyes to keep us in the Premier League when he should have done and had most definitely failed miserably in my view to get us back with the strongest squad in the Championship.

So in the week I thought about it I came to the view perhaps he was right to want to leave. But perversely I had reservations. Yes, I was bored with his antics and outlook but then 'better the devil you know', as the saying goes. When all was said and done, Dowie had been the only manager to date who had given me a modicum of success.

I spoke to him a week later and he seemed in an immeasurable hurry to get this matter resolved. He was now resolute about going back up north, even rescinding the ludicrous offer to stay until we appointed his successor.

We had a £1 million compensation clause in his contract and by releasing him I was effectively waiving that. Of course, then we wouldn't be held to paying up the remainder of his contract. But this was his agenda. Purely out of empathy to his wishes, given he was playing the family card so strongly, I agreed to waive my compensation rights and release him from his contract.

I was to fly in on Monday 22 May to hold a press conference to announce his departure. As I have said before there are very few secrets in football and soon the rumour mill began to reach my ears.

I got a phone call on Friday 19 May from Neil Ashton of the *Daily Mail*, a staunch Crystal Palace fan who I knew well. He asked what the press call was for and when I said 'wait and see', he told me it was to announce Dowie's departure, which slightly irked me as I wanted to announce it. He then said: 'You do realise that Dowie is nailed on for the Charlton job?'

I don't know whether it was arrogance, naivety or just plain stupidity, but I found it difficult to believe that Dowie would have the gall to lie to me in such a barefaced way. I phoned him to just check again about his 'going up north to be with his family' but got no answer. So I spoke to his brother Bob, who told me that there was no way to his knowledge that he was going to Charlton. So I left it there.

I flew in and met Dowie in my office prior to the press conference to sign the compromise agreement, which nullified the contract in its entirety. When I got to Palace, Dowie's lawyers had changed the agreement. My HR director Kevin Watts, my rock of all things employment, was on a flight to Dubai and unable to be contacted.

Dowie and his lawyers wanted a specific clause about the removal of compensation in the compromise agreement, which was totally unnecessary as the compromise agreement did precisely that. It set off alarm bells and I suggested we did the press conference and sign afterwards, as by that time Kevin would have landed in Dubai.

Dowie pleaded with me to sign, and as the press were now waiting I asked him straight out: 'Are you going to Charlton?' and he categorically assured me that he was not. So I relented and signed, thus releasing him and waiving our £1 million.

In nine days' time I took a controversial action as the depths of Dowie's treachery became evident.

12

YOU HAVE TO WONDER WHY

'Un-fucking-believable. Who does he think he is?'

That was my reaction as the news filtered through to me that, three days after being released from Palace and despite his promises and protestations to the contrary, Iain Dowie was going to be unveiled as the new Charlton Athletic manager in a press conference scheduled for the Tuesday after the May bank holiday weekend in 2006.

I couldn't believe it; well, I suppose I could because he had no shame. Dowie knew he was going to Charlton and, using his family as an excuse, played on my better nature to get himself released from a contract that had a £1 million compensation clause in it. There was no way I was going to take that up the backside.

Dowie should have known me better. But as I have said football people live in a cosseted environment, outside the normal rules that govern society and think they can do as they damn well please.

Over the years I spent many hours with lawyers and many millions of pounds fighting legal injustices so there was no surprise when my legal representation received my call. My lawyer, Mark Buckley, was aware of the Dowie departure and the manner in which it had manifested itself and now he had been informed that Dowie was to be the new Charlton manager. I wanted something done and I wanted to be told how I could address this outrageous abuse of trust.

Mark Buckley came back with two words: 'fraudulent misrepresentation'.

Aware that Dowie would be presented as Charlton's manager at a press conference with his new chairman Richard Murray I decided to get a writ served on him live on national TV.

It was drafted over the weekend and was ready to be served. There was a private detective who I used regularly, Stuart Page, and I instructed him to pose as a reporter going to the press conference. Once he was in, at the most opportune moment, I told him to serve it upon Dowie in front of millions of watching eyes.

I sat in front of my TV in Spain watching Dowie being unveiled as the new Charlton manager – the post he said he would never take – and only about six miles north of Palace. I waited patiently for my guy to deliver my leaving gift to Dowie, but as the press conference went on, I listened to certain parts where Dowie blatantly lied and Murray ridiculed me, but there was no sign of Stuart.

My phone rang. 'I can't get in, I couldn't get a press pass.'

'Hold tight, Stuart, I'll get you in.'

I phoned one of the Sky guys and told him that if he wanted to see something unique and interesting to get my guy in.

Stuart Page burst into the press conference with a writ in his hand from CPFC for fraud against Iain Dowie. The place descended into mayhem. Dowie looked gobsmacked and Murray bemused, perhaps thinking it was some kind of prank from *Candid Camera*. Eventually my guy got manhandled out by security. Meanwhile, I sat in my front room, thinking, 'OK, Mr Dowie, you wanted to lie and cheat, now you have something else to consider.'

My phone lit up like a pinball machine as newspapers and radio stations bombarded me with calls, but I wanted to speak to Sky live to ensure everybody knew what and why this was going on.

Jim White, the Sky anchor, who considered himself something of a roving investigative reporter, tried to portray my actions as taking football to a new low. I agreed wholeheartedly and said that when a man lies and cheats his way out of a contract and betrays people, football *has* reached a new low!

OK, it was theatrical and unnecessary to have served the writ in the manner I did but I wanted to ensure that Dowie got his just desserts. He had hoodwinked me; Charlton, our now fiercest rivals, had got him for absolutely nothing, and unlike most others in football, I was not going to sit back and let that happen. As with Steve Bruce before him there was a consequence. In the world outside of football, there were consequences for managers who behaved unethically, and I didn't see why football should be any different.

Once the furore died down I discussed the next move with my lawyers and was horrified to be told that the charge I was alleging against Dowie was one of the hardest to prove and they had reservations about its success. My grandstanding had the potential of becoming a big custard pie in my own face. 'Bit bloody late to tell me that now,' I said, 'and not what you said when we decided on this drastic course of action. You got me in this with your advice, you better get me out of it one way or another.'

And with that we put together a case that was to create legal history.

As I have mentioned many times before I didn't want to constantly be in the way of confrontation but I wouldn't avoid battles when they were necessary. Despite putting myself under enormous pressure I only stepped up when it was the right thing to do. Iain Dowie had betrayed me and all the Palace fans who had supported him when he was at the club. Why shouldn't he be held accountable for his treachery?

During the summer of 2006 I distracted myself with getting involved in other projects. I'd always been interested in the restaurant business and with a partner launched the soon-to-be-award-winning Club Bar and Dining in the heart of Soho. I also decided to sell my 50 per cent shareholding in the very successful motor car magazine I had launched just over three years earlier to Felix Dennis, one of the country's leading publishing moguls.

Returning to football I was always looking at ways to increase Palace's reach. I had previously considered buying Northern Spirit, an Australian Club, also coming close with the Auckland Kingz, a New Zealand side playing in the Australian Major League, only to pull out when I discovered that they were being booted out of the league. This had been represented differently to me by Phil Alexander, who had a personal agenda because he wanted to run the club.

Following on from that theme of trying to increase Palace's reach wherever I could, I started up a venture in America: Crystal Palace USA. We were to be the first English club to have a subsidiary in the US and would be based in Baltimore, just outside of Washington DC, and play in what was the Second Division of American Major League Soccer. The idea was to have a club where we could discover new talent for CPFC UK, as well as a venue for our young players to gain invaluable experience before joining our first team. It was a revolutionary move and one that could have had big potential.

While the long arduous task got underway with the lawyers on the Dowie case, I started the search for yet another manager. Incredibly, I had still kept on Bob Dowie, despite the situation with his brother. He assured me that he still wanted to work and

273

I felt Bob would be advantageous to have around to help select a new manager.

I met Graeme Souness in Marbella for dinner to discuss the Palace job. I liked Graeme as he had been great with my dad when he had open heart surgery in 2005, talking to him about his own experiences of it. I admired his forthright nature and the passion he exuded. We had a good chat but I got the impression that he was done with club management. I have to say that would have been an interesting relationship between myself and Graeme.

In a night out with friends in Puerto Banus, I bumped into Mike Newell, the former Everton and Blackburn striker, who was then managing Luton Town. When I say 'bumped', Newell lumbered over, drunk as a skunk, plonked himself down next to me and told me he wanted an interview with Palace. I got the impression he actually expected one there and then! I told Newell that Bob Dowie was doing the selection process and if he wanted to be considered he should go through Bob.

You would have thought that I had just told him I had slept with his wife, given the offence he took. 'Charlie big fucking bollocks, too important to talk to me,' he raged. I thought he was going to hit me, especially when I told him that it was an impressive interviewing technique, standing in front of a potential employer pissed as a rat. Unsurprisingly, he never got his interview and was filed under miscellaneous with Stan Ternent and trolled off back under the bridge whence he came.

Someone, somewhere mentioned the former Palace player Peter Taylor, and for the life of me I can't recall who it was or how it came to be otherwise I would have probably served a writ on them as well as Dowie with the benefit of hindsight. For some reason Taylor became a serious candidate. I held a long-standing opinion that Taylor was a coach, not a manager, and had conveyed as much to his chairman at Hull, Adam Pearson, a friend who I saw a lot of in Spain. Adam always told me how much that irked Taylor. Following Trevor Francis's departure I had an opportunity to talk to Taylor when he was the Leicester manager in 2003. Peter had expressed a serious interest in the Palace job, but I had heard that he was nervous at Leicester and if they started badly he would get fired so was thinking of jumping before he got pushed. My reaction to that was, 'What a bloody loser.' Why would I want someone managing my club who forecasts failure?

With all that in mind I still interviewed Peter after Bob had met him and given me a good report on him. Given the absolute waste of time this appointment was to be I jokingly assumed that this was Iain Dowie's parting gift to me: getting his brother to advocate Taylor's appointment.

I liked Peter. He is a very affable man and does a very good Norman Wisdom impression. Unfortunately, I didn't expect him to take that into our dugout when he was appointed. He spoke of his love of the club – as a player, he had been a hero there, becoming the only Third Division player ever to play for England; he felt as if it would be in some way coming home.

I confronted him with my usual barrage of difficult questions, but somehow he convinced me. He was easy-going in a determined way, had learnt a lot from his experiences at Leicester, where he had failed shockingly, and rebuilt his reputation at Hull. He was also the England under-21 coach, and I felt that would allow us to have access to perhaps a lot of loan signings of young talented players at the top Premier League clubs. Perhaps most persuasive of all was his claim that he wanted to work with his chairman, not against him. After two and a half years of Iain Dowie's difficult attitude that was what probably sealed it. I wanted someone who I could bloody get on with.

Needless to say I had approached Adam Pearson seeking permission to open official talks with Taylor and was advised there was a £300,000 compensation fee to release him from his Hull City contract. Unlike others, I paid it. I tried to chip Adam but he wouldn't shift. I managed to get only one caveat in the formal compensation agreement. As Adam Pearson's dress sense was so shocking that I was embarrassed to stand next to him in Puerto Banus, I got a clause put into the agreement that 10 per cent of the compensation payable must be invested into Pearson's wardrobe! And he actually signed it, although to date I have seen no improvement in Adam's dress sense.

In between all the controversy of a manager leaving and writs flying about and a new manager coming in it was with immense regret that I had to make good on my promise to sell Andrew Johnson if we failed to win promotion. We had a number of interested parties with three firm bidders: Everton, Bolton and Wigan. Andrew wanted to go to Everton and after pushing Bill Kenwright the Everton chairman to breaking point – as he put it – I agreed to let my favourite player, my surrogate footballing son, go for £8.6 million. I could have got over £9 million from Wigan but I stayed true to my word, very rare in football, and let him choose his club.

Ironically Everton had bid £7 million for him when we got relegated from the Premier League and he had finished as the highest English goal scorer; now they paid £1.6 million more after a season in the Championship where he had picked up a serious injury and had his worst year as far as goals were concerned. The business of football decision-making defies logic but if a football manager wants a player, who cares? It's not his money he's spending.

With Taylor now secured in the managerial post the team headed off for a pre-season tour in America. Naturally we were to play our own team Crystal Palace USA, as well as LA Galaxy in the pre-Beckham days. I flew from Spain to London, picked up my suitcase packed by my right-hand man and driver John, and jumped straight on a flight to Washington with Bob Dowie and my brother Dominic. The two of them had been the architects of this American deal. When we landed in the capital of America it took us three hours to go twenty-five miles in rush-hour Washington traffic. I had spent eight hours on a plane, so more travel time was not exactly welcome.

When we arrived in Annapolis we stayed in the town's best hotel, which was a marginal step up from a Travel Lodge. They had no English tea, no valet, no adaptors to charge mobile phones and, with humidity levels off the charts, the air conditioning in my room had broken. And when I opened my suitcase, virtually all I had packed for me were heavy woollen suits. I wasn't being a precious little swine, I was absolutely exhausted and at this point my humour had completely deserted me.

Previously I never went on any pre-season tours, and the only reason I had gone on this one was because it was big news in the States that an English club had invested in US football, and a series of press conferences had been arranged. When I awoke in the morning to head off to speak to the media I was jet-lagged and in a filthy stinking mood. I had managed to dig out from my unwanted luggage one light tan Prada suit so to cap it all I now looked like the bloody man from Del Monte.

All the way to the press conference I did nothing but moan and groan. What was I doing here? What kind of godforsaken place had we landed up in? Was this really a good investment? But as soon as I was in the press conference and the lights and cameras of ESPN were up and rolling I went into a 180, extolling the virtues of this wonderful country, fantastic city, incredible opportunity and how excited I was about embarking on this project. Once the cameras had stopped I was back to full-on moaning and groaning. 'Media hound', was how my brother described my moth-to-the-light performance for the cameras.

Next stop was the biggest radio station in Washington for another round of interviews and one in which I sat next to Hasim Rahman, the former heavyweight champion of the world who had beaten Lennox Lewis. After talking about football I quipped to Rahman live on air that I'd seen Lewis beat him up like he had stolen something, which made for an uncomfortable ten minutes as this seventeen-stone former heavyweight champ glowered at me in the studio. I have to say at this point I gave serious thought to wondering if there was something wrong with my mental state to provoke a man-mountain like Rahman.

Paul Kemsley, the Spurs vice-chairman and a personal friend, asked a favour. During a holiday in the Bahamas, he had met and taken a young player under his wing and asked if I would take him with my team to America and give him a shot as in his view he wouldn't be good enough for Spurs. Not rising to that comment I agreed to do him a favour. We took him on a trial but Peter didn't rate him and in his honest expert opinion didn't feel he was good enough. The player's name was Jay Boothroyd, who went on to play for England a few years later.

My first impression of Peter's managerial prowess and outlook was that he was a little bit of a whiner. Nothing seemed right. As I watched the players train the atmosphere wasn't good. Apparently some of them didn't want to come here and a couple of disenfran-chised players who had asked me for transfers and been given short shrift were now sulking and causing a negative effect. Taylor picked up on the disharmony and it concerned me that he did nothing to address it. You would have thought players would want to create a good impression with their new manager but clearly, with Taylor, for some reason they didn't think they had to!

As a result I thought, 'Sod it. I don't need this self-indulgent negativity.' I had enough on my plate and left Dominic to deal with our American partners and Peter to do his job and get his team together, and flew back home to Spain.

The players and management returned from the States amongst reports from Bob Dowie that Peter Taylor was quite a difficult character to deal with and had been quite fastidious over there. I soon saw that side of Peter. Within weeks of being back he and Dominic were dealing with the travel arrangements for the impending season. We had a preferred travel agent and coach company but Peter wanted to use a firm he had a personal relationship with and when he didn't get his way he spat his dummy out. Out of the blue I got a phone call from him. 'Chairman, I am going to resign,' insisted Taylor. After ascertaining what the problem was I was incredulous that something so inconsequential could cause such a reaction and told him so in no uncertain terms. Peter went full circle and apologised for 'acting like a baby'. I began to wonder quite what I had employed.

After selling Andrew Johnson it was not my intention to weaken the squad further but I had various situations forced on me. Fitz Hall, the club captain, had a £3 million release clause in his contract and Wigan tabled a bid of £3 million and a pound. As the player wanted to go we had to let him. Emmerson Boyce had been one of the truculent players in America and from being a model professional he became petulant and difficult to deal with as I wouldn't let him have a transfer. He became so negative that Taylor came to me and asked me to sell him, which we duly did for £1 million, again to Wigan. And finally Mikele Leigertwood wouldn't sign a new contract and as he was under twenty-four we got compensation of £600,000 from his move to Sheffield United.

At Peter's request we went into the market and bought quite heavily, bringing in eight players and spending nearly £6 million. Whilst it may have appeared we had generated some significant cash most of it was used in either buying players or paying wages. Despite having one parachute payment left and significant transfer funds generated by the Johnson, Hall, Boyce and Leigertwood sales, I had also invested £12 million back into the team in the previous twelve months.

Hull City prospered as not only had I coughed up £300,000 for Peter's services, we went back and paid a million for their centre half Leon Court, as well as buying another player, Stuart Green, for £100,000. I have to confess the reason why we bought Green beggars belief. Peter's daughter was dating Green and he wanted him down in London to make his daughter happy. So, to support Peter, I did it. Back in 1999 I had spent £100,000 on a marketing campaign with Palace as a result of a date with the advertising manager and this time I spent another £100,000 so someone else could have a date!

On the seemingly endless conveyor belt of players I had to buy year on year was the highly rated Scott Flinders, who was the England under-20 keeper from Barnsley, who we bought for £600,000. His inept performances were to earn him the unwanted nickname of 'Flapper Flinders'. We bought Carl Fletcher from West Ham for £600,000, Tony Craig from Millwall for £200,000, the ex-Liverpool player Mark Kennedy arrived on a free transfer from Wolves and our marquee signing was Shefki Kuqi for £2.5 million from Blackburn!

We also signed Jamie Scowcroft from Coventry for another £800,000 as another striker to partner Kuqi. The fact that these two had scored 198 goals in 771 games between them appeared lost on Taylor and more fool me for allowing these signings. If they continued the way they were, I worked out that our strike force would only contribute eleven goals per season. In fact, they did even worse than that, scoring thirty-one goals in 161 games between them, an average of nine goals per season. So we hardly had a strike force to put the fear of God into the opposition. Although we did have Clinton the 'Pest' Morrison to back them up.

Despite all that the season started impressively under Peter Taylor as we won our first three games and went top of the Championship. But that was where it began and ended and like Forrest Gump: 'That's all I have to say about that.'

In September I had a change in my personal life and started dating the model Sophie Anderton, which inevitably drew the attention of the media. It was a short-lived liaison and as much as she was fun she did have a short circuit somewhere. One night we were dining out in the London restaurant Zuma and bumped into Paul Gascoigne. I liked Paul and he was charming although I have to say a little worse for wear that evening. Sophie had just done a TV show with his stepdaughter and certain unproven allegations had been made by her concerning Paul. When he joined us for a drink Sophie said she didn't want to speak to him as she believed what Bianca Gascoigne was alleging. This greatly upset Paul and it also enraged me and I forcibly dragged Ms Anderton over to apologise, and that with a host of other eventful excursions was soon to bring the curtain down on my relationship with her.

No sooner had I ended my relationship with Sophie, I became involved with a beautiful lady called Suzanne Walker. Ironically Suzanne was the soon-to-be-ex-wife of former England goalkeeper Ian Walker, who Dowie had wanted me to sign at the beginning of the 2005–06 season but we had been unable to agree personal terms. Fate has a funny way of intervening in people's lives. Suzanne was soon to give me the greatest gift in the world, something money couldn't buy.

By October 2006 the team's performances were pretty diabolical. After the heady heights of being top for two games we had now slumped to eighteenth and had been knocked out of the first round of the League Cup by Notts County.

But I had a bigger fish to fry. Ron Noades was selling the stadium to a property speculator, David Pearl. When I met Pearl I asked why he was buying it, why he hadn't come to talk to me as the anchor tenant and what his plans were. What I heard didn't make for good listening. Pearl controlled a property investment fund and they were not overly concerned if Palace stayed there. In fact, they preferred we didn't, as they quite fancied the idea of building houses on the site and unlocking the real estate value!

We had four years left on our lease with the mistaken belief that Noades would never find anyone else to buy the stadium besides the owner of the football club. The ground had severe planning restrictions designed to ensure that the use of that land was only for football. Noades, being the individual he was, and seemingly without the slightest regard for the club he regularly professed to care about, had found a property speculator willing to pay £12 million for it. David Pearl couldn't care less about restrictive covenants on the land and would simply wait for them to lapse after he had booted the club out when our lease expired. By taking a ten-year lease when I purchased the club, which had been designed to put us in the best position to take advantage of a raft of possibilities, including locating a new stadium in the borough, or getting Noades to become realistic and give us a fair price, especially as time pressed on, I had inadvertently got myself into a bit of a conundrum. Clearly I needed to do something pretty sharpish.

The solution I came up with looked great at the time but caused me some significant difficulties, embarrassment and damaged my credibility. It appeared to some people that I had misrepresented certain things and was ultimately to be for me like jumping 'out of the frying pan and into the fire' at huge personal cost!

My pal Paul Kemsley, the Tottenham vice-chairman and owner of a massive property company, Rock Investments, was my solution. The valuation of the stadium was only £6 million, which meant that I couldn't get funding for a £12 million purchase without using a big fat slug of cash. Kemsley, however, could get the funding as he had a vast line of credit with HBOS.

My idea was this: Paul and I set up a company and used HBOS's money to buy the stadium from David Pearl, who we would give a 'drink' to for stepping aside. I would service the borrowings, give Paul a small margin on that, and would work very hard to find a new stadium location in the borough where we could move Palace. Kemsley and I would then be free to split the property value of Selhurst Park on a 70/30 ratio in our favour and Palace would get a brand-new stadium, paid for out of the proceeds of the sale of Selhurst Park, the development value of which was estimated to be at the time upwards of £32 million.

So that is what we did and I announced to the world and a very surprised Ron Noades that I had in effect bought Selhurst Park. The reaction from the fans was one of delight and given that all I had got Paul to do was help with the funding via HBOS – no different from someone getting a mortgage for a house – I was happy with what I had done, for a few moments, anyway!

But like everything in football, nothing seemed to run to plan. Firstly the company that was set up never formalised the relationship that was agreed, and then within a matter of months Kemsley was expressing disappointment that we hadn't found a new stadium.

He was being ridiculous. He knew it would take substantial time to get a new location. Besides, I was paying the mortgage on the loan but he was being clever with me. Our relationship began to deteriorate and he suggested we moved out and shared a ground with Millwall. I suggested Tottenham do the same with Arsenal! To cut a long and complicated story short I agreed with Kemsley to buy the stadium out of the structure we had created. All I had to do was to find a new funder as I was not prepared to put up £12–13 million of my own cash, as by now I had already invested over £30 million in Palace and I wanted to do what everyone else did in property – use a funder!

This transaction bit me on the arse. I had done it with the best intentions and motives and with Kemsley running around telling anyone who would listen he owned Selhurst Park, I got to look a bit of a fool and a liar. In a desperate attempt to secure Palace's future, get the stadium away from Noades, I had dropped myself in it and now had a major problem.

As the months rolled by and I still hadn't secured funding, the world began to collapse as the financial crisis began and borrowing money became more and more impossible. After a confrontation with Kemsley outside a London casino where I told him I had enough of him ridiculing me about the ownership and reneging on our original deal, I agreed to sign a twenty-five-year lease and a bloody high rent and I personally paid him £1 million premium to rectify the position. I got vilified for this in certain quarters. In the long run this was to prove an absolutely massive thing for Crystal Palace FC, but not for Simon Jordan.

To be blunt, football-wise, this was a very dull and uninspiring time. Try as he may, Peter just didn't get the team going. We were eighteenth at the end of October, November and December. Industry wisdom purports that where you are at the end of December is often where you end up at the end of the season and as a rule of thumb it does have the ring of truth about it. So this was not quite the Peter Taylor effect I had hoped for. It was more like Peter Failure, as he was fast becoming known amongst my cohorts.

*   *   *

As a welcome distraction from Taylor's failure to lift the team on the football pitch, in late 2006 I signed up to do a television series on ITV. Having been with Max Clifford for a couple of years and done various media work it was perhaps a natural progression. I had in fact a year or so earlier had the opportunity to do *Dragons' Den* but I turned it down, not really grasping its concept. Why would I put up my money for the BBC to get viewing figures? More fool me!

Prior to the ITV show Max got me to do something with Sega games as they had introduced a function in their computer game *Championship Manager* called something like 'benefactor button'. Given I was indeed a major benefactor of a football club with a high profile I agreed to do it. It was a press launch and suffice to say I got them a lot of headlines due to my strident views. I got paid £5,000, which I donated to a children's hospice in Guildford.

The hospice was introduced to me by Max Clifford and touched my heart. I subsequently had a long relationship with it. Every piece of media work I got paid for I donated, as well as the damages payments I received from every inaccurate story written about me, which were many. I also made personal donations and got certain wealthy and influential people to do the same. I involved the football club, getting the players to go there every Christmas and we had a 'siblings' day every year, where the children could come and raid our club shop and take whatever they wanted – and they did, the little rascals! They also stayed, had lunch and watched a game. These are the things that make you proud to be part of a football club as it is an integral part of the community and makes a difference to people's lives.

The TV show I signed on for was *Fortune: Million Pound Giveaway*. Seven hour-long prime-time shows at 9 p.m. on Monday evenings. It was similar to *Dragons' Den* but giving away money not just for business ideas but also for appeals based around life-interest stories. I did the show with Duncan Bannatyne, Jeffrey Archer, Kanya King and Jacqueline Gold, daughter of David. We shot seven episodes in six days at Three Mills Studios in front of a live studio audience.

Straight away it was obvious that there was not harmony between the five millionaires. Jeffrey was a little smug, Duncan abrasive, Jacqueline and Kanya were gentle and cuddly, and then there was me.

On making myself comfortable in my dressing room on the first day I decided to put on some music and have a cigarette. Jeffrey Archer marched down the corridor and ordered me to turn my music down and to stop smoking. As you can imagine the volume went up and I advised Archer that insofar as my smoking was concerned I was surprised at his objection. Given that where he had just come from cigarettes were currency! That went down like a lead balloon with inmate Archer. Yet over the course of the week Jeffrey was quite charming to me and even brought a set of first-edition copies of his books signed for my mother.

There were other confrontations. Duncan, who I got on famously with, was a notorious camera hog. All the others complained, whereas my attitude was more fool you for having nothing to say. Jeffrey acted up immediately and during one session of filming told Bannatyne to shut up and let others speak. Duncan was raging in my dressing room afterwards and Jeffrey popped in and foolishly announced that he found the show a bit difficult as he was nothing like us and not an entrepreneur. Duncan agreed with him and said there was a vast difference between him, me and Jeffrey. And then went on to qualify that in language not even I can repeat! That was the end of their relationship and incredibly I found myself acting as a mediator.

As the basis of the show was to give a million pounds away to people that came forward with business ideas, community projects or life-interest matters, every time a contestant produced a hard-luck story, plausible or not, or if children were involved, Jackie and Kanya immediately voted yes. To get the money required you needed three of the five of us to vote yes. Given most of the time the contestants, whether merited or not, had two of the three votes required, this took the intrigue and possible misdirection out of the programme and was the subject of many a heated debate back-stage with Duncan and myself upsetting the girls.

The show was hosted by Richard Madeley and to be honest was not particularly good. And whilst there were some very deserving individual cases that got money, on the whole the majority of the contestants were poor and difficult to get any grasp on. If some bloke comes on and asks for £500 as he has 'ponced' off his mates for years and wants to get the money to take them for a slap-up meal, or a guy who has lost all his money on the horses has decided he wants to buy one rather than bet on them, it does not take you too long to tell them to piss off, and that doesn't make for great TV. One person who stood out was a twelve-year-old boy called Liam Fairhurst who suffered with cancer and raised £50,000 from us for Clic Sargent, a cancer charity. He was a fantastic young man and went on to raise much more money elsewhere and be recog-nised in far more auspicious surroundings than a TV show. Tragically, Liam died two and a half years later. If nothing else, doing that show gave me the opportunity to meet that splendid young man.

After filming the television series I was sitting in my office at Palace. I was busily looking through paperwork on my desk, perhaps stealthily trying to avoid signing any cheques for players in the transfer window, when I happened across a file containing information on the *Telstar* play. In it I found a screenplay for a potential film version. Since the critically acclaimed run had ended in 2005 I had stored the stage set under the main stand at Palace, with a view to bringing it back to the West End at a later date. Reading the script I had other ideas.

I decided that I wanted to bring *Telstar* to the silver screen and would fund it all myself. Why not? funding a football club was so easy! Why not go into another expensive and notoriously difficult industry? With my friend Ray Winstone I had executively produced and part-funded the BBC1 drama *Sweeney Todd*, so I did have some experience. I set about contacting Nick Moran in Los Angeles, who was filming an episode of *CSI Miami,* and asked him if he wanted to make this film. 'Of what?' he asked.

'Well we don't have enough subject matter to make your life story, you buffoon,' I replied. '*Telstar*, of course.'

At the time of deciding this I was invited onto *Soccer AM* for the second time. The first time I had taken Terry Hall in 2005 to announce the likely re-formation of The Specials. This time I took Nick Moran with me as I was going to talk about amongst other things the intention to make *Telstar* the movie. What I did was get myself into some hot water.

On this edition of *Soccer AM* the resident fans of the club who sat in the studio were Brighton and Hove Albion, Palace's fiercest rivals. Having me on the show was manna from heaven for them and gave them an opportunity to hurl abuse at me, which I took in a good-natured way. But when we got onto the subject of *Telstar*, I described the film and its storyline and, totally tongue in cheek, used one of the scenes to make fun of the Brighton fans. They were taking the mickey out of me, so I thought I would do the same to them.

It was a fantastically powerful drama, about an innovative record producer in the 1960s. What I said was: 'In one scene Joe Meek is found "importuning" in a public toilet with another man and this should no doubt appeal to the Brighton fans.' Brighton is known as the gay capital of England. Tim Lovejoy, the presenter, cracked up laughing. He immediately covered Sky's backside, no pun intended, by saying this was not the view of Sky. Fortunately, the meaning of the word 'importuning' went over the Brighton fans' heads – traditionally they're not the sharpest tools in the box.

I sauntered off after the show and right into a media melee with newspapers, radio stations and journalists demanding I qualify my comments. Fortunately I had Max Clifford to deal with it as certain factions had taken great exception to my tongue-in-cheek remark, demanding I be rebuked and disciplined in the strongest fashion. Perhaps the punishment they had in mind was to send me down to the very same toilet I had mentioned to be in-appropriately dealt with by Brighton's gay community? I refused to apologise. It was a joke and I am in no way homophobic. I even got contacted by the FA Homophobia Advisory Unit, whose chairman was none other than Martin Perry, the CEO of which club? Brighton and Hove Albion! This kerfuffle soon blew over and I put it behind me.

I had hoped for good things from Peter but the team was just flat, with no real inspiration. Yes, the second half of the season was better. In fact, we picked up thirty-nine points from our last twenty-three games, which was play-off form, and if we had not been so poor in the first twenty-three games we could have reached them again. But the football we played was unimpressive, and the fans seemed jaded. It had been two years of having a go at getting back into the Premier League and our time at the top was receding into distant memory.

Despite Peter's history with the club he did not seem to fit. The supporters, despite a level of enthusiasm at the beginning, hadn't taken to him as I thought they would. Behind the scenes he had reshuffled the staff. Bob Dowie had departed, inevitable given what was going on with his brother, and Peter, despite my unhappiness, had dismantled elements of our scouting network especially our representation in Europe. Due to personal differences, he took out our chief scout Gary Seward, someone I rated quite highly, and replaced the scouting network with a group of his incompetent mates.

Taylor and I rarely had a cross word until the back end of this season. As the season was clearly going nowhere I hoped that Peter, given his under-21 and youth development background, would look to blood some of the younger players who were emerging stars in our academy. There was no substitute for first-team experience, but Taylor flatly refused, citing that it was important for his reputation that Palace finished as high up the league as possible. This didn't sit well with me at all and told me all I needed to know about where Peter really was in the great scheme of things.

As the season wound down I found myself playing in two more games where my burgeoning reputation as a not-bad footballer was cemented. In the first of two matches organised again by Geoff Thomas for his leukaemia charity, I played in the first-ever game at the new Wembley in March 2007. I played alongside such luminaries as Graeme Le Saux and Neville Southall. We won 2–0 in front of 20,000 spectators. Mark Bright scored the first goal and I believe he was texting the world before the ball hit the back of the net. And I, to my eternal delight, scored the second. Say what you like about me, that fact is indelible. No one could accuse me of not being a real pro: I played in this game, and, before the next one against Liverpool – a restaging of the 1990 semi-final, I had cortisone injected into the base of my spine.

In the second game my expectations of myself were very high, playing against a Liverpool team consisting of the likes of John Barnes, Jamie Redknapp, Bruce Grobbelaar, Jan Molby and Steve McManaman. Again I played very well if I do say so, nutmegging Steve McManaman and laying on the pass for Mark Bright to score again, in the vain hope of halting his endless comments about scoring the first-ever goal at the new Wembley.

Ridiculously, these were the two high spots in a footballing Sahara of a season. The real team finished on a high, rounding off the season with back-to-back wins and giving me a straw to cling onto for next season that maybe, despite my nagging feelings, Peter Taylor may well come good . . .

But most things based upon hope rather than substance rarely come up trumps. Besides, I had the small matter of a High Court trial with Iain Dowie, the commencement of filming of a major movie, a landmark birthday and a monumental event in my adult life, all about to happen over the summer of 2007.

13

DOWIE ON TRIAL

Since issuing the writ on Iain Dowie back in May 2006 my lawyers, together with a senior QC and a junior counsel, were preparing one of the most difficult court cases in English law to prove: fraudulent misrepresentation. The case was meticulously prepared over a year to ensure that when we arrived in court the case did more than get media attention, but delivered the appropriate verdict based on Iain Dowie's conduct.

The court case took place in May 2007, almost a year to the day after he had left Palace and was served with the infamous writ in the press conference. It was scheduled to be an eight-day hearing at the Royal Courts of Justice at the Strand in London. The basis of our case was Dowie had told lies to get released from his contract, thus circumventing a £1 million compensation clause.

Before the trial had even begun, the legal costs had already exceeded £500,000. This was the financial risk I was prepared to take in being so resolute in my belief that Dowie should be held accountable for his deception. In the media, much was made of the fact that part of my motivation was my intense dislike of Charlton Athletic, their chairman and directors as a result of their actions in our fateful game against them in May 2005 when we were relegated from the Premier League. In point of fact, that was a peripheral motivation. Naturally it irritated me that Charlton had avoided paying compensation like every other club for a manager but my focus was always on Dowie and his actions.

The main players in this case were the well-respected Judge Tugendhat, my QC John Davies, an expert in his field who was supported by a junior QC Stuart Ritchie. On the other side were Iain Dowie and his counsel Michael McParland, a protégé of the famous trial lawyer George Carman. Also in attendance with Dowie were Charlton Athletic's chairman Richard Murray, his chief executive Peter Varney and their legal representation. Quite why Charlton were there besides being possible witnesses for Dowie was beyond us all and quite why they needed legal representation again was a curiosity as the action was being brought against Dowie, not Charlton. But as the case unfolded those reasons became apparent.

The first day of the trial was a media circus with camera crews and press photographers swarming outside the High Court and journalists thronging the public gallery. It started with both parties presenting their legal arguments and then very quickly moved into certain areas of legalities. My lawyers had demanded the handing over of Dowie's laptop he used at Palace and once we secured it we had to ask the judge to make a ruling that we could send his hard disk to a computer specialist to re-create everything that had ever been written and deleted. After much toing and froing we were given permission to send the computer's hard drive to the experts and when it came back it made for some very interesting reading.

Once the legal complexities were argued through it was time for the witnesses to be called. Given the nature of this case, which to a large degree hinged on one person's word against another, witness evidence was going to be crucial. What we were seeking to establish was the timeline in which Dowie effectively entered into managerial dialogue with Charlton Athletic and, as we were to discover, a number of other clubs. Given that our argument was based upon a fraud being perpetrated by Dowie whilst in the employment of Crystal Palace, which resulted in him being released from his contract, if it was established that Dowie had, in fact, no intention of leaving Palace to go back up north, but was in fact merely saying that to get released from his contract with the specific intention of going to Charlton Athletic, then the leap to find him guilty of fraudulent misrepresentation – alongside evidence from myself and others – was not going to be that great to make!

So with that in mind an unusual list of suspects appeared on the witness stand giving some interesting testimonies for a variety of different motivations.

My current manager Peter Taylor was the first witness called and he proceeded to describe events back in that May of 2006 when he was the manager of Hull City. He gave evidence that he was contacted by Charlton and invited to attend a meeting described as 'having a cup of tea'. This of course meant that Charlton were speaking to Taylor without the permission of Hull, which contravened football's rules and illustrated that although Charlton were not on trial here, they operated in a certain way.

James Price, a lawyer who represented the then manager of Preston Billy Davies, further supported Taylor's testimony. Davies was first offered an informal meeting that became formal as Charlton were thinking about appointing Davies and eventually sought Preston's permission to talk to him and agree compensation . . . perhaps compensation being the key word.

What we established was Charlton were speaking to a variety of managers about their availability and were doing it without first seeking the permission of the clubs these managers were employed by, which frankly I did not in the real world consider a major crime, but it flew in the face of how Charlton liked to portray themselves. As soon as we put Dowie on the stand we established fairly quickly that he had spoken to Charlton and a number of other clubs before we had even agreed to release him from his contract.

Peter Varney, the then chief executive of Charlton, took to the stand and went on to describe his version of events and claimed that Charlton acted with integrity and good faith! So far as he was concerned Charlton hadn't contacted Dowie prior to his release from his contract. To be fair to Varney, my QC John Davies was pretty confident that he was telling the truth. It was more than likely Richard Murray was having discussions with various managerial parties and that may not have been within Varney's line of vision.

My moment arrived and I took the stand in front of a packed gallery. I was to spend nearly two days being interrogated by Dowie's counsel Michael McParland.

There was a marked difference between the two lead lawyers. McParland was a physically big man with a puffed-out chest. He had a barnstorming, theatrical quality to his questioning. John Davies, on the other hand, was a much smaller man, who reminded me of the actor Patrick Troughton who played the second Doctor Who. He had a more considered manner: when he made a point it was not a dramatic revelation preceded by a big drum roll. John had an air of confidence and substance and never really raised his voice, although he was quite sinister in his Rottweiler-like pursuit of the answers he demanded. It was no surprise to me when I learned that John Davies had wanted to be an actor in his early years at Cambridge and was part of the famous Cambridge Footlights.

There is in fact a large amount of theatre in the High Court, from the packed media gallery, the audience of friends and colleagues who come to watch to the bewigged lead lawyers in their black gowns; the protocol of the court standing and bowing every time the judge enters or leaves the courtroom to the conduct of the witnesses on the stand.

The court clerk, to my horror, was a bloody Millwall fan and even though I wasn't on trial I had visions of me getting the chair if he had his way. He regularly came out to the non-smoking hallway as my QC John Davies and I hid cigarettes behind our backs with a plume of smoke appearing over our shoulders with a pile of cigarettes at our feet while we vehemently denying we were smoking.

McParland's strategy when I got on the stand was to try to establish that I was a tyrannical boss, abusive to the point of unbearable, and had effectively hounded Dowie out of his job. He wanted me to admit to him that I had brought the case against Dowie maliciously, and that I was motivated by money. I was confident in myself and also had the added advantage that I knew I was telling the truth! But ringing in my ears was the advice of John Davies to not be clever or cocky or lose my temper, as this is exactly what his opposite number was attempting to achieve.

What McParland confronted me with was trial by newspaper articles. He attacked every aspect of my character by bringing up every controversial or outspoken remark I had ever made. As I had been manna from heaven for the newspapers he did have a lot of subject matter to point to. I had bundles of court files in the witness box and was constantly directed to a particular section where inevitably there would be a newspaper article where I had made some strident comment. He made a particular meal over the *Sunday Times* article from my time in the Premier League and poured gravy all over it. It got to the point in the questioning where before he had even finished a question I was asking what bundle he wanted me to go to and 'Oh yes, another newspaper article, what did I have to say here?' would be my cocky yet slightly exasperated comment.

It was like a joust with McParland. He wanted to grind me down so that he would get an outburst from me in a way that would advance his case. But, as John Davies told me during the breaks, my conduct had little to do with whether Dowie had lied to me or not, and I was to keep answering the questions without being clever or facetious. But my nature got the better of me.

After almost a day and a half of repetitive questions surrounding my character I was becoming very fidgety in the witness box. I was sitting on a bloody uncomfortable chair and had a dead bum. I let out a yawn, which McParland saw and asked if I was OK.

'I am OK, thank you, just a little bored,' was my unwise response.

'Bored?' he boomed. 'How dare you be bored? You have a man on trial here facing conviction of fraud and you are bored?'

So I topped and tailed it. 'I am not bored of the proceedings. I am frankly bored of you and your repetitive newspaper articles and character assassinations.'

This got a smirk from McParland and a glare from John Davies so I apologised to the judge for my comment and enquired, to the great amusement of the court gallery, if I could have a cushion if I was going to stay there much longer as my backside was asleep.

McParland continued with the newspaper articles and used one rather cleverly against me. He asked if I considered myself to be a Machiavellian character, a fact I immediately dismissed. He followed that up with: 'If not in character, do you act in a Machiavellian way?' and again I responded robustly that under no circumstances was I Machiavellian. Then he took me to a newspaper article where in my own words I described an action I had taken as being Machiavellian.

'Hmm,' I mused. 'That's not very helpful for me,' I said ruefully. To which I got a grin from my interrogator.

The final exchange of note was around the financial position of both Crystal Palace and myself. He alleged that Palace and I were in severe financial difficulty. He based this on his assumption of how much money I had and Palace's accounts over the last two years, and on both fronts he was very wide of the mark.

He said it was a matter of public record that I had stated I had spent £30 million-plus on Palace to date and went on to conclude that, given I was a 50 per cent shareholder in The PocketPhone Shop which had been sold for £75 million, I would have got £37.5 million, thus I had spent the bulk of my money. What he didn't know was I had a completely different deal with my ex-partner in that business and I was bound by a confidentiality document of non-disclosure and I was not going to divulge that to him! He demanded the judge order me to disclose, at which point I spoke directly to Judge Tugendhat, saying that I was not prepared to breach that legal agreement even if it risked contempt of court. Despite McParland's blustering the judge upheld my position and ordered that we move on. Although I did quickly add that in fact I did get significantly more than £37.5 million!

McParland then attacked Palace's financial position, saying that in the last filed accounts from 2005–06, turnover had dropped by £11 million from the previous year and the club was in dire financial trouble. He could not have got it more wrong. What he had neglected to understand from the balance sheet was that despite losing turnover, profits had gone up from £5.1 million to £11 million in those two years; ironically and incredibly helpfully in this instance these were the only two years in my tenure the club posted anything resembling a profit. He misunderstood the construction of a balance sheet: player transfers didn't go to turnover, they went straight on the bottom line for accountancy purposes; in 2006 I had sold in excess of £12 million worth of players.

I painstakingly pointed this out to him and very quickly he wanted to close this subject. But I couldn't resist labouring the point and asked would he like me to help him read a balance sheet, as I was concerned that his lack of understanding could jeopardise his client's position. When I asked again, for the benefit of the mirth-filled courtroom, whether he was certain he didn't want me to help him to comprehend the figures in front of him, he responded angrily: 'Mr Jordan, I ask the questions not you!' And once that exchange was over I was very shortly dismissed from the witness box.

Soon enough Iain Dowie was called but not before his brother Bob took to the stand in his defence and proceeded to contradict himself left right and centre. He had given two statements, one directly after Dowie had joined Charlton and he was in my employment, and an entirely different one some eight months later when he was not. My QC poked and prodded and got Bob to admit that the first statement, which was more favourable to us, was likely to be the more accurate. In effect, Bob had gone on the stand and had hindered rather than helped his brother's case!

From the moment Iain Dowie went on the stand it became clear that if a question asked of him was one he liked or advanced his position he could recall exact dates and times. But if the reverse applied, he'd immediately reply with 'I do not recall.' During the majority of the questioning my QC was greeted with that unhelpful response from Dowie.

At one point it got so ridiculous that Dowie, when asked if he had a diary, didn't recall if he did. John Davies persevered and said

'A desk diary, perhaps?' And still no recollection from Dowie. It was only when John produced a desk diary, with the label 'Iain Dowie's desk diary' printed on it in his handwriting, that he suddenly recalled owning one.

Throughout his time on the stand Iain was as upright as ever. I genuinely think he had convinced himself he was absolutely in the right. As I have said, he avoided answering behind a blanket of 'do not recall's but was constantly pressured by John Davies into giving more forthcoming answers, despite objections from his own barrister. It is difficult and somewhat intimidating being in the witness box but Iain approached it with his customary confidence. He even developed a ludicrous way of answering questions with 'My learned friend' at the beginning or end of his answer, which of course is how the legal profession address one another and is not how witnesses answer questions.

The difference between the questioning of me and Iain was that John had the evidence to confront him with. We had phone records and computer files; they had newspaper articles and allegations of abusive management, which for the record were not true!

Via the computer records we established that Dowie had produced a number of reports for clubs with potential vacancies. All of them had been written even before the compromise agreement to release him from his Palace contract had been agreed and were entitled: 'Reinvigorating the Rams' for Derby County, 'Fuelling the Foxes' for Leicester City and 'Advancing the Addicks' for the vacancy at Charlton – the club he assured me he was not joining!

John forensically took him through his phone records, which were in our possession as Iain had submitted them for expenses at Palace. We had investigated various numbers. Two days after a conversation between Iain and me in Spain he had a series of calls with Mike Horton, the chief executive of Derby County. When questioned on this Dowie explained that he had been asked his advice on how to restructure their club!

Then we moved onto the critical area of the case: the contact between Charlton Athletic and Iain Dowie, when it occurred, what it contained and what Dowie had said to me prior to me signing the release agreement. In essence the whole case turned on these facts.

My evidence, which was not contradicted by Iain when on the stand, was that I asked whether he was going to Charlton on Saturday 20 May, and asked him the same question again two days later on Monday the twenty-second, prior to signing the release agreement. Both times he emphatically denied that he was. Given what we were able to substantiate, this was very damaging to Dowie's credibility. Even more so when at the press conference announcing his appointment as Charlton manager he said: 'No contact whatsoever and I am fully comfortable I have covered myself in lots of integrity.' This, quite apart from not making sense and being shocking English, was a blatant lie!

We had phone records that showed that Dowie spoke to Richard Murray the Charlton chairman on 17 May, 19 May, twice on the morning of 22 May and again directly after the press conference that announced his departure from Palace and his release from his contract.

Also, on 19 May at 11.57 he created the 'Advancing the Addicks' document and amended it at 12.57 on Monday 22 May. We had Richard Murray's phone records, as well as those of Mick McGuire from the PFA, who represented Dowie. These records showed calls from Murray to McGuire and McGuire to both Iain and Bob Dowie straight afterwards. In his witness statement McGuire told how Murray had phoned him to ask about Dowie's position. All of this from a man who stated he had no contact with Charlton whatsoever prior to his departure from Palace or knowledge of their interest in him.

Under intense questioning, Dowie said the telephone conversation on the seventeenth with Richard Murray was to do with the Charlton chairman asking his advice on Palace players who might be for sale. From this point on John Davies turned the temperature up on Dowie and began to piece the phone calls together, analysing each one. He was beginning to make statements rather than ask questions. In one of the breaks he said privately to me that he wondered if at any time in this trial Dowie was going to tell the truth!

Davies took that sentiment into court after the break and on the penultimate afternoon of the trial questioned Dowie about every phone call, questioned the likelihood of his answers, and forced Dowie into admitting that what he had said in the Charlton press conference about no contact 'whatsoever' was untrue. Then, out of the blue, John Davies ramped up the rhetoric and openly called Dowie a liar in court.

Once Iain got down from the stand there was one more witness, Richard Murray the Charlton chairman, and this provided a little bit of a sideshow. He had sat adjacent to me and throughout the case attempted to befriend my father, much to my distaste. At one point when I was absent from the courtroom Murray then changed tack and told my father that he should be ashamed to have brought up such a disgraceful liar of a son. I repeatedly reminded Dad of this man's conduct two years earlier.

Under questioning from McParland, Murray was confident and assured and made a number of disparaging comments about me, much like he did in that press conference. When he was faced with John Davies the confident demeanour remained, but the facts did not. In taking him through his witness statement John tripped him up on a contradiction. Murray admitted he had only speed-read his statement and signed it, which John seized on. 'Read and signed? Do you not mean written or dictated?' Murray misunderstood where he was going and asserted he was a busy man and had many documents to read.

The point John made was that Murray did not appear to know what was in his own statement, asserting that this was a statement prepared by someone else, made to fit the circumstances and was merely speed-read and signed by Murray. By doing this and getting him flustered, John had discredited pretty much everything Murray had to say.

When John had finished we were treated to a stunning outburst from Murray in the witness box. When asked by McParland if he had anything else to add, which was strange in itself given that he was a witness and not there to make statements, he raged: 'When we win this case I will be bringing an action against Simon Jordan for £50 million, which is what we have lost as a result of the distraction of this court case and our relegation.' I have to confess I burst out laughing at this bizarre statement. The fact that he used 'we win this court case', when the action was against Dowie not Charlton, was not lost on the courtroom. Perhaps it explained why the Charlton chairman was there for the entire case, as well as bringing legal representation along with him.

We had the closing statements of the opposing lawyers and then it was over. Now all we had to do was to wait for the judge's decision. Whilst we were confident, we couldn't be entirely sure which way the ruling was going to go.

On 11 June we were handed down the verdict three days before it was made public. I breathed a huge sigh of relief. We had won, and not just won, but in tennis parlance we had won 6–0, 6–0,

6–1. We had just received a landmark verdict, and once again showed the football world that there were consequences outside of its seemingly protected and unaccountable existence.

Despite being denied leave to appeal by the judge, Dowie was granted an appeal by the Court of Appeal. His new legal representatives offered to settle, which in the interests of time and questions surrounding Dowie's ability to meet his increasing costs, I took. When the substantial settlement finally arrived I was only surprised that it wasn't from Charlton Athletic's bank account!

14

LIGHT AT THE END OF MY TUNNEL

No sooner had the season finished and the drama of the court case with Dowie concluded than I received the biggest and most monumental news of my adult life. Suzanne was pregnant and I was going to be a father. Initially I was shocked. I mean honestly I was only thirty-nine and having my first child at such a young and tender age! The relationship with Suzanne, although relatively new, was very passionate, and now we were bringing a child into the world together. In my mind I had been looking after a group of children for seven years in football so it would be much more rewarding to have one of my own, and one who might actually love me!

During the summer I had hoped against hope that Peter would come back with a fresher perspective and the next season would be one of achievement and getting back to contending for a place in the Premier League, which was the very reason why I brought him here.

Peter wanted to change the personnel around and freshen up the playing squad to stamp his authority on the place. Players who had been here for a while and become stale needed to move on so a number of senior players left Palace in the off season. We also sold Jobi McAnuff, as he had been one of the disgruntled players who had wanted to leave the previous summer. Relegated Watford agreed a £1.75 million fee and McAnuff left.

As we had a reasonably sized squad and made quite significant additions over two years I felt Peter needed to get the best from the squad he had, not least the players he had spent heavily on last year, before we started more spending. In football, managers will tell you that when they spend your money they will spend it with the same care as if it were their own. Then they proceed to spend it however they want and if they get it wrong they come and ask you for more.

Despite that, my ambition to achieve got the better of me and I still allowed Peter to spend the best part of another £1.5 million on players, bringing in Neil Danns, José Fonte and Jeff Hughes. Our parachute money had run out so funding was now entirely dependent on me.

Significantly reduced gates further depleted our finances. In the space of three years 7,000 fewer supporters per game were following Palace. In the previous season alone there was a £1.6 million reduction in the gate receipts and this trend was to continue. Falling attendances reflects a lack of success, yet as I have said clubs that had been relegated and were achieving far less were still pulling in far more supporters than us giving them a significant financial advantage over us. To compete with them and ultimately achieve promotion back to the Premier League the onus fell on me, which I accepted as a consequence of owning a football club.

We had a playing squad that had cost about £12 million to assemble, a wages bill of £9 million on players, before bringing anyone else in, and a turnover of just £12 million, which meant that the costs associated with trying to achieve success were frankly ludicrous in relation to the turnover of the business. But that was football. In fact, in that financial year to the end of 2008, the actual losses were £8.1 million so I already had a bloody huge headache as the beginning of the world's financial crisis began.

As a nice respite from thinking about the economics and problems of my football club I played in the Soccer Six tournament, which was televised and held at West Ham United's ground. Given my football prowess (!) I was made captain of a team, which, amongst others, included Nick Moran, Bryan McFadden from Westlife, Steve Norman from Spandau Ballet and actors Tamer Hassan and Danny Dyer.

Steve Norman's presence caused great amusement to Nick as I had often been likened to the bass guitarist because of my long blond hair, and not in a complimentary way. We were a competitive lot and not bad at all, with the exception of Nick, who was an asset for every other team apart from the one he played for – he's a talented actor but even he couldn't pull off impersonating a footballer! We won all our group games.

Danny Dyer and Tamer turned up late, severely hung over, brandishing a bag of five-pound notes they had just received for a public appearance in Plymouth. Frankly I didn't particularly much like either of them at the time. I had come across Danny Dyer socially in my restaurant and thought he was a poor man's Ray Winstone. I left Burke and Hare on the bench counting their fivers, even preferring Nick to them, and still won. In the quarter-finals disaster struck as our star player – besides yours truly of course – Bryan McFadden, pulled a hamstring and featured no more. We were playing Babyshambles, who were quite a strong side, and made up of the members of the band including the infamous Pete Doherty, who was quite a good footballer. I was forced to resort to Danny and Tamer, who were bloody useless. Danny in particular would have difficulty trapping a bag of cement although in his mind he was Wayne Rooney – Mickey Rooney would have been more appropriate. We were knocked out and our dream was over. The only satisfaction I got was winding up Doherty, firstly by waving profusely to his then girlfriend Kate Moss, who I knew via my relationship with Meg Mathews, and secondly when, after one particular scything challenge I enacted on him, he got up in my face full of testosterone and I suggested, 'There was no need to get the needle,' referring to his much publicised heroin addiction.

Back to the serious football. Palace played Anderlecht in a friendly and drew 1–1, had a quick tour of Sweden and finished off playing Everton, which saw the return of the crowd's hero Andrew Johnson in a game that was part of the deal when he was sold. Playing Everton enabled me to fulfil a little boy's dream. He was the son of a friend of mine from Chester, and was a massive Everton fan. We made him their mascot, walking out on to the pitch holding AJ's hand, as well as giving his parents an executive box for the game and getting the Everton boys to come up to the box afterwards. This is one of the good things about owning a football club: watching a young man's face light up as he meets his heroes.

As well as the imminent approach to what I saw as a critical season given the cost implications involved, I also had the added distraction of my approaching fortieth birthday and a lavish party I had chosen to mark it.

I had invited 600 people and sent out invitations with 'Oh Shit, I am Forty' on the front and on the back the strapline: 'The only present required is your presence.' Inside it had a collage of images from a newspaper shot of me taken after Palace had scored the winning goal in the 2004 play-off final, to pictures of the Club Bar and Dining, images from *Telstar* and *Octane* magazine, Aston Martins and Ferraris, The Specials and glamorous women, all the supposed components or interests of my life.

The party had a budget of £600,000, and was held at a venue alongside the Thames. I hired a £35 million boat to take my guests to the event, and had organised a fireworks display in the middle of the Thames, taking place against the backdrop of a lit-up Millennium Dome, which resulted in the world trade boat being forced to stop for fifteen minutes waiting for the display to finish.

The venue was the last working lighthouse on the river, which had been used for television shows and celebrity events. The theme was music, as it is one of my great loves. I hired Kid Creole and the Coconuts to sing on the boat taking us to the fireworks display and the venue.

Inside the lighthouse, each room was decorated in the style of a different decade. A sixties lounge full of Mary Quant-dressed waitresses, a seventies kitsch lounge with hanging chairs and an eighties lounge with power drinks and so on. Each lounge served the drinks of the time, and each environment was revealed at the same time as a musical act of the decade played. The Boot Leg Beatles for the sixties, Imagination played for the seventies and Curiosity Killed the Cat for the eighties. We had the largest video bank screens in Europe and a pre-recorded video hosted by Nick Moran talking about each decade with messages from friends. As my *pièce de résistance*, I had two acts. All summer I negotiated with Bryan Ferry to play and after agreeing to £90,000 for forty-five minutes, he promised to do me a favour, after initially refusing, and sing 'Avalon', my favourite Ferry song.

Finally four years after I first mooted the idea and twenty-six years since they last played, my friends The Specials started my much-dreamed-about re-formation in earnest and played for me for free. The guest list included movie and television stars, footballers and models, all the people from my life, from Kevin Spacey to one of my dearest friends, Deano, a builder from Sheffield who I had known for twenty years. My most special guest came to the party and was very quiet, but she was there, my soon-to-be-born beautiful daughter!

I had come a long way: I had built myself up from starting a small business to owning a football club, a restaurant group, a magazine, a film company, a Spanish property company. I had investments all over the world and was able to throw a party like this attended by A-listers from media to movies to money. This party showed where I was in the world. One thing I should have remembered: as quick as things come, they can go!

Telstar, the film, was in production during this time. Set in the 1960s, *Telstar* is a biopic of the music producer Joe Meek who gave the world the song 'Telstar' and a host of other hits. Nick Moran came on as the director, and I hired Guy Ritchie's producers Adam Bohling and Dave Reid to work alongside me to make the film. The six-week shoot kicked off in July 2007 at Twickenham Studios.

It was the first British movie in forty years to be independently funded and produced. I had decided that I would approach the film world in the same way as I had approached the football world: trying to 'knock the world out with my chin'. By making the film in the manner that I wanted I did not want to involve 'sales agents', nor partner up with an investor or film distributor. I backed myself and my project, and took all the risk, believing I would produce a successful film.

The original budget was around the £800,000 mark but by the time I had looked at it and understood what it took to make it high quality it was up nearer the £2 million mark. Not only did I take on two top producers, I wanted a great cast and we set about hiring one. Con O'Neill, an Olivier- and Tony-winning star, took the role of Joe Meek in the play and was so startlingly good he was a shoo-in for the lead.

We auditioned many people including James Corden, who read for the part of Clem Cattini, the famous drummer. When Corden came in he was great in the read-through, which I sat in on, but I felt he was slightly too heavy and suggested, to the horror of the producers and director, that he train with the fitness instructor at Palace to lose weight. The horrified response was that he was an actor not a footballer! We asked him politely to drop some weight if he wanted the part, and it was an indication of how much Corden wanted the role that he duly did – that is, until the on-set catering kicked in!

As well as Corden we hired Ralf Little, Pam Ferris and JJ Field, who went on to appear as Union Jack in the *Captain America* film. We took on some well-known British actors: Rita Tushingham, Jess Conrad and John Leyton. The young Leyton actually featured as a character in the film and was played by another actor. We hired Jimmy Carr, Marcus Brigstocke and also took on two big-name musicians – Justin Hawkins from the Darkness and Carl Barat of the Libertines – to play pop stars of the era.

Finally I wanted some gold dust, a marquee 'signing'. We looked at a host of top-name actors, including Tom Hanks who had seen the play, loved it and actually came backstage to visit the cast. Tom considered it but he had scheduling issues, as did Anthony Hopkins and Bill Nighy. But one of my favourite actors, and someone I had met through Nick Moran, was pursued with vigour. I made it clear in a terse call from Spain to Nick and the producers, that no head-line name, no film. Within an hour Nick came back and said he had secured Kevin Spacey. I can only imagine what Nick had to do for that! But Spacey was whom I really wanted and we were now in business.

As well as the on-screen talent, you need talent behind the scenes and we hired some of the best. We had a brilliant production manager in Russell De Rozario, the BA Baracus of production design. He was able to build anything from anything and if we forgot something in a particular scene he would go and 'procure' it; his only shortcoming was that he was a Chelsea fan.

The film business has a great number of similarities to football. Your manager in football is your director in films and your players are the actors. Like their footballing counterparts they are well paid, often very young and full of themselves.

And the similarities don't end there. As with football you have an endless amount of back-room people from cameramen, produc-tion designers, make-up artists, line producers, electricians, grips, best boys to runners; a bit like physios, fitness trainers, masseuses, sport scientists and kit managers. And then you had my favourite similarity, the line: 'We don't do things that way.'

As I had in football, I had a desire to make something I was involved in the very best it could be but at the same time 'sweating the asset'. I have told stories of big monies being spent and some-times wasted but behind every pound I spent was an intensity in other areas to generate the best we could from everything we did. Along with Dominic I drove every aspect of commerciality at Palace: we monitored and analysed every part of the business, from ticket sales to merchandise, from programmes to hot dog sales, and the operation was slick and dynamic.

I wanted to do the same with the film: there was significant investment from me, from the cast assembled on to the excellent personnel hired and even the film we shot on. As always I backed myself on this film, believing in Nick Moran as a first-time director, and in the story as being compelling and powerful. I had the added advantage of knowing some extremely influential and powerful people in the film business including Paul Higginson, MD of 20th Century Fox, a big Liverpool fan who I had got tickets for whenever they played Palace; Stuart Till, soon to be head of Icon, one of the biggest film distributors and a former director at Millwall; and Peter Rice, head of Fox Searchlight in America, an Englishman living in LA who was a big Palace fan. And I believed this would enable me to fast-track this film. All I had to do was ensure we shot and edited it well, and bingo!

I decided that I didn't need the dreaded agents – this time sales agents in the film world – and I didn't overly need distributors from the outset. I thought that I would deal with them after the film was shot. I made my life on this film, as I had sometimes in football, very difficult, as there was an established way of doing things. Sometimes you just have to accept it is not always about 'breaking eggs to make omelettes', sometimes the established way of doing things is the right way.

We took an ambitious, take-no-prisoners approach to making the film, from the fluidity of having the producer/money on set so decision-making was easy, to guerrilla filming, where we filmed without licences or stayed eight hours when we were licensed to film for two; doing such things as getting people to dress as policemen and illegally stopping traffic on the Holloway Road whilst we filmed a key scene that had overrun by many many hours. There is a better way of doing things than just always going 'balls out' and I was to find that the film business is even more brutal, unforgiving and disingenuous than football.

Despite that, the bond between cast and crew was great to see. Everyone shared the same desire: to make a great British film. On the first day of shooting I called everyone together, from actors and directors down to runners, gave everybody a glass of champagne and made a speech about ensuring that this project was the best it could be. I made a toast to: 'The good ship *Telstar* and all who sail in her.' My words had the desired effect and the commitment from everybody on this project was 100 per cent.

The 2007–08 campaign was fast approaching and I was a busy boy with plenty of things to occupy my mind like parties, films, court cases and the arrival of my first child. But, as it had for the last seven years, football took centre stage. I had grown over the pre-season a little disinterested in Peter. This sounds like a strange observation to make but I think I knew that it was only a matter of time before I fired him.

At the end of every season senior players would come and have a chat with me. It was not something I encouraged, but I listened to their views and made up my own mind. Dougie Freedman was a player who usually came to see me. We had known one another a long time. I wonder how Dougie would feel now, given he is the manager at Palace, if his players were going off to see the chairman without his knowledge!

This summer Freedman was scathing about what was going on at the training ground and pleaded with me to come and see for myself. He said that there was no discipline, the training was poor, Peter was not involved and the fitness regime was a joke. I took it all on board but I couldn't go to the training ground as it would be undermining the manager. I would see the endeavours and abilities of the training ground at 3 p.m. on Saturday. But as Freedman left it did strike a chord as the team had been poor the previous year. The players didn't appear as fit as they had under previous regimes and we also seemed to be getting more than our share of soft muscle injuries. So whilst I appeared to ignore it, Freedman's complaint stuck firmly in my mind and it was not going to take much for me to take drastic action.

Just before the new season was underway we were faced with a very curious set of circumstances. Gabriel Heinze the Manchester United and Argentinian international defender wanted to leave Old Trafford and was being publicly courted by their arch-rivals Liverpool. Alex Ferguson, supported by his board of directors, said he would never consider selling Heinze to Liverpool. Phil Alexander received an approach from someone called James Green who purported to represent a South American football agency caller Soccer SA.

The gist of the conversation was that this agent wanted Crystal Palace to buy Gabriel Heinze from Manchester United and then immediately sell him on to Liverpool, thus circumventing United's position, and we would be paid £1 million commission or in my eyes receive a bung for participating in this unsavoury affair. My stance was no way were we getting involved and I told Alexander to contact David Gill, Manchester United's chief executive, and tell him of these attempted shenanigans, which he duly did. Of course I took the opportunity to get Phil to advise Gill we would like them to remember the favour. The upshot was there was an ongoing Premier League dispute between Heinze and United and we were required to give evidence and this strange and murky set of affairs was resolved by others!

Our opening game of the new season was away to Southampton and brought a convincing 4–1 victory. Miracle of miracles, Jamie Scowcroft scored a hat trick. As I left St Mary's I got waylaid by a group of disgruntled Southampton fans who wanted to tell me that: 'Palace were shit and not fit to grace our pitch.' The fact that we had just trounced their team 4–1 seemed to elude them. The perverseness of emotional fans never ceased to amaze me. Of course, I told them if we were indeed as bad they thought then God only knows what it made their team, or words to that effect. That made for a very brisk stroll to my car.

That was the last time we were to record a win for nearly two months and by September normal service resumed under Taylor's uninspiring leadership and we were languishing in sixteenth place having already been as low as twenty-first. My relationship with Peter was cordial but I had lost my faith in him and rumours were circulating in the newspapers about Neil Warnock coming in. When I invited Peter to my birthday party along with Steve Bruce, Trevor Francis, Steve Kember, and Neil Warnock, Peter declined to go, and that said everything about where our relationship was.

During that period we had played newly relegated Charlton Athletic for the first time since the fateful day in May 2005. The bad blood had increased with the Dowie court case and an article I wrote in the *Observer* in August of the same year about the conga-dancing celebrations of their fans at our relegation! I remarked that I felt they behaved like morons. A spokesman for a Charlton's fans' group said: 'They were astounding comments from an ex-Premier League chairman.' He demanded an apology he never got. He did add the rather perceptive comment: 'There were 24,000 Charlton supporters at the Valley that day, including myself. That's an awful lot of morons.'

My response was: 'In retrospect, of course I regret calling them morons, imbeciles would have been more appropriate.' This of course fuelled the flames and the bad blood so the atmosphere for this game, which was always explosive, had more of an edge. Their buffoon of a chairman, Richard Murray, was notable by his absence in a game we lost, much to the joy of the Charlton fans.

Unfortunately there was trouble after the game. The spectre of football violence hasn't disappeared, it just doesn't get as much coverage as it once did. Many a time I sat in the police control room at Selhurst Park watching the CCTV cameras on the away supporters, horrified by the threat of imminent violence, most notably with Millwall fans.

It appeared that some Charlton fans, including young supporters, were attacked on their train journey home by a mindless element of Palace fans. This was reported by Kelvin MacKenzie in his column for the *Sun*. I had had no time for MacKenzie's opinions when he was editor of the paper and I had even less time now he was a columnist. His piece condemned the cowardly Palace fans, which was difficult to disagree with, but then went full tilt into blaming me for the attack, suggesting comments I had made two years ago were the catalyst. I took this very seriously and considered legal action against the *Sun*.

The only other match we won in the first eleven games of the season was against Sheffield United and given the events that followed there was a significant amount of irony in that win.

Coming into October we played Plymouth away and quite frankly I made more effort getting to the game, by train, plane and automobile than the team put into the match. The performance was horrible, one of the worst I had seen, and I knew then that Taylor was a dead man walking.

The last match Taylor took charge of was against the team I had taken him from sixteen months earlier, Hull City. Frankly I had no interest in the result. In fact, for the first time I wanted us to lose as, come rain or shine, I had no further requirement for Peter Taylor's services. As it was we played quite well and actually should have won but drew 1–1. I left the ground immediately after the game not wishing to speak to Peter. What I did do was phone the one manager I had coveted for a long time and tell him in no uncertain terms that his services were required!

On Monday 8 October I went down to the training ground to see Peter. He was having his annual meeting with the League Managers Association. He was sitting in with Ray Graydon, the former Walsall manager, when I cut short that interview. I asked Peter for two minutes and told him that with immediate effect I was relieving him of his duties and advised him that Kevin Watts would take it from here. Taylor took it with good grace and even made a joke as he walked back into Graydon about the irony of having his annual managerial chat and getting fired!

I think part of Peter was relieved. For me, there had been a tinge of regret or reflection with virtually every manager I had fired or parted company with. I felt neither with Peter and it was certainly not because I disliked him. I had always felt in my gut that he was a coach, not a manager, and he had proved to me that that was all he was – if that. Frankly I was agitated after wasting sixteen months, significant monies and allowing a general downturn in the morale of the supporters.

Without delay I made the move for the man I had wanted for some time. It was to prove to be my best football decision. I brought in a manager who finally showed me what owning a football club could and should mean. An all for one and one for all mentality. A togetherness and support and a complete respect for others' acumen. My new manager would not give me two and a half years of total success but the most enjoyable rewarding time. How ironic it was to be my last appointment that brought me that!

I appointed Neil Warnock as my eighth and final full-time Crystal Palace manager on 11 October 2007. Prior to the appointment we had a little haggle over money. Neil wanted more than I wanted to pay. I had to pay off another manager in Peter Taylor and wanted to keep managerial costs in perspective yet at the same time pay Neil what I thought was right. I convinced Neil to come for the right reasons, telling him that he and I could fly together and if we did, money would be the last of our issues. The only concern raised was by his lovely wife Sharon, given we were friends. If it didn't work out then she didn't want us to lose our friendship. My only comment to Neil on that was: 'Are you going to ever lie and cheat me?'

'No, of course not,' he replied.

'Then whatever happens we will always be friends.'

The press conference on 11 October was one of the most relaxed I had done. I was genuinely delighted to have Neil with me. Certain segments of the media couldn't get their head round it, describing it as a 'a marriage made in hell' and 'the two most combustible men in English football sitting side by side'. What they failed to take into account was that our relationship had been forged over years of friendship. Neil and his family stayed on my yacht in Marbella for holidays and we were very close confidants. All in all we knew one another well and wanted to work together.

I never really went to the training ground after the first season and a half of my ownership, as there was little point. My relationship was with the manager and his with the players. The training ground was the manager's domain, and my view was that the chairman coming on to it undermined his authority. If I felt the need to check up on my manager on the training ground then I should not have him in the job in the first place! When I did go down, more often than not, it was to fire the manager!

Often it is the case when a new manager comes in that he will automatically make stock comments about the players not being fit enough and this and that being wrong and laying the blame on his predecessor by inference. But in this instance I took it upon myself to look at the training ground after Taylor's departure and it was a diabolical mess. Players' standards were low, medical records that were a must hadn't been maintained, the scouting network and reporting was scandalously bad and the fitness records of the players, key indicators to how successful fitness coaches were, were all over the place. I was horrified at the state of that department. My mind flashed back to the conversation with Dougie Freedman in the summer, but the results on Saturday had indeed told me everything I needed to know.

Unlike previous managers, the first thing Neil did was to find a house and a school for his children and move his whole family down to south London. It showed me everything I needed to know about how committed he was to the job.

I had taken Peter Taylor out during an international break and Neil had ten days to get his bearings before his first game at Blackpool. During that time he proceeded to look at the squad and facilities. Neil brought in his own team, which I sanctioned, despite the costs, in order to support him, Mick Jones as assistant manager, Keith Curle as first-team coach and Nigel Cox as physio.

I felt genuine excitement approaching the first game of Neil's reign, away to Blackpool. I flew in from Spain and watched us play in freezing cold conditions, initially irked by the fact Blackpool came out onto the pitch to our signature tune, 'Glad All Over'. I was far from glad all over. We were disappointing and quite poor. I'd hoped for a rousing start because of Neil. We scraped a 1–1 draw. I felt genuinely deflated as for the first time in a while I had felt energised again, but as Neil told me at the time: 'I am a good football manager not a bloody magician.' He might have been wrong on one of those scores. The next two games were at home to high-flying Stoke City and table-topping Watford; both games resulted in convincing defeats.

Neil looked at the squad and, believing in using young players, gave a debut against Watford to a fifteen-year-old who had been raved about in our academy. Said to have inspired interest from Barcelona, he was one of my future stars and a player who was to cause me consternation, young John Bostock. He'd been with the club since he was nine and had proclaimed himself a future Palace captain. After this game and the manner in which we were comprehensively outplayed, my mood was one of reflection. Watford were top of the league and the club had high expectations of the season; in the two years since relegation, we were nowhere, struggling, with no expectations. I contemplated sadly how it had come to this and after that game my mood was very low, strangely lower than when we had been relegated from the Premier League and lost in the play-offs so badly in 2006.

Neil decided to change the dynamics of the team after these opening three games. He was unhappy with the ethos and personnel. Paul Dickov, who had joined in the summer with the promise of repaying me for my help when he was arrested in Spain in 2003, was shipped out on loan as his performances on the pitch were poor. There was also an incident in training when he had gone over the top in a tackle and Neil decided he wanted him gone. Neil brought in a host of loan signings and also decided that he was going to use the younger players in our squad who in the previous season had been overlooked, which was music to my ears. Neil was unimpressed with some of the senior players, saying privately to me that the younger players couldn't do any worse than the so-called senior pros. He decided that our £1.25 million centre half Leon Cort was not for him, saying at the time that he liked his centre halves to have scars and battle wounds, implying that Leon was soft!

He suggested the idea of selling Cort, which I said was his call.

I awoke the next day to see he had sold Cort for an agreed £1 million to Stoke City, who ironically Cort had played his last Palace game against. It's funny how two managers see the same player differently. We had taken Clint Hill, a slightly injury-prone centre half, the other way, who became a warrior for my club, on an initial loan deal to become permanent in January. The fact that Neil had gone and done it with no recourse to me whatsoever made me laugh, as in the past I would never have allowed such a thing, but such was my faith in him and his take-charge approach.

Despite these decisive actions Neil did express some reservations about achieving anything with what he had as a playing squad. I gave him the answer I gave him many times over the next two years: 'Good job I have you!'

My enormous faith was not misplaced as I was about to discover, but even I was staggered by the transformation of this team. From my depths of depression after the Watford game, what started as a mentality that we must stop conceding goals turned into a fifteen-match unbeaten run spanning three months. After our turgid but dogged 0–0 draw on 3 November away to Scunthorpe, which left us second to bottom of the table, not even I could see this coming. It took us from twenty-second in the table to fifth, winning nine games and drawing six and taking thirty-three points. That form would have won any league in the world.

He got players who had previously been poor to really step up and play at a level I had never seen from them before. He took our young players, two of whom were Victor Moses and Sean Scannell, and put them in the first team. We also brought in a raft of loan signings and two players really pushed us into gear. Scott Sinclair, a tremendous talent, was brought in from Chelsea and, as Neil wanted a midfield player, I suggested we look at re-signing Shaun Derry from Leeds, and he was a revelation. These factors, combined with the particular rise of young Victor Moses, were pivotal to our success.

In amongst this was a most satisfying win for Neil away to Sheffield United on 29 December. It was his first return to the club since his departure in the summer. In my view he had been shoddily treated by the club's owners.

In fact, every time we went to Sheffield United, the lack of empathy towards Neil as their manager from the United fans always surprised me given he was a Blades fan through and through and one of the most committed individuals you could have. But in his new incarnation as Palace manager he was given an ovation from the Sheffield United fans on his return to Bramall Lane, and I remarked to his wife Sharon, 'Shame they didn't give him that support when he was here.' And she nodded knowingly. I know this win pleased Neil as he had a point to prove, but at the same time he was sad, as under Bryan Robson, the then United manager, his beloved team were in decline.

During November I had some other pressing matters. The filming on set of *Telstar* had virtually been completed and we had one piece left to do in Spain as the central character took a holiday there in the script. So I flew the lead actor Con O'Neill, another actor, Sid Mitchell, and the director Nick Moran to my house in Spain hoping to catch some sun in which to film. The weather was unpredictable but at 8 a.m. the day after they arrived in Marbella I looked out my window and into the November sky and saw sun. In a frantic rush I got the actors out of bed, and myself and Nick spray-tanned them, and dashed them off down to the nearest beach to film a scene in their swimming trunks. It was sunny, but it was still pretty cold. We had no licences or permissions yet managed to film for the duration of the day.

As we sat over dinner contemplating the ridiculousness of the above scenario, I got a phone call from my now heavily pregnant partner Suzanne, who said her heart was racing at a phenomenal rate. When I asked her what it was she told me it was beating at 170 according to her count. 'Christ, you are seven months pregnant, call the ambulance, darling,' was my frantic response.

Fifteen apprehension-filled minutes later she phoned me back and I spoke to the ambulance medic, who told me that her heart rate was now at a staggering 230 beats per minute and they were immediately taking her to hospital to stop her heart, inject her with adrenalin and restart it!

Can you imagine being told that this is happening and your partner and unborn child are at risk? I was in a state of complete panic. After I had hung on by the phone for nearly an hour in abject terror, Suzanne's chirpy little voice came on the phone: 'Everything is all right; I'm fine.' That certainly put life into perspective; it also put Suzanne in the Portland Hospital – with no expense spared – for eight weeks after she had a recurrence not long afterwards! It seemed that the reason for the attacks was that Suzanne had been taking the wrong dosage of her medication for ME.

After the scare in November and Suzanne being 'locked up' in a luxurious room at the Portland Hospital, on 18 January 2008 at 9.02 a.m., and weighing seven pounds and two ounces, my beautiful little girl Cameron was born. And in a distinctly un-Jordan-like way she didn't utter a murmur for days. Cameron arrived in the world via a Caesarean and the previous evening Suzanne and I had discussed the birthing music. I had wanted 'The First Cut is the Deepest' and Suz suggested 'Strangers in the Night'. We ended up settling for 'Glad All Over', the Palace theme tune. Of course we didn't, even I couldn't get away with that. I am pleased to say I have an adorable but wilful little girl who is the light of my life, especially in recent times.

Just a week after my beautiful little girl was born, my father had to have a second huge operation on his heart. He had had a quadruple bypass in 2005, which astounded us all at the time as he was such a fit man. He came through that operation with flying colours but this time round the operation was fraught with complications. The first operation had lasted almost five hours, but this was getting on for ten and as time dragged by Dominic and I became more concerned.

We had been waiting for news but after hearing nothing we went to the hospital, and were told there were serious complications. There was internal bleeding and they couldn't sew up his chest and had to leave him in the theatre overnight, on a table with his chest packed with ice and gauze. The next day they managed to stop the bleeding and sew him up, but he was now on a ventilator and in a very serious condition and was not getting better. This was the first time I saw my father in such a vulnerable state and there was a very real possibility he might not survive: his blood pressure was almost non-existent, his oxygen content was incredibly low and his lungs were collapsing. Over the next three days this situation got worse rather than better.

Dominic and I sat by his bed day in day out; my father was kept breathing by the ventilator and so heavily medicated that he was only partially aware of us. I spoke to him about Palace, about anything to try and engage him. It was heart-wrenching for us, but nothing compared to what he was going through.

After about five days of doctors shrugging when we asked what they were going to do next for my dad, I exploded in the intensive care unit to such an extent they threatened to throw me out. I wanted something done and I didn't care how they did it. The specialist said there was an American who was an expert in these circumstances they could get in. 'Get him in, then!' I exclaimed. It took a day or so for him to arrive and after what appeared to be the turning of a few valves and the pushing of some buttons, within hours my dad was sitting up, coherent, still on the ventilator but talking and on the road to recovery. But what if I hadn't had that emotional outburst?

Back to the comparatively trivial business of football.

We reached the end of January still unbeaten but then surrendered inexplicably away to Leicester and then lost two more games on the bounce, one of them away to Charlton. It was the first time I had been to the Valley since May 2005 and relegation from the Premier League. The game was moved to a Friday night due to police intelligence of potential crowd trouble and I was instructed that I was going to have a police escort into the ground, which I duly ignored, and stewards sitting next to me, such was the bad feeling between the clubs, and more so from the Charlton fans towards me.

I went with my entourage of six friends who now accompanied me to most matches. They were always frustrated by my desire to be at the game only five minutes before kick-off so as not to fraternise with the opposition, whilst they wanted to sit in boardrooms quaffing wine and eating laid-on meals. The atmosphere as I walked in was intense and very quickly I was surrounded by stewards and police. I got to enjoy the spectacle of the Charlton fans singing the words of the song I now knew well: 'Simon Jordan is a wanker, is a wanker.' Worse than that I watched us get beat 2–0 with some rascal little kid sat in front of me in his Charlton scarf, turning around taking pictures of me on his camera phone, which amused me no end!

It did however become serious when the police instructed me to stay in the ground for an hour after the match. No way was I sitting around in that stadium and I told them so. I was escorted, along with my friends, by stewards and police who scrummed together and virtually lifted me off my feet and through the crowd as bottles and abuse rained down. Even I had to consider that was a little scary and perhaps I should have taken their advice.

In December 2007 I had travelled to Barnsley to watch us play. We had received a request from the wife of an ardent Palace fan who lived in the area. Her husband Carl had terminal cancer and wanted to see his beloved club and to meet me. I met Carl Lewis before the game and had a long chat, and this man's indomitable spirit moved me so much that on leaving him I instructed Phil Alexander that whenever Carl was free, I wanted a private jet sent for him and his family to fly them to London, and for them to be put up in a hotel, to meet the players, sit in the dressing room before the game and be my guest at a game of his choice.

But early in the New Year, my PA received an email from his wife Jane. I still have it today, it reads:

Could you please forward this to Simon from me. Simon will never know what it meant for Carl to meet him at Barnsley. Carl was so looking forward to being a guest in the boardroom and meeting Simon again, but unfortunately that will not now be possible. Carl was discharged from hospital three weeks ago because he was given a prognosis of two to three days at most. I didn't want him to die in hospital so brought him home.

Carl is now very poorly and I don't expect him to last more than a few days. I would like Simon to know that the first Palace match I went to with Carl, I looked across at this man with longish blond hair, a fur coat and a mobile phone in his hand. I asked Carl who he was to which Carl replied, 'That's God!' Quite indignant that I didn't know. So Simon, I can't thank you enough for allowing Carl to meet his God and only wish he could have had his lunch with you that he was so looking forward to.

This email made me cry, as it does even now as I am writing this, and I have never forgotten Carl. For someone to suffer this way and to think of me in the manner he did was humbling and it showed how important football was to people and how privileged I was to be held in such regard.

I emailed the letter to Neil Warnock with the accompanying message. 'Neil read the below. This is the reason why I stay in football and am determined to succeed because of people like this. Heart-breaking!' I wanted Neil and the players to know about this man and how much he loved his football club and what they did.

It looked as if the wheels had come off this phenomenal turn-around under Neil as we set off to play Bristol City on a freezing cold Monday night in February with a team decimated by injuries. There was a little niggle between the two clubs as when we had played them a month earlier in January and beaten them 2–0, they had bitterly complained that we were over-physical. This game was not without controversy and was delayed for fifteen minutes due to floodlight failure. As the game was live on Sky the referee came on television and explained the delay and it has to be said he looked very strange, his eyes were as wide as saucers.

The game eventually got under way. We were flat in the first half but came flying out the blocks in the second and scored through our seventeen-year-old left back Lee Hills, making his first start for the club. We were still in the lead at ninety minutes. But then, after a disgraceful decision – and not the first we got at Bristol City – the referee awarded four minutes of injury time and with no events in the those four minutes to prolong that period, proceeded to play another minute in which Bristol City got a corner and scored.

Cue outrage from the manager and the chairman. In the boardroom after the match, the Bristol City chairman, rather than be magnanimous about this highway robbery was doing a celebratory dance. As I glanced over with the red mist descending, he reminded me of some demented Morris dancer. This resulted in a coffee cup being flung at the TV by me. Perhaps I should refrain from going into boardrooms, I thought. Neil went on TV and had a rant about the referee, being funny in an outraged way, saying at one point he thought it was a bit strong that the referee punched the air in celebration when Bristol scored!

Neil was charged by the FA for criticising the referee and I suggested he put down his mitigating circumstances in writing and I would read the letter before it went off. I can write and say some outrageous stuff but Neil accused the referee of everything from being 'The third gunman on the grassy knoll' to an outlandish suggestion as to what may have caused his strange appearance on TV before the game. Even I couldn't let him write that and toned it down, to no avail as he still got fined and I got to pick up the tab.

We lost again on the Saturday at home to Wolves, a team we had annihilated 3–0 away a month earlier and dropped to eleventh, and it looked as if we had fallen away. But not this team or, more to the point, this manager. We put in another Herculean effort to win six and draw four of the next eleven games and went into the last match of the campaign needing to beat Burnley at home to secure a play-off place.

In the just under ten years of my ownership this was my favourite day. Naturally there had been significant highs that preceded it.

The play-off final win in 2004, the League Cup semi-final victory over Liverpool and a variety of other big days. But this was the day I will always remember. It was what I always wanted from my ownership of the club, a day when owner, manager, players and supporters were in complete harmony.

We thrashed Burnley 5–0 to take our place in the play-offs with our young star Victor Moses opening the scoring. The stadium was a scene of unbridled joy as Neil took the players for the customary lap of honour in the last home game of the season. He took the microphone on the pitch and applauded the players and the fans for their tremendous efforts and then out of the blue announced that the person who should be thanked the most was the chairman.

It was the most embarrassing and gratifying moment I had in football. Not because I needed the plaudits but because the manager, a person in other guises I had nothing but strife with over the years, had publicly stated such support and gratitude. It meant an awful amount to my family and defied all the people who had said that the relationship between Neil and me was doomed from the outset.

Whether or not we won or lost in the play-offs this achievement was by far and away the best. Unlike in 2003–04 when Dowie inherited a very talented but grossly underperforming team, this squad was made up of a mixture of tremendously talented young players from our academy, some senior players who had not covered themselves in glory prior to Warnock's arrival and a raft of inspired loan signings. And they all shared an incredible bond and a will to win, which had been instilled in them by Neil Warnock and his management team.

Now we were facing Bristol City in the play-off semi-final, with the added pressure of being favourites to secure promotion back to the promised land and all that meant. Not least of all the release of the tremendous financial pressure on me.

15

STOP THE TRAIN, I THINK I WANT TO GET OFF!

After the euphoria of getting into the play-offs it never really entered my head that we wouldn't get past our opponents Bristol City in the semi-finals. This was not arrogance, it was just that I had never seen all the parts of the football club working together so well, as beforehand there was always some sort of dissension within the ranks. I often said that I could buy the best player in the world, build a brand-new stadium and sell tickets at half price and someone, somewhere, would complain the hot dogs tasted like shit. But not this time: fans, owner, manager and players were in complete harmony.

We lost the play-offs against Bristol City, not in the pathetic manner we had whimpered out in 2006 but with a fully committed performance in both games. In truth, in the first leg at Selhurst Park, we met inspired opponents and were slightly under par and got beaten 2–1. After going a goal down we equalised through a penalty from Ben Watson but they scored a world-class goal with virtually the last kick of the game.

The second leg was on the Tuesday, and although history dictated that no team that lost the first leg had ever progressed, I felt anything was possible with Neil. He was slightly irritated as the

Bristol City players and fans had, in his view, over-celebrated on the Saturday, but this just seemed to increase his determination.

Driving to the away leg I listened to talkSPORT, who were carrying an interview with the Bristol City chairman. He was talking about the game and their hopes for success. He also mentioned me, saying I was a strange person, not overly friendly, and would only speak if I were spoken to. It was a rather unnecessary comment, I thought, as well as stupid, because he had not actually spoken to me so by definition he was guilty of the very thing he was accusing me of! I sincerely hoped I had the opportunity to speak to him after the game and give him my commiserations.

The atmosphere was incredible but with so much at stake it was also very tense. We were brilliant and at half-time were 1–0 up through Ben Watson, who scored as he had in the first leg. Bristol City were all over the place and the weight of expectation from their fans seemed to play heavily on their players' minds, and if this continued in the second half, there was only going to be one winner.

Bristol City fans are very fervent, as I had heard first hand when we had played them earlier in the season. This time I got to see it first hand at half-time. As I went outside the directors' entrance to have a cigarette with some of my friends I was confronted by a couple of hundred of their supporters. They stood in front of me screaming – and I do mean screaming – abuse at me inches from my nose. Stewards tried to get between them and get me to go back in but I was going to finish my cigarette.

So I stood there, smoking eye to eye with these hate-filled fans. They were standing so close to me that when one of them was screaming at me, bits of the burger he was eating flew out of his mouth and hit me in the face. Charming. But I stayed there. I was dying to say 'One–nil' but I kept it to myself. I was not moving or backing down. When I eventually finished my cigarette, I gave them a wink and thanked them for the generosity of their kind words. Just as I was about to leave my friends behind me broke into a chorus of: 'You're Welsh and you know you are, you're Welsh and you know you are.' Apparently this is a massive insult to Bristolians. We just got through the doors before being lynched.

In the second half the team got even better and in the seventy-second minute we were awarded a penalty. Looking down to the dugout I caught Neil's eye and we both knew our time had come. Bristol City were out cold, their fans in virtual silence, and if we scored there was no doubt in my mind we would go through. I watched Ben Watson, a young player who had come from my cherished academy, step up to score his third goal of the tie – and he missed!

This penalty set in motion a sequence of events that would ultimately end in the direst of consequences for me!

That miss, as it often does, reinvigorated the other side and appeared to sap everything out of us. The team gave everything to get to that point, now we were flat on our feet. We struggled through to extra time as the scores were level on aggregate and then completely ran out of gas as Bristol City scored twice and ended the dream.

There were no recriminations between Neil and myself, just a feeling of what could have been. There was mutual respect between us. We were a unified double act, and the only competition between us was who could say the most controversial thing in the media.

A week or so after the play-off loss I went to lunch with Neil and we discussed the future. Neil, being something of a crafty bugger asked me a question that took me into a theoretical cul-de-sac: 'Do you think I am the best manager in the division?'

Innocently, I said: 'Of course you are, Neil.'

'Well, how come Dave Jones at Cardiff is getting paid more than me?'

'I guess he won't be any more!' was my response.

That was the quickest £250,000 pay rise Neil ever got. He was delighted and called his wife Sharon and in his broad Yorkshire accent said: 'You'll never guess what chairman has done?'

So that was Neil and I wedded together as far as he was concerned.

As at the end of every season I was handed the budgets for the following year and the cash flow forecast made for bleak reading once again. We had lost significant monies in the last year and the same was forecast for this season, but more importantly than losses we were now showing a significant cash call.

Losses don't always mean cash calls. They do in the end but losses in football clubs can come from areas such as player depreciation on your books or, in some instances, sales of players for values that are less than they are valued on your balance sheet. Players are valued in accounting terms by the amount you pay for them, reduced every month by the period of their contract. So for example a player you buy for a million who signs a four-year contract depreciates at £250,000 per year, so after twelve months that same player would be on your balance sheet at £750,000 and so on. On the converse, young players from your academy carry no value, as they have cost nothing. Of course, when you sell such a player you show gains.

This year the budgets and cash flows showed a cash call of just under £5 million to stand still. This was the inevitable cash flow catch-up of the losses of £2.6 million and £8.1 million of the two years just gone. By now I had nearly £35 million invested in Palace and whilst I was still very liquid in cash terms it was getting towards the red-line area of my finances that I had promised myself and my family I would never cross. I decided I needed to get some funding and looked for a likely source.

In 2007 I had met Jason Granite, who was a senior figure at Deutsche Bank in the high-risk lending division, which was what lending to football clubs is classified under. I had looked at doing a deal with Jason on some funding but it never materialised. By early to mid-2008 Jason had set up a hedge fund called Agilo, which had a lot of money under management and was looking to lend into potential high-risk sectors with the requisite interest charge. There were no other traditional methods of raising money for football clubs outside of the Premier League besides third-party investment via selling equity, and there was no queue of people for that.

My relationship with Jason was very good. He asked me for advice on some investments they were looking to make, namely the acquisition of the Sports Café group of restaurants which had gone into administration, given I knew the previous owners and had experience in both sport and restaurants. More importantly though, he said if I ever required some funding we could do a deal.

Following the play-off loss and being advised of yet another huge cash call for the next season I made good on his offer and borrowed £5 million, payable back over four years at a rate of 15 per cent. Yes, it was expensive, but it was the only money available and I needed it. Costs were coming a little more under control as certain big-wage earners were coming off the payroll. Coupled with the team's performance of last season and the management team we had I could see that in the next eighteen months our costs were going to reduce dramatically without us losing our ambition and having to sell all our best assets to keep feeding the ravenous beast that is a football club.

The final part of the decision for me was that I wanted to use the money we borrowed to fund the shortfall that would merely enable us to stand still. Any money I had available I wanted to use to advance the club and keep supporting Neil. The paperwork for this deal was immense, the security required was belt and braces. They took charges over all the club's assets and finally I had to give a personal guarantee. The paperwork was so arduous and detailed and the personal guarantee so comprehensive that, while I was signing everything I made an offhand remark to my long-term lawyer Jeff McGeachie, who had worked with me when I bought Palace in 2000. I remarked: 'Could this be the deal that finally undoes me?' I put it out of my mind as soon as I had said it, believing that I had signed a deal that funded the club. In fact, I had signed my own death warrant.

Not long after that I had another issue that would dramatically change my mind-set. Our media-hyped and potential superstar John Bostock had been developed for six years by my treasured youth academy. His stepfather had promised us faithfully that John would sign his first professional contract with us when he was legally able to at seventeen. But this promise meant nothing. After all the time and energy many others and me had put into this young man, he rejected our offer of a scholarship, which took him to his seven-teenth birthday with a pro contract attached to it, and decided he was going to sign for Tottenham.

After failing to agree a reasonable fee with Tottenham we went to a tribunal which awarded us £700,000 for a player who at the time was widely considered to be one of the best in his age group. Players like Theo Walcott, who were only marginally older, were going for £11 million, and for seven years of dedicated develop-ment and support we got £700,000 and some far-off Mickey Mouse add-ons. That just wasn't right. Yet again the system had not protected my club, my investment and hopes for our future success from the pillaging and lure of so-called bigger clubs. I found this insulting and demoralising: not only was the club haemorrhaging cash and I was having to borrow money, not only were the crowds diminishing but I couldn't even get the benefit of keeping the young players I saw as my sanity and saving grace!

One of the things that always amused me in a kind of frustrated way was the unwritten rules surrounding football. Top of the pile was the one surrounding the inner sanctum of the dressing room, this mythical place where alchemy is conjured and troops are galvanised to put their lives on the line by fire-breathing call-to-action generals.

On the whole this is utter nonsense. I came to the conclusion that the reason it is called the inner sanctum, a place never to be entered besides by the chosen few, is because actually there is not a lot going on in there. I have been in the dressing area many times, most of the time spent in the room adjacent to it, the physio room, in order to hear what's going on out of sight. And to be blunt I very rarely heard any supposed Churchill-like speeches. In fact, in my previous life I had heard more rousing speeches from my twenty-something area managers speaking to their salespeople.

My forays into the dressing room were a regular thing, as they are with most owners who have the presence of mind to actually steer their club and the confidence to ignore the ludicrous taboo perpetuated by the media of chairmen entering this inner sanctum. I went in there to see my charges, wish them luck and look into their eyes, as winning was everything to me, then departed, leaving the manager to prepare his troops, or not as the case may be. The only manager I heard who combined wit with steel and great leadership, the only manager who I remember thinking that this was someone I would play for if I was a footballer, was Neil Warnock. During my time I met a lot of managers, most of whom had been players and came up through the system. I have to say that there were very few who impressed me. The perception of players being selfish and disingenuous pales in comparison to a vast number of managers.

This leads me to players themselves. Often the public perception of players is one of two diametrically opposed types. Either they are selfish, unruly and as thick as two short planks or they are all-out role-model superstars. Of course, most players are neither. Most players now come through academies and youth development schemes and a very big part of their time is spent with the clubs providing significant academic support in order for these boys to ditch the stereotype of the 'thick footballer'.

Let's face it, football players are institutionalised: they live in a cosseted environment and are made to feel special, which does lead them into certain codes of outlook and behaviour. But to be frank, which one of us at twenty-one with £10,000, £20,000, or even £100,000 a week in our pocket and grown men chanting our names by the thousands in adoration would not be affected by that and lose perspective every now and then? Yes, there are terrible examples of bad behaviour but there are also great acts of kindness and generosity that never seem to get reported. I always found once players reached their late twenties they became much more rounded and aware of their privileged position. I remember writing an extremely disparaging commentary on Craig Bellamy only to bump into him a few years later, whereupon he marched up to me. Expecting the worst, I was taken aback to be told by Mr Bellamy that he had agreed with what I had written and how much he would love to play for a chairman like me.

When I first came into football, the 'best chairmen' were

apparently the ones you never heard from, and anyone who dared describe football as a business was lambasted. Look at it now: people demand to know their clubs' owners and want them to hear their views and woe betide you if you do not oblige. Also, managers were only deemed to be capable of being managers if they had been top footballers and could put their 'caps on the table'. Tell that to José Mourinho or Arsène Wenger.

Despite finally having a manager who was totally with me, I felt after the Bostock tribunal decision in July 2008 that I had finally had enough. I had lost my enthusiasm and desire and I felt Palace should have an owner who had the same determination and freshness I had when I came in back in 2000. I made a formal announcement that I wanted to sell the club and I was prepared to listen to offers. I gave interviews, ensuring that my desire to sell was right in the public domain so it was not a secret, and engaged a firm of so-called experts to handle the club's disposal. Of course wanting to sell a football club and being able to are two different things entirely. Football can be very easy to get into, but bloody hard to leave!

I decided to engage Seymour Pierce, and specifically Keith Harris, to sell Palace and went to meet him at the Carlton Tower hotel in London to discuss the mechanics. It may have seemed like a strange choice, given the acrimony that had existed between us when he was the Football League chairman during the ITV Digital affair as well as the strong words of dislike for me that he expressed at his departure from that role. But Harris had a reputation as somebody who was effective at selling clubs. With the experiences I had with him and Seymour Pierce it is difficult to understand where that reputation emanated from or what it was based on.

Harris dispelled any bad feelings over matters of the past saying that's where they were: the past. He was keen to help sell Palace and said he had about ten parties around the world who would be interested in buying the club. He was adamant there would be no problems securing a sale and gave me an indication that he felt the price for Palace, debt free, which was not a problem as most of the debt was to me, and including the stadium, was circa £35 million.

This price surprised me but they based it upon a variety of calculations and that was their expert valuation. Before instructing Seymour Pierce I gave them one more set of parameters – that my 'legacy was as important as my tenure'. I wanted legitimate buyers with genuine intentions for Palace and with that understood, in August 2008 I formally engaged them and set about giving them all the information they required to produce a glossy information pack and sales brochure for potential purchasers.

Neil Warnock was fully supportive, both privately and in the media, believing that I was entirely right to want to sell. Personally there was a level of disappointment seeing as we got on so well but he knew if I got the club sold it would be done with the club's and his best interests at heart.

My modus operandi was business as usual so we set about preparing for the new season with the ambition, as always, to be successful. We sold one of our young players Tom Soares to Premier League-promoted Stoke City for £1.25 million and, rather than bank the money as most sensible people would have done, I backed my manager and allowed him to go out and spend nearly £2.5 million on players!

We brought in Paddy McCarthy for £500,000 to replace the club captain Mark Hudson, who left on a free transfer after contract negotiations broke down. I was told he deliberately made ridiculous demands because he never had any intention of signing a new deal once his existing one had run out. This was because when he had signed in 2004 Iain Dowie promised he would be our starting centre back in the Premier League, but nothing ever came of that promise. So I lost Hudson, who had originally cost us £500,000, for nothing to Charlton! On top of that Neil signed their centre half for £500,000! So Charlton managed to get some of the money back they had to pay in legal fees on Dowie's behalf over the lost court case!

We also signed Alan Lee, a big centre forward from Ipswich, for £650,000. The most curious signing and one which Mr Warnock was entirely culpable for was Nick Carle, an Australian international. We paid £1 million to Bristol City to meet a release clause in his contract. Carle was sold to me as Bristol's key player, a free-scoring midfielder according to my management team. I do remember him being mentioned as the player to stop when we played Bristol in the 1–1 draw in the controversial League game back in January.

So I sanctioned the investment and when he scored his first ever goal in English football for Crystal Palace early in the season it came as something of a surprise to me. He started with such promise but virtually disappeared and was nothing like the player I had been led to believe I was buying. His hefty salary aside, he was, shall we say, a bit of a disappointment and not one of Neil's finest moments.

We also signed two other players and a raft of loan players from Premier League clubs, such was the belief I had in Neil. Unfortunately for this season it was to prove a little misplaced. Perhaps it was my announcement to sell that unsettled the club, or maybe it was a hangover from the disappointment from the play-offs last year, yet it was a surprise to me that we started the next campaign so poorly given that we had significantly strengthened our side. It took us five games to record our first win and at the end of August we were in the bottom three and had suffered an embarrassing 4–0 away defeat to then League One Leeds United in the Carling Cup. The performance at Elland Road was abject, and that's being kind, which was surprising given how Neil, as a Sheffield fan, viewed Leeds.

Tragically in late August I lost my dear friend and publicist Aroon Maharajh. We had been working together for about eighteen months and had become very close. In one of life's strange co-incidences I had met his wife Teresa some twenty years earlier as she worked for Mark Goldberg and was responsible for my first ever computer contract. Aroon was one of those people who made a room light up. He had an infectious personality and a wicked sense of humour. He was thoroughly on my side, albeit frequently encouraging me to do things I never wanted to do! On my phone the first picture I have is Aroon in my house in Spain in March 2008, holding my six-week-old daughter Cameron. He died seven months later after suffering a massive heart attack. I gave a eulogy at the packed church for his funeral. He is still sorely missed. Shine on, you crazy diamond.

Throughout September we stayed in and around the bottom three. The only bright spot of any note was playing Charlton Athletic at home, where we got to achieve a long overdue win. Craig Beattie, a loan signing from West Brom, scored the winning goal in front of a euphoric Selhurst Park crowd. Beattie proved to be an inspired signing, and in October and November we started to fare better. By the end of November we were mid-table, still not where I had expected us to be!

By now the sales document from Seymour Pierce had been circulated to potential purchasers for Palace and, according to Keith Harris, we would start to see some interest very shortly.

The launch of *Telstar* in October at the London Film Festival was greeted with great critical acclaim and by now I had decided to use a leading film sales agent, Fortissimo, who had very high hopes of sales. They gave me three forecasts of what they were expecting internationally and in the UK market. The top-end forecast was just under $10 million, the most likely was $6.5 million and worst case was $4.5 million. What this told me was at best this film could make me over £4 million on my £2-million-plus investment, worst case maybe half a million. This was from one of the leading and most experienced internationally reputed big sales companies so it should have meant something. The fact the forecasts weren't worth the paper they were written on emerged sometime later.

In the same month I was invited to co-host my favourite radio show on talkSPORT with the copper-headed one Adrian Durham. I always enjoyed being a guest on the show as I liked talking to the fans on the phone-ins, discussing any weighty issues of the time and regaling the world with my opinions. But this was a co-host slot and involved a different set of parameters. I had to try and be a proper radio presenter, which wasn't that easy as I had no benchmark working alongside Durham.

But I enjoyed it. On the three shows I did I invited Lynval Golding and Terry Hall from The Specials to talk about football as well as the recent re-formation of the band and how and why it had come about. On the last show I invited Nick Moran on so we could shamelessly plug our film *Telstar*. Whilst I was discussing the film, and during a round of banter, Adrian asked me if I would consider the now actor and ex-footballer Vinnie Jones in any future film projects. My sarcastic comment in response was only in the event that the dialogue consisted of a series of Neanderthal-like grunts.

This was fed back to Mr Jones, who somehow got confused.

Vinnie Jones had worked with Nick on the hit film *Lock, Stock and Two Smoking Barrels* and upon hearing this bit of mickey-taking he jumped to the conclusion that it was Nick and the producer of *Lock Stock*, Matthew Vaughn, who had made fun of him. Thus a bemused Matt Vaughn received a series of explosive phone calls from Jones, and Nick Moran, in fear of his life, phoned him to apologise. Oh well, all in a day's work for me!

In autumn 2008 the world was gripped by the current financial crisis and I was becoming extremely exposed. Since 2001 I had used an overdraft to fund Palace's trading. The long-standing reason for this was that in the unlikely event I was ever able to take money out of Palace, reducing an overdraft was seamless, whilst taking money out would inevitably lead to criticism from certain fans! The overdraft was fully supported and secured by my cash, which was put into an investment vehicle. The borrowings my cash supported were at £12 million but my portfolio was at circa £14.5 million so I had plenty of headroom, or so I thought. In three short months that portfolio was to lose in excess of £3 million as a result of market volatility.

The forecasts at the beginning of the season for Palace that had shown the £5 million hole, which I had plugged, were now proving to be wrong. The recession was biting into our attendances, and the team's slow start didn't help: for the fourth year in a row our crowds dropped substantially. This, coupled with a big downturn in corporate spending with the club, meant that our income was actually coming in at several hundred thousand per month less than anticipated.

On top of that I had several million invested in the Spanish property market, which by now had gone soft. I had bought twenty-three properties in 2003 and the developer had been late completing them. I had only managed to sell nine, and as the market worsened the potential of selling more receded; furthermore, twelve of these properties lost their planning permission – and I had invested a significant seven-figure sum in them. I had been suing the developer for nearly fifteen months to get my money back when the company, Fadesa, one of if not the biggest developer in Spain, went into administration with debts of €1.5 billion, which meant getting my money back became even more difficult.

To compound things further the Club Bar and Dining business was ailing and my relationship with the partner I had founded it with had now deteriorated. I was concerned at his lack of hands-on involvement, and it seemed that company funds had been misused. This business now had cash demands and the only place to get the money from was me!

Around this time I was due to go to America to look at the marketing opportunities and key sales of my film *Telstar*. As I was preparing for this my best friend in the world, someone whose judgement I trusted in unreservedly, came up with an investment opportunity. My lawyers and accountants looked at it, and the information we gleaned suggested it was a sound investment. It was based upon buying shares in a Nasdaq-listed company at a certain price which were going to move to the London AIM market. Going to another exchange meant that the shares would then increase in value – a huge opportunity for gain with seemingly no risk whatsoever! So with that I placed a seven-figure sum into this investment!

By November 2008 my liquidity was at its lowest in eight years and below the threshold I had said I would ever go under. I had just under £10 million in the bank but I remained asset rich. I had a football club supposedly worth £35 million that I was potentially about to sell, a film that wouldn't only get my £2 million back but also generate a good return, a portfolio with £3 million excess cash in it against the borrowings I had for Palace and a house in Spain with £2 million in equity. Whilst slightly problematic, there was also a seven-figure sum claimable by me also in Spanish property and a lucrative investment with a close friend, plus sundry assets like boats and luxury cars. So all in all, whilst I had alarm bells ringing, I had the asset base and wherewithal to see out the problems I had. How wrong one person can be!

The team's performance in December improved markedly and we troubled the top six for the first and only time that season, going to fifth in the league. Even the forgotten £2.5 million Shefki Kuqi was back in the team and scoring goals and despite the threats on the horizon, this gave me cause for optimism. Wrong again!

Each year I threw an annual Christmas party for the staff and players. And this year, irrespective of the financial pressures, was not different. These parties were big affairs with over 250 guests and most years were held at the Grosvenor House Hotel. We had top-drawer entertainment from comedians like Jimmy Carr and Bradley Walsh to music acts such as Lemar and the Sugababes. These parties cost me in excess of £100,000 a year, but were a great opportunity for me to show the staff how much I appreciated them for all their endeavours over the past twelve months. This year, my customary speech at the opening of the evening was touched with a tinge of sadness as, given the club was up for sale, it was likely to be the last one. Well, I had to get something right!

Despite being told in October and November that the sales document for Palace had been produced by Seymour Pierce, I finally saw in the New Year what was going to all the supposed interested parties in Palace. My faith was a little diminished as to date Seymour Pierce had proved to be all talk and no action, but there had been one interested party. They themselves were of course represented by a third party. In the third week of January, with the team two points off a play-off spot, I flew with Tom Sheldon, one of Keith Harris's staff, to Paris for a meeting.

By now we had established that the interested party was a French–Israeli consortium. I met them and their representation in Charles de Gaulle airport for a two-hour meeting. They appeared knowledgeable about football and purported to be interested in owning the club solely for footballing reasons. After going through all aspects of the club they announced they would be making a bid of £25 million but both Seymour Pierce and I said the document had said we were looking for £35 million, which now seems a touch avaricious but no one takes the first offer. If I had done that back in 2000 for the sale of my mobile phone business I would have got £40 million less.

One of them, a Middle Eastern guy whose name escapes me now, asked to speak privately with me. He said he could make the offer £30 million but £5 million would need to be paid in cash as they wanted for their own reasons to book the sale at £25 million. This concerned me, as whilst the number was very acceptable the fact they wanted to pay in cash didn't sound right. I stated that whilst he might not want to make such offers in front of his own representation I most certainly wanted mine to hear and called Sheldon over.

I expressed my discomfort at being paid a significant proportion in cash, mainly because it smacked of money laundering and could be a possible sting. We agreed to look at how we could work such a deal, bearing in mind taking £5 million in cash was not plausible, and Seymour Pierce would get back to them.

I was hoping these people were real and legitimate but I realised that if they were I would need to be careful as I had to acquire the stadium from Paul Kemsley's HBOS-backed company. Even though I had signed a lease he had flatly refused to put a maximum buy price into the agreement and the last thing I wanted was for him to get me again! But I considered that was only worth worrying about when it was necessary to do so.

In early February I received, via Seymour Pierce, an offer of £30 million from the Israeli consortium, using their company United Mizrahi Financial Corporation Limited and supported by a letter from their bankers Mizrahi-Tefahot Bank Limited, an FSA-regulated UK-based bank, saying they were good for the £30 million. It was very encouraging but the correspondence was a little flaky and I was hopeful more than expectant. By the end of February my suspicions were confirmed when the consortium disappeared off the face of the earth. I looked to Seymour Pierce to up their game, which was fruitless and a complete waste of time.

With the offer falling away so too had the team's performance. What had looked very promising at the end of December was now turning into a damp squib of a season. We had dropped down to fourteenth in the league with two thirds of the season gone. When I really needed Neil to push the team on and get us back into the play-offs or at least competing, the exact opposite happened and just compounded the ensuing problems.

The financial pressure was now increasing and by March there was a hole in the immediate cash flow of £2 million and growing. It would have been even worse if I had not sold one of our younger players in January. Ben Watson was in the last year of his contract and refused to sign a new one, so we took the commercially sensible decision to sell him to Wigan for £1.5 million. It is an irony that if Ben had scored that penalty we may well have been in the Premier

League and not under these huge financial pressures, rather than transferring him to a Premier League Club at his request!

Clearly this season was going absolutely nowhere. I spoke to Neil in private about the enormous financial pressure building on me. He encouraged me to get out, but that was appearing unlikely as the only enquiries we were getting were from tyre kickers. In order to weather the impending storm that looked like it was going to batter me on all fronts, I needed to focus and couldn't be distracted by the team's performance, so I asked Neil to keep the team in the best position he could while my attentions were diverted.

What I now faced was the most difficult and harrowing period of my life. And as a seasoned gambler I was about to bet it all on red.

16

AND NOW THE END IS NEAR

When I took the £5 million loan from Agilo in June 2008 I knew it was merely plugging a cash-flow hole for a year. I believed a lot of things could happen in that period of time. The team had been narrowly knocked out of the play-offs and there was good cause to be optimistic for the following year. At the time I had reasonable liquidity personally and a host of different commercial opportunities that I considered likely to bring me back some significant cash!

Also, when I took Agilo's loan, I knew that the cash calls on Palace for the following year, i.e. the 2009–10 season, had been vastly reduced. We had less outstanding transfer fees to pay and a shrinking wage bill coupled with a highly rated young squad as well as an increase in Sky monies. And if push came to shove I might be able to sell a young player like most clubs invariably did when they required funding.

What I couldn't legislate for was the meltdown that happened in the world's financial markets in October 2008, which hit me in every area of my investments. And with a club urgently requiring cash injections from me, as unbelievable as it may sound, this was just the start of my problems.

All of a sudden the landscape changed completely. I was no longer trying to sell Crystal Palace, I was trying to find funding to keep the club going to afford me the opportunity to sell it. Seymour Pierce along with a number of others were now tasked with finding investment, which given it was football and the world was going to hell in a handcart wasn't going to be easy.

In March 2009 I was in serious trouble as my financial position came under enormous threat. I had a portfolio that had lost £4 million in five months and was now £1.5 million underwater, and the bank had started to apply pressure on me to rectify that.

The £2 million I had invested in *Telstar*, despite the film's huge critical acclaim, was failing to show any sign of a return. The sales agency, Fortissimo, failed to deliver on any of their projected forecasts. We had no UK or US distributor and only a handful of foreign countries buying the film. To add injury to insult the £200,000 the film generated had been swallowed up in marketing costs by the agency.

The Spanish property market had completely collapsed and the millions I had locked in were unlikely to be seen for some considerable time, if at all. The restaurant was in turmoil as I was forced to remove my founding partner and was left having to try and turn this ailing business round – which meant devoting to it time and funds I was running out of – or sell it.

The problems kept coming. The investment in the stock-market-changing oil business had fallen on its arse and I had lost my seven-figure investment. I had an extremely high cost base of personal expenses running at over £100,000 per month, which included the salaries of staff in the UK and Spain. All these problems were surmountable if you didn't have a football club haemorrhaging money and requiring further investment merely to stand still.

I had managed to fly by the seat of my pants when it came to cash flow at The PocketPhone Shop; I was going to have to do the same at Palace. To get Palace's cash flow under control I either had to bring in some significant income or reduce the outgoings in some shape or form. From a personal point of view I needed to do this rather than call upon my rapidly depleting financial reserves. The traditional method of bringing in cash required selling players but this wasn't an option as the transfer window had closed and wouldn't reopen until the end of May.

So the only option was to reduce outflows and the only place to go was the Inland Revenue. We were a large payee and National Insurance contributor given the salaries on our books, paying HMRC £450,000 per month. I decided to use a newly introduced government edict to help businesses with cash-flow problems to put a proposal to the Revenue that allowed me to defer the next six months' worth of payee payments, circa £2.7 million, and then to pay that off in equal amounts over the next twelve months. It would give me cash flow and the chance to find funding opportunities, player sales or any other things I could exploit to inject cash into this business.

Their response was a resounding no. We showed them the cash-flow hole and explained we had nowhere to go given the time constraints to get funding so it had to be a yes in some form. Their advice was go to a bank and borrow the money. What bank would that be then, the Bank of Neverland!

HMRC's blunt and unhelpful no was never explained and our circumstances never taken into account. HMRC had a hard-line approach to football primarily because back in 2003 they had lost their position as a secured creditor and now they were going to war with the game. It was irrelevant that clubs contributed large amounts of tax, were often funded by individuals and were part of the fabric of a community. HMRC couldn't care less and had

football firmly in their sights. If it meant forcing clubs into administration and only getting 10p in the pound rather than helping
cash flows and getting all their money then they seemed to prefer
the former!

Although I wanted to work with HMRC I was prepared to use
commercial shotgun tactics and quite simply not make the payments
anyway. My view was by the time they caught up with me hopefully I would be in a better cash position.

Whilst I was grappling with HMRC and trying to find a deal I
was working with Seymour Pierce to find a funder. They came up
with a new football lender called the Hero Fund which apparently
had £125 million at their disposal, and had a revolutionary way of
lending which resulted in repayments only being made if and when
players were sold, which in real terms was a unique and very palat-
able way of getting funding.

While I was fighting these many battles my biggest enemies were
yet to show themselves.

The relationship with Agilo throughout the year had been very
cordial. They got paid their £65,000 interest every month on time.
There had been a change of management in their business: Jason
Granite, who I knew well and had a very good relationship with,
departed and I was now dealing with a Serbian-American, Milos
Brajovic, who I had met before and had done some of the negotiations with on the original deal. He appeared a perfectly amiable
kind of guy and I initially got on quite well with him. But that
was all to change!

So as the football season ended with Neil Warnock and a disappointing eight-year low in performance finishing fifteenth in the
league, at the end of May I approached Brajovic with a short-term
proposal. Agilo were due a bullet repayment of £900,000 on the

loan on 15 June. Palace didn't have the cash so I was going to have to personally pay it. I asked Brajovic if I could split the payment in two, paying £450,000 on 15 June and the other £450,000 on 31 July and pay any interest penalties. By doing this it gave me a chance to raise some funds before the second payment fell due. As far as I was concerned, we had a verbal agreement to this effect, which I assumed would be confirmed in writing soon enough.

On 15 June I paid the £450,000, then on 26 June I received a default notice from them, calling in the balance of the loan three years early. They cited the non-payment of £900,000 and completely ignored the agreement in principle I'd made with Brajovic. More sinisterly, this notice arrived after the seven working-day window I'd had to remedy any breaches. I hadn't thought there were any.

If Brajovic couldn't agree the £450,000 deferral to 31 July he should have said! I would have paid the £900,000 in one sum, as I eventually ended up paying the other £450,000 out of my own pocket because Palace's cash flow was still shot to pieces. By not telling me of any issues with our agreement, Brajovic had lulled me into a false sense of security, and then served me with a default notice.

Calling in this loan would add even greater problems to my increasingly worsening financial situation. After speaking to Brajovic he confirmed the default, said it was designed to protect their position and was merely a piece of bureaucracy which he had to go through. When asked as to why he hadn't told me if there was a problem, he assured me he had no intention of 'fucking me over'. But, rather conveniently, he did admit his hedge fund was under redemption pressure and he wanted to work with me to get this loan, which was only twelve months old, repaid as soon as possible.

By now Keith Harris had introduced me to the Hero Fund,

which had this alleged investment fund for lending to football clubs. The security they took was charges against your playing squad and ostensibly the younger players. It was innovative and creative as their margin was taken from player sales. What this did was enable a club like mine to keep their younger home-grown players, who traditionally were on significantly lower wages than players you signed in, for much longer. It also enabled you to keep them whilst their potential value became more tangible, get the benefit of their abilities, and then pay the Hero Fund their monies and profit back through the increase in their value at a later date.

The only problem was that the Premier League had already outlawed this funding vehicle as they considered it bordered on third-party ownership. Following the furore over the Carlos Tevez affair at West Ham they were extremely cautious. Another issue was they didn't understand it and had no wish to.

The Football League had followed suit and would not approve this type of funding for their members. So, given that I could see no buyer on the immediate horizon and that there were no other funding opportunities besides emptying the entire contents of my bank account into this football club, somehow I had to get the Hero Fund in a position so they could lend.

In June 2009 and against a backdrop of increased pressure from HMRC and almost daily cash calls on me from Palace and other areas of my business portfolio, I went to a Football League meeting for the first time in seven years. It was the year-end conference, held in Portugal, three days attended by the owners and CEOs of all seventy-two League clubs. My sole reason for going was to convince the Football League board, its chairman Lord Brian Mawhinney and the other clubs to approve funding from the Hero Club.

I flew out to Portugal with Theo Paphitis, who, along with

Deloitte's, was giving a keynote speech about football finances. Upon arriving I was greeted by the League officials with a degree of suspicion as to why I was there and what trouble I may be seeking to cause. It was not without grounds as at the last meetings I attended I was the ringleader in the outcry over the ITV Digital debacle and a staunch critic of the League's chairman of the time, one Keith Harris, and over the years since been very outspoken in my criticism of the football establishment.

The League meeting was its usual scenario of small-minded nonsense dealing with minutiae of rule changes and the same old endless circular argument over why the lower leagues apart from the Championship got such a small percentage of the Sky money. I ingratiated myself straight away by pointing out that I had been absent from such meetings for years and the same crap was still being debated, adding that frankly nobody was remotely interested in watching Darlington v Lincoln live on Sky; it was the Championship that generated the monetary interest. The other leagues should pipe down and accept that and work with the Championship to squeeze more money out of Sky and the Premier League.

The subject turned to football finances, the very reason I was there. Theo and Dan Jones from Deloitte's gave a doomsday speech about the spiralling costs in the Football League and the lack of funding available. Lord Mawhinney spoke about revenue streams and getting costs under control and deals with the Premier League for the future. Once he had finished speaking, the floor was opened up to all seventy-two clubs.

I was about to lose the will to live when John Madejski, the Reading owner, piped up with his particular cure for resolving spiralling costs. He suggested the Football League board implement a rule change allowing all clubs to unilaterally immediately reduce players' contracts by 50 per cent! The unrealistic nature of John's outburst gave me the platform to intervene and speak after Madejski's stunning cure for all ills.

'Chairman, after we have got John back from Narnia, where he is playing in the wardrobe with the lion and witch, and back into the real world, where players have fixed contracts and they can't be changed and people like the PFA would stamp all over such a decision, I need to talk about football funding.' I embarked upon a speech that I knew had to be a call to action.

I told them football was facing financial Armageddon outside of the Premier League and funding was desperately needed. I said that a vehicle like the Hero Fund had to be legitimised. Clubs were desperate for money and banks were closed for business. While I accepted the board needed to implement changes to ensure clubs controlled their spending, this was an issue for another time. Without third-party investment there was nowhere for clubs to source funding if they needed it. The Premier League could afford to adopt a pious attitude towards such funders, but their poorer cousins couldn't. Any reasonable source of funding had to be made available and it was the responsibility of the board and the chairman to legitimise it.

My words had the desired effect as clubs rose to applaud. More importantly Lord Mawhinney understood what I was saying and knew how critical the financial situation surrounding many clubs outside the Premier League was at that time. He jumped on my words and asked the clubs if he was being mandated to achieve my objective. He was almost unanimously given the all clear. I had just taken a giant step to getting the Hero Fund into play and moved a step closer to solving my financial problems.

I had a conversation with Lord Mawhinney afterwards, who was very complimentary about what I had said and observed it was rare to see something so unanimously supported by clubs, adding that despite what I might think he was a huge fan of mine, which took me by complete surprise.

I flew back from Portugal in an upbeat mood and informed Keith Harris about the news, who in turn relayed it to the administrators of the Hero Fund. It was agreed that when, rather than if, it happened the first deal they would complete was with Crystal Palace as there was a whole raft of clubs in the queue – Leicester City, Sheffield United, Hull City and Cardiff amongst many others – who were chomping at the bit. And given Lord Mawhinney's enthusiasm it was my belief that this would happen sooner rather than later.

Back in England I had the release of the film *Telstar* to contend with. So far Fortissimo's ineptness over pricing left us unable to secure hardly any deals and we didn't even have a UK distributor. So I decided to self-distribute in order to get a box office release which would give us the platform for a significant DVD release thus making some inroads into returning some of my investment in this film. In order to get this box office release I had to put up £250,000 as a 'sprat to catch a mackerel' for marketing and materials. We had chosen an opening date of 19 June and according to the scheduling there were no other films due for release.

Within weeks of us setting the date, the producers of the new *Transformers* film selected the same release date. It was a different film entirely but we were now competing for screens with a huge-budget studio film. To add to our problems, *The Hangover*, released some weeks earlier, was smashing box office records and still going strong.

We opened in thirty-two screens around the country and, despite further critical acclaim, the £250,000 brought limited media space and even less time in the cinemas. You opened on a Friday and over the weekend if you hadn't taken what the cinemas considered decent money you were out of commission a few days later. Given we had to have certain regional cinemas that traditionally had low attendances, five days later we were out of fourteen theatres and shortly afterwards all of them. The only exception was reasonable success in the Warner Cinema in Leicester Square.

The £250,000 I spent was an educated marketing campaign to promote awareness, more reviews and support the DVD launch at the end of September. I had signed a deal with a distributor, G2, which was putting the film out on DVD via Momentum, one of the country's biggest film companies. Given supposedly expert industry projections I hoped the DVD sales would be significant and enable me to recoup some of my investment, but as ever nothing worked to plan.

As soon as the film was released a man called John Repsch hit me with a lawsuit. He claimed that the film's screenplay was adapted from a book he had written. This court action would block the DVD distribution deal, which was set for release in September 2009, and the very reason I had paid for a film release was to support the DVD release. The claim was spurious. After a legal review by my lawyers they considered he had no grounds for action.

But what Repsch had managed to do was get a CFA (conditional funding arrangement) with a set of lawyers, which in essence is a no win no fee scenario. The lawyers he used knew they had the leverage, as the release of the DVD would be held up by a pending legal claim. They suspected that it would be more economical for me to settle this grotesque claim than fight it for two years regardless of whether I won, and lose the opportunity to reclaim some of the £2 million-plus I had invested in this film.

After being forced to get my head around the reality of this situation, and trying to deal with gutless distributors who refused to market the DVD because of this farcical claim, I reluctantly made a commercial decision to pay a man who I had never met and was advised had no case against me in excess of £100,000 to ensure the DVD release in September went ahead. After all of that, incredibly, it was all pointless: the launch handled by Momentum, who had wanted no input from either me or the director, was a commercial disaster. At that point in time everything with this bloody film seemed to conspire against me.

By now the relationship with Agilo was deteriorating and they were becoming far more aggressive. They were no longer asking when the loan was going to be repaid; they were demanding to know, using a disputed default notice as leverage on a loan that was up to date and yielding a massive 15 per cent return! I was still attempting to reach an ongoing agreement with HMRC surrounding a payment plan for the arrears Palace were accumulating, aware my failure to pay represented another material breach in Agilo's agreement, this time a legitimate one. And if that wasn't enough I was now paying in around £500,000 a month just to keep Palace afloat.

I now embarked on the most brutal four months of my life. I descended into a hell of trying to save the football club and pumped fortunes of my ever-depleting financial reserves into it. I had to try and contain the increasing aggression of Agilo, get the Hero Fund into play, attempt to address my personal income streams and monies owed to me as well as becoming increasingly aware that there may be other agendas at play here!

I had managed to negotiate a deal with the Revenue for some payments and the balance of circa £1.8 million to be deferred until at least the end of August when the transfer window had closed, which would allow me to sell some players to raise some funds.

In negotiating with the Revenue their constant threat was to wind up the club. Their leverage was they knew how much money I had invested and how much the club meant to me so they used it to apply an inordinate amount of pressure. But now the cash drains on me were enormous in relative terms. From May to the opening of the new season I had put £4 million in Palace alone and I was in serious financial trouble. I soon realised that even if I got the Hero Fund in place the money would merely come in and go straight out to pay off this bloody hedge fund.

In the summer of 2009 I sat in my house in Spain with my father. I was being confronted with a very bleak future. I had been in tough spots before but nothing like this. I was like King Canute commanding the sea to go back, swamped in a tsunami of battles, which, in hindsight, were frankly unwinnable.

I was fighting on so many fronts that this was the time to take control of my own destiny, save myself and make the decision before it was made for me. At this time I should have put Crystal Palace in administration. I was the biggest creditor and I could have had a degree of control over events. But as I spoke to my father, who as he does today, had an unswerving belief in me, despite knowing the truth that the game, if you can call it that, was up, I once again backed myself to win, or at least come through all this adversity.

After many battles fought on their behalf by Lord Mawhinney and me the Hero Fund was approved at the end of August. We eventually got it past a suspicious FA with some very lateral and technical thinking and adapted the League's rules to get the fund into play.

Now it was time for them to honour their obligation by putting the funding up for Palace as they had promised. They had completed all their due diligence and all that had to be decided was the quantum and commercial terms. To keep Agilo and their increasingly aggressive Brajovic at bay I had told them about the Hero Fund, whose deal with me would pay them and finally get rid of them!

HMRC had been paid some money but there were still seven-figure sums outstanding and I was negotiating with them again as unbelievably, despite our best efforts, we had been unable to sell any players during the August transfer window.

My personal circumstances were becoming ever more dire. I was running on fumes. By September I had put another £1 million into Palace. None of my deals were bearing fruit. I couldn't get my money out of Spain and the portfolio of money supporting the overdraft was not recovering to give me any working capital. The bank was becoming increasingly concerned and switched me from a bank manager that I had for twelve years to a new recoveries division. Whereas before my relationship with the bank had often been on my terms, given the assets and cash I had, the balance changed and they were now applying enormous pressure on me and wanted to know the ins and outs of everything.

Palace had started the season slowly but the results were coming despite the backdrop of the pressure I was under, as well as the media reporting on a daily basis about cost-stricken Crystal Palace; it was testament to how strong we were as a unit that the team was focused on winning games. Normally, under these circumstances, the first thing to go is the results. But this wasn't the case.

In the Carling Cup we drew the now Sheikh Mansour-fuelled Manchester City, who were spending money as if they were printing it themselves. Before the match the press billed this as the battle of the 'haves against the have nots', which was a little galling for me to read under the circumstances. They compared the cost of the two squads with Palace coming in at about £9 million and City circa £173 million. However, we got to showcase some of our young talent, notably Victor Moses, who we believed was worth £5 million of anybody's money. He was outstanding on the night and regularly showed the England full back Micah Richards a clean pair of heels. Moses immediately caught the attention of Brian Marwood, City's main recruitment officer. Was this our get-out-of-jail card if all else failed?

As often is the case in football when you are low on luck it completely deserts you. We played Bristol City away and relations between the two clubs were cool. More controversy ensued as Freddie Sears, our recently acquired loanee from West Ham, scored a legitimate goal that wasn't given. The ball went in the net and bounced off the hoarding at the back of the goal and while everyone else witnessed it the referee decided to award a goal kick! There was uproar for five minutes to no avail and then with virtually the last kick of the game Bristol City scored a winner. Neil and I were outraged and lashed out in the media. I went a little further than Neil and accused the Bristol players of being cheats and promptly got charged by my close personal friends at the FA!

By now my finances had evaporated in liquidity terms. The bank was so concerned they wanted to appoint an external set of accountants to look at Palace's financial position and Agilo tried to deploy the same tactics. I was not keen for either party to come in but especially not Agilo, given the disingenuity of their conduct and their clear agenda to get this loan repaid early. Also, the arrears with the Revenue would have caused another default notice. They knew I had a case to argue as they were pressing for payment on the back of a spurious default notice, but if they knew I was in arrears with the Revenue, they would no longer be pressing, they would be demanding.

As I was waiting for the promised term sheet from the Hero Fund and an agreed sum of money, I was working on other initiatives. I asked Phil Alexander to approach a selection of wealthy fans, some of whom were already sponsoring Palace in certain areas, and set up meetings with them. I thought that perhaps I could sell some of my equity to raise some cash to help the situation. Alexander in the past had been quite successful getting monies into the club for commercial properties such as shirt sponsorships or big advertising deals; he was an inveterate glad hander and I was to become well acquainted with someone on that list.

After being pushed, Alexander came back with nothing. Apparently none of these so-called big hitters and fervent Palace fans even wanted to sit down and have a chat with me. It struck me as strange as I know football fans, especially wealthy ones, and if nothing else, morbid curiosity would have got the better of them. This was when I began to feel that Phil Alexander and I were perhaps no longer singing from the same hymn sheet. I got the impression he was easing back, waiting to see if I failed and protecting his position. I also began to have an even greater sense that agendas were being drawn up by certain factions, nothing tangible just an insidious feeling.

Finally, as I was driving up to Cardiff for a game on 17 October, Keith Harris phoned to announce that he had agreed a deal with the Hero Fund. Due diligence had been completed and a term sheet had been agreed. Although they failed to offer us the £10 million I was after, they agreed to meet our backstop figure of £7.5 million. The margin they wanted was reasonable and all in all it was a great deal. I could now pay down Agilo, this difficult, aggressive and dangerous creditor, and still have £3 million plus of working capital to move forward on.

I asked Harris if this was the real deal and he was adamant it was. In fact he suggested we met in the Hero Fund's office with one of their principals, Damian Roberts, on Tuesday to sign off the term sheet. The relief I felt was incredible and it looked as if I had just pulled out the proverbial rabbit.

Around this time I had developed a prolapsed disc and was having a series of epidurals in an attempt to avoid back surgery. So when I met Damian Roberts and received the signed term sheet I declined the opportunity to go for a drink to celebrate their first ever deal in football as I had a hospital appointment. I departed clutching the signed term sheet feeling infinitely more relaxed. I was told the money would be available by the end of October or beginning of November and went off to wait for the formal contract and the money, and wait is what I got to do: I waited and waited!

In November I decided to let the bank appoint Deloitte's, and specifically Lee Manning, to come in and see what the state of play was as well as look at any solutions to ensure the business was able to go forward. I had known Lee for many years. He had undertaken other work for me in the past when he was at a firm called Kroll Buchler Phillips. There he was with David Buchler, the Spurs director and the person I had introduced Mark Goldberg to as a potential administrator some ten years ago. I rated Lee and trusted him.

When Agilo, or more to the point their increasingly erratic principal Brajovic, found out I had allowed the bank in I got my first taste of this man's true character. He went absolutely berserk. He was raging about being the secured creditor and claimed that the bank was in a better position than he was by being allowed in. What he failed to understand was that the relationship with the bank was strong, and Manning knew football well and could quite possibly bring the bank onside to support me, which might mean paying Agilo their money. I sought to placate Brajovic with that in mind but by now the previously cordial and work-together mentality was gone.

The vile threats began and never really stopped for three months. He wanted to call in this four-year loan that was sixteen months old, fully up to date and earning a huge yield!

An unlikely casualty of the financial crisis was Paul Kemsley. His business Rock Investments, one that he frequently bragged was so successful and had a £500 million line of credit with HBOS, failed and was placed into administration. Now I have to admit I didn't shed a single tear for him. What I did was stop paying the rent to try and aid our cash flow, requested a new deal as the one I had done with Kemsley was done under duress and, as this asset was in a company that was in administration, I started to negotiate with the administrators for a vastly reduced purchase price and rent on the lease while it applied.

Lloyds Bank had been forced to buy HBOS, which meant that the actual owners of the stadium in funding terms were now Lloyds, the club's bankers. This was fabulous news as Lloyds wouldn't want to be difficult with Palace, primarily because of their relationship with me, but also no bank wants any adverse publicity surrounding a football club.

This situation, which I had inadvertently engineered and then suffered from at the hands of Kemsley, came full circle for me, with a huge opportunity to renegotiate the whole lease and better still finally get a realistic price for the stadium. This position for Palace was to prove of paramount importance and provide another nail in my coffin!

It had now been brought to my attention that Agilo, as well as putting a 'full court press' on me, were actually seeking to sell the debt to anyone they could. I had tried to find commercial ways to satisfy them. The Hero Fund was still in play, or so I thought, and

I also tried to discount future TV revenues to help cash flow and pay down some of Palace's debt to Agilo. After a series of fraught meetings with Brajovic he announced that he might be selling the debt to Ron Noades, which for me was like lighting a blue touch paper.

If Noades bought the debt he would, to some degree, have control over the club and me. It enraged me, although I knew at the time it was an unlikely scenario as it would have meant that he would have to put his hand in his pocket, something he was not prone to doing. But as information filtered through to me I became conscious of the fact that there were people – and some of them on the list of individuals I had asked Alexander to approach – who were plotting to take advantage of the situation. This was disturbing to say the least. In the discussions with Brajovic he told me that unless I paid down their loan pretty quickly Agilo would come after my personal guarantees. My response was I had committed so much money to Palace in the last twelve months, as well as being battered in every other area, my personal liquidity was questionable, and so he may do as he pleased on that front! Wouldn't it be better for him that we resolved his problem of wanting a loan repaid three years early? That suggestion brought to an end any rapport I had with him and he decided to unleash everything he had to get what he wanted.

Incredibly, after all the hard work to get them into play, the Hero Fund deal stalled without any reasonable explanation. They went into hiding, refused to return phone calls and gave lame excuses to explain away the delays. A term sheet that had been signed in October, with the likelihood of monies available in two weeks, now turned into nothing over the weeks of November and early December. All this was going on while Brajovic and Agilo were threatening to put the club into administration on a daily basis, and as a secured creditor they had the leverage to do that.

Agilo changed offices and summoned me to a pointless meeting where they issued further threats. I recognised the address for some reason and when I arrived I realised why. They were renting a serviced office in the same building as the Hero Fund, in fact, directly above them. Given the Hero Fund were now back-pedalling from the deal they had offered to me, was this a horrible coincidence or was there more to it than that? I still haven't worked that out.

In mid-December, some eight weeks after signing the term sheet, I had a heated and very bad-tempered meeting with the Hero Fund, their two principals Damian Roberts and Nick Hely-Hutchinson, and Keith Harris, where they backtracked from what they had said in the term sheet and to me. They needed to get more funding and wanted to do more due diligence on Palace. They had signed a term sheet subject to contract, not due diligence, and by signing that agreement they had acknowledged they had done the due diligence. I knew, as I sat there listening to what I can only describe as utter bullshit, there was no deal with these guys. I had spent time getting them in play, put more of my money into Palace on the basis of my agreement with them, and they were not going to come through!

After Deloitte's had been in they produced a report of a relatively well-run club in commercial aspects but one that needed funding to get out of its current predicament. They noted the club had the asset value in the playing squad to do this and given the new incomes coming in the future in the season 2010–11 and after the cost reductions, would be in even better condition. The club had debts of circa £30 million but £23 million-plus was to me, £4.3 million to Agilo and the other £3 million-odd was HMRC, other creditors and football clubs on transfer deals where the money was not due in some cases for eighteen months. So in real terms the club's finances were far from disastrous, primarily because I had just kept on funding it; we had just lost cash flow and had a secured creditor change his agenda.

The immediate short-term issue was with HMRC. They had decided to issue a petition to wind up Palace that was due to be heard on 28 January 2010 for around £1.2 million. This could be easily cleared up with a small player transfer in January but the overwhelming problem was Agilo. Where Lee Manning and Deloitte's were going with this report was to explore the potential of Lloyds Bank stepping in now that they had the stadium to provide funding to pay Agilo their money.

In December I engaged Denton Wilde Sapte, ironically the lawyers who had acted for the administrators of Crystal Palace and in whose offices I had arrived nearly ten years earlier to buy the club. I wanted them to help with the legal aspects of the pressure that Agilo were applying and to ensure I was acting appropriately, given the legal position with the Inland Revenue and Agilo, and to try and protect my other directors from any allegations of wrong-doing around the trading of the company.

Lee Manning came to a meeting with Agilo to try and work out a solution to their loan. The idea was to allow me to get to January and pay both the Revenue and Agilo as much as possible through player transfers in the window. In the meeting he got to see Brajovic in action, who from the first whistle was hostile and incredibly aggressive. He stated in no uncertain terms he was not interested in the well-being of the club; he was not interested in solutions or working together. 'I will get our money; this is the business I am in. I will do it whatever I have to and am not interested in any more fucking discussions.'

The hostility from Brajovic was pretty jarring even for someone as experienced as Manning and he immediately saw that we were not dealing with someone with a rational perspective to resolve an issue. This was someone whose constant threat was administration, someone who was hell-bent on doing something even if it meant he was cutting his nose off to spite his face. It had become personal for him. The language he used was what it was, and while I am certainly no shrinking violet this was not what Deloitte's had expected, even though I had warned them of Brajovic's temperament. I listened to him threaten and rant and tried to hold my temper. After leaving this meeting, which frankly was just a forum for Brajovic to vent his spleen, we tried to work up a solution.

By the end of December I had involved Lord Mawhinney as the Hero Fund had all but reneged on everything. He wrote a withering letter to them about their conduct and implored them to honour their deal. It was very pleasing to have such support from Brian; he of course may have felt a tinge of embarrassment as he had lobbied hard to get them into play. But it fell on deaf ears – they just came up with more lame excuses!

To avoid forcing the club into administration and to give me the time in January to raise the funds to pay them, Agilo demanded I sign over all my shareholder loans to them. This meant that if they did put the club into administration in the event that I failed to pay them, if the club were to be bought out via a CVA (company voluntary agreement) – the only way the club would exit administration and get Agilo their money – I couldn't block said CVA. Given that I was the biggest creditor and could therefore block any deal I saw as unfair on unsecured creditors and that my shareholder loans would be a major obstacle to Agilo putting Palace into administration there was no logic to their demands. No rational person would threaten, let alone do it!

But I was not dealing with logic. Brajovic insisted he would put the club into administration if I didn't sign these shareholder loans over to him. It would be signing my own death warrant with these people again unless I did it with some agreement in place that gave me at least the January transfer window to raise the funds. And there we reached an impasse. I was reluctantly prepared to sign over my shareholder loans, but only in exchange for a standstill agreement until the second week of February in order to give me time to sell players, get Lloyds involved or find some other funding!

There was of course the added problem of HMRC, and their petition to wind up was due to be heard on 28 January 2010, three days before the transfer window closed. If the Inland Revenue didn't agree to step down the petition or defer it for a period of weeks, then the club would be wound up on that date. Of course, Agilo wouldn't allow that to happen and would have pushed the club into administration before then as a secured creditor to protect their position.

As December wound down we desperately sought an agreement with Agilo and believed we were close to one. I would sign over my shareholder loans, again completely backing myself in exchange for a standstill agreement and also getting the Revenue to defer their petition to wind up. But on 23 December Brajovic announced he wanted to invoke a clause in the loan repayment called 'make whole', which involved paying them all the interest they would have earned if the loan ran its full term. Therefore they wanted another £900,000 on top of the outstanding balance. This was unbelievable. The agreement only provided for this if we voluntarily repaid early, not if they called the loan in. The flimsy truce broke down and I was told unless I signed up they would put the club into administration the next day!

Conventional wisdom from both Deloitte's and Denton Wilde

Sapte was that Brajovic would never do it and it was all bluff. If he did it was very unlikely Agilo, given I was the biggest creditor and the banks were secured by more of my money, would get their money repaid. But it didn't stop Brajovic and Agilo's legal advisers, DLA, again ironically people well known to me as they had represented me and commanded huge fees for the 121 court case, turning the screw, assuring us they would do it. It was a case of who blinked first. I didn't, and late on Christmas Eve we received an email saying that it would be better for all parties to consider their positions and talk after the Christmas period.

No sooner had I breathed in than Christmas was over and I went to watch Crystal Palace at Selhurst Park on Boxing Day 2009. It would be the last home game I ever watched as chairman of the club, but I didn't know it at the time. And there was no respite as Agilo and DLA were making more threats about administration and assuring me there would be no second chance if I didn't sign over the shareholder loans. I stood my ground again. 'Give us the standstill agreement,' I said, 'remove the ridiculous make-whole demand and I will do it.'

Rachel Anthony of Denton's and Lee Manning desperately tried to make Agilo see sense. Trying to reach an accord, we had managed to agree the terms of the shareholder loan sign-over and the standstill agreement but they still insisted on this extra £900,000. On 30 December DLA advised us that their client would put the business into the hands of the receiver on New Year's Eve if I didn't give in to their demands. Once more I was playing Russian roulette and at the last minute once again Agilo backed down. For the first time in weeks Brajovic picked up the phone to me and spoke directly, saying the lawyers were getting us into a mess and we needed to work it out together. He, of course, was instructing his lawyers to act this way but we agreed to pick this up in the first days of the New Year. This second climbdown gave Brajovic further substance to Denton and Deloitte's insistence that Brajovic wouldn't make good on his threat to put the club into administration. They were guilty of sorely underestimating him.

January 2010 was a blur of legal toing and froing, a minefield of threats and legal obligations. The bank insisted I went to court to get something called a validation order to ensure any payments I made were sanctioned legally, given HMRC's wind-up order. Without this they would freeze the club account even though they had the security of my cash. Agilo also demanded this, so with Rachel Anthony and Lee Manning at the helm with me we went to court and got the order, which involved high-level legal representation and costs.

Neil Warnock was aware of the predicament I was in and was very supportive. I even got a high-spirited message from him and his assistant Mick Jones on my voicemail over Christmas telling me how much they loved being at Palace. Neil had also identified players he felt we could sell and command good fees for and not necessarily halt our progress on the field, which despite all the problems was pretty good.

Agilo eventually agreed to drop the make-whole monies but I had to get HMRC to withdraw their petition, which was easier said than done. But I convinced them during a conference call that in effect they were not dealing with me but a very dangerous and serious secured creditor who was threatening to put the club into administration. If this happened, the Revenue would get little if any of their money. We made them see sense, but not without some concessions.

Because of the precarious legal position, certain parts of any monies received from such things as transfer receipts had to be put to one side, meaning not every penny we got in could go to Agilo. We had to put a percentage into the working cash flow of the business and an 80/20 split was agreed in favour of Agilo, with the funds being held in escrow with Rachel Anthony at DWS. We still hadn't signed an agreement on the shareholder/standstill agreement but commercial activities came into play. We believed we were just about to receive a £5 million-plus offer from Manchester City for young Victor Moses, even more so after they came and watched us play Plymouth away and Victor scored a wonder goal which we thought had clinched the deal, but an offer never came. We sold a player for a million to Southampton. Not all of it was paid in one tranche. As is often the way in transfer deals payments were spread out over a period of time, so to get the balance paid immediately I had to do a discounting deal with a funder, who would advance the rest for a fee.

The trade-off with HMRC was to ensure the payee position got no worse and also to make a payment towards some of the arrears. Our cash flow provided for the monthly payee payment but they wanted an additional £200,000. So I used the VAT on the player transfer that was due to be paid over to HMRC in three months to pay that amount. In other words, I used the Revenue's own money to pay them. This decision prejudiced no one, came from no cash-flow loss but was to be the precursor to the final explosion.

Brajovic suggested to me he had someone who might be prepared to buy out their loan, but it needed my consent as the loan could only be sold to an FSA-registered organisation, unless I agreed. The person he wanted me to talk to was someone Phil Alexander had spoken to who had apparently shown no interest in talking to me about the financial position at Palace but was now interested in buying the Agilo loan. It was Steve Parish, the chief executive of a firm called Tag, who had a smallish shirt sponsorship deal with Palace.

I had never met or spoken to Parish before but that was all to change. In the interests of keeping Brajovic appeased I spoke to Parish, who confirmed he was interested in buying this loan. What he suggested was he would pay Agilo the £4.3 million outstanding, take over the loan and I would pay them £6.3 million by 26 June. In other words, if I failed to make the repayment in five months Parish, who intimated there were other parties involved in buying out Agilo's loan, would take the club.

Effectively Parish and his backers wanted circa 120 per cent interest secured against the £35 million I had in Palace. Despite the appeal of being able to rid myself of this man Brajovic I can't say I jumped at this deal. In speaking to Parish, it was clear to me he knew a lot more about the exact financial position at Palace than he had any right to. I wonder – who could have told him that from my board of directors? My brother Dominic? The fiercely loyal Kevin Watts? Or my chief executive Phil Alexander, he of the 'the king is dead' mentality? I suspected Parish and the others he alluded to were involved had been speaking to Agilo for some time!

On Friday 22 January a highly irritated Brajovic phoned me late in the evening and asked me to assure him I hadn't paid any money to the Inland Revenue. 'Of course I have, Milos. It is in the court-approved validation order, and I had to pay them money to get them to delay their petition hearing until February, and the extra bit I paid was their own money, the VAT on a transfer fee that they would be getting in three months' time. What's the problem with that?'

Brajovic exploded and told me that was it. He wouldn't listen to reason, and stated I had no business paying HMRC. Of course, I didn't want to pay the Revenue at this time but I had to, but he was not interested. He was in a demented rage, finishing his rant with, 'You just fucked yourself. You have until Monday to pay down this loan or your club will go into administration.'

I took this phone call seriously but once again it was considered by Rachel Anthony and Lee Manning to be another example of irrational behaviour and likely to be more bluster.

The next day I travelled with friends to watch the team play Premier League Wolves in the third round of the FA Cup on a cold blustery day in the Midlands. I sat and watched a goalless first half and as it came to an end my mobile phone rang. It was Milos Brajovic again. I took the call and spent the entire half-time break in the foyer at Molineux having what can only be described as a very heated conversation. I tried to talk sense into this man but he was raging about this payment to the Revenue.

The temperature of the call rose and rose as he became more and more aggressive. He threatened to ruin my club, ruin me personally, take my possessions and put my family on the street. Once it reached that point, I had had enough, and I exploded. I told him that if he ever wanted to speak to me like that again, to make sure he had the courage of his convictions and do it when he was standing in front of me.

After the call concluded I went out to watch the remainder of the game. We were now winning 2–1 and I had missed all the goals. I sat down for the final twenty minutes or so and the last goal I got to watch as the owner of Crystal Palace was the Wolves' equaliser!

The next day was my daughter Cameron's second birthday party, which I never got to enjoy, as outside the house were paparazzi. One of Suzanne's guests was Vanessa Perroncel, who the newspapers alleged had an affair with the England captain John Terry. I spent the majority of the afternoon on the telephone to Rachel Anthony at DWS trying to prepare ourselves for the inevitable onslaught that Agilo would throw at us on Monday.

First thing Monday morning it came. Do a deal with Parish in twenty-four hours or the club goes into administration. The deal Parish was offering was even worse than Agilo's but I now had to explore it. Frankly, to this day I do not believe that Parish had the money himself, or money in place elsewhere to do the deal he was proposing, or any deal full stop. I think he was just stirring the pot and seeing what came out of it and how best he could position himself, but what- ever he did was very unlikely to be of any benefit to me. We tried to liaise with Agilo and their lawyers to introduce the potential of Lloyds stepping in with funding, but we were getting nowhere.

The number of emails flying back and forward on Monday, starting at 7 a.m., between me, Parish, Agilo, Lee Manning and Rachel Anthony, was vast. But still the opinion being put forward by my advisers was that Brajovic wouldn't do it. It made no sense to put the club into administration; he wouldn't get his money; he is just raging because he wants to push you around!

DLA, Agilo's lawyers, were not responding to phone calls to confirm whether they had been instructed to file for administration, which led Rachel Anthony to believe they would not. She also suggested that Lloyds Bank, who didn't want CPFC to go into administration, should phone DLA as well as some of the big insolvency firms to state that they would take a very dim view of any such action.

At 11 p.m. Brajovic told me he was close to doing a deal with Parish and was selling him the debt for a 10 per cent discount and expected me to sign a deal to pay Agilo the £400,000 balance. My advisers were outraged at this and suggested we left it till the morning, so at half an hour before midnight we all stood down.

The next day Lloyds phoned around as, despite their disbelief, the feeling began to permeate that this threat might now be carried out. They reached Grant Thornton, an insolvency firm, who advised

Lloyds they were offered the administration two weeks earlier and turned it down as they 'did not want to be a patsy for Agilo', meaning they knew this was a bad administration for them to take: there was no money being offered to fund the club through administration, however long that might take, and they knew I was the biggest creditor.

My advisers and I scrambled to see if we could do a deal with Parish, who by now was very much in bed with Agilo, and as the morning wore on a deadline was set for 2.30 p.m. to either conclude a deal with Parish or get Lloyds to agree to pay Agilo. Agilo said they had the papers drawn up for the court order and would file by 4 p.m., when the courts closed

Still Rachel Anthony suggested this was utter nonsense, stating that if the papers were drawn up it would take five minutes for them to file and they wouldn't need to wait another one and a half hours until four – and in any case the courts closed at 4.30 p.m. In her email to me at 13.18 she said it was 'bullshit'. The problem was, she was wrong!

Lloyds got through to DLA, who refused to confirm or deny that they were going to file, and refused to advise which firm was going to be appointed as administrators if they were. Once again this suggested to my advisers that the threat of administration was a ruse. Time ticked by. At 14.30 I was on a conference call with all my advisers and still sending emails to Brajovic at 14.56.

At 15.02 on 26 January 2010 the football club I had owned for ten years, the battle I had fought for eight months, was lost, but as yet I didn't know this and neither did my advisers. Even at this stage we were still trying to get Agilo to engage with us and work out a deal, before anyone else knew, but somehow Steve Parish did. He phoned and told me that Agilo had filed.

With dread I phoned Rachel Anthony, who checked her in-box. I could hear the disbelief in her voice as she confirmed she had the court order and that indeed the club was in administration. Time exploded and space contracted. I was choked. I had to conclude the call as my emotions got the better of me.

I had lost.

17

THE AFTERMATH

My first reaction upon hearing the news I never wanted to receive – the news that Palace was in administration – was one of complete and utter desolation. It felt like someone had ripped my guts out. For a moment I was inconsolable. When I received the news, I was alone and so no one got to see me that way. I wouldn't wish that feeling on my worst enemy, and at the time I felt there were a fair few candidates to fill that spot. It was the single worst moment in my entire life.

My phone went into meltdown. One call I did answer was from my mother, but I was very distressed and didn't want to talk. Yet in the twenty-five minutes it took her to drive to my office in Park Lane, I had recovered my equilibrium and was now speaking to my advisers about finding a way to get the order set aside or even getting the bank to back me to buy the club back. This is just how I am. Adjust to something and then move forward. In this instance it was a coping mechanism, nothing more.

I phoned my brother Dominic to break the news to him but I was too late: he already knew as the administrator had wasted no time assuming immediate and complete control of Palace. I phoned

Neil, who was just getting off a plane with the team as we were playing Newcastle United away. He was emotional and deeply upset and wanted to resign there and then, which was testament to our strong bond. But I made him promise to stay as Palace would need his help.

I then phoned the appointed administrator Brendan Guilfoyle and advised him that I was available if he needed me and that I would do as much as I could to help him do his job, which was to get the club out of administration.

Palace was in administration for just five months and during that time those agendas that I had become aware of in the months leading up to the loss of my club became all too clear to me. Initially I was considered the largest obstacle as I was the biggest creditor and could vote down the CVA and subsequently block any sale. I met Guilfoyle days later and he asked if I was recording the conversation, which struck me as odd, but what he said next clarified the reason why he had asked. Firstly, he asked me if I was prepared to fund the administration! And then, jaw-droppingly, stated that he should never have taken it on. It broke his personal rules of administration, taking into account who was going to fund it and what the exit strategy was. He went on to add that Palace should never have gone into administration. In my opinion this made him little better than an ambulance-chaser. It was scant consolation to learn from Guilfoyle that he had taken the job on the fly because not one of the major firms wanted to touch it.

When Palace went into administration we were in eighth place in the League and a few points off the play-off spots. The club was said to be £30 million in debt, but as I have said £23 million of that was to me and I wasn't calling it in. And also it had a playing squad independently valued at £27 million. So, as Guilfoyle himself stated to me, the business should not be in administration. All I had done in the last eight months was pour millions of pounds into reducing debts. I had kept the playing squad and also inadvertently got the stadium priced in the best way it would ever be – and all for the benefit of others.

Soon Parish approached me as I was the biggest creditor. He wanted to do a deal, rolling the debts to me into a new structure with him and others to bring the club out of administration. I looked at his proposal but before I even had a chance to really consider it everything changed!

Agilo were now forced into funding the administration as the business had cash calls and administration meant any monies coming in from transfers had to pay down football creditors first. So the likelihood of them getting their money even if they, or Guilfoyle, smashed out players in the remaining days of the transfer window appeared extremely unlikely. All they had been told and had ignored was now dawning on them, but again this was of little consolation to me.

Victor Moses was sold and the administrator announced he had secured a £2.5 million fee from Wigan, which was not true! My information was that Guilfoyle even tried to press-gang players into leaving. Apparently young Nathaniel Clyne was told he had to be sold to Wolves. I understand from Neil that they got the upstanding Phil Alexander to advise this seventeen-year-old boy that if he didn't go, the rest of the players wouldn't get paid. If so, this was a shameless tactic, and not even true. I phoned Neil to get him to speak to Clynnie as well as Neil Danns and Darren Ambrose, two others who were earmarked for the fire sale, to tell them not to go.

I watched from the sidelines to see how events would play out, though I knew what was going to happen. Given that the club had ten points deducted and were now in a relegation battle, I knew that a cut-price sale could send Palace down. Agilo didn't give a toss and would have sold everybody and everything to get their money, irrespective of what that did to the club and how it would look in the eyes of a potential buyer. Also the administrator, despite protestations to the contrary, was most probably doing the bidding of Agilo. Brajovic had put the club into administration, now he had to fund it, and ironically rather than reducing his debt he was increasing it.

I saw Palace a week later beat Wolves in the televised FA Cup replay. Then they drew Aston Villa in the next round, which again would be on TV and got a replay too, which would generate circa £1 million in unbudgeted income for the club's administrators. Bloody sod's law!

I now knew that Parish really wanted to buy this club. He hinted that there were others involved and I suspected that he needed these others financially. His original idea was to include me in the equation as I controlled the CVA. But I had personal guarantees in the club for several million for leases and advance season ticket sales and as soon as Parish became aware of this the whole situation changed! It seemed to me that he now felt I was superfluous to requirements. He played the role of reluctant buyer brilliantly, convincing everyone he didn't really want to buy the club and would do it only if he absolutely had to!

As I watched Parish manoeuvre and manipulate circumstances towards achieving his end of owning the club or part of it, albeit as a 'reluctant owner', I tried to ensure that I and the other unsecured creditors got the best return they could. Many people purporting to want to buy the club out of administration approached me but where had they been when I had it for sale?

Anyway, they were all complete time wasters. One who approached me and I nearly vouched for was the owner of Croydon Athletic

Football Club, a wealthy young sports agent. I was introduced to him by Robbie Earle the ex-footballer, and he came and met me in the Dorchester and talked a good game. He even upon request produced proof of funds for £15 million. But this was to prove a red herring as despite being a successful businessman, Mazhar Majeed was soon arrested as the ringleader in the match-fixing scandal surrounding Pakistan Test cricket.

Parish had picked my brains during the early period of administration, validating cash flows and getting to grips with the business when we had looked at a possible future together. Now he and others decided that there was no need to do a deal with me but they would 'reluctantly' still buy the club but only in the event they could get the CVA through. That could only happen if the bank and I voted for it and given that the bank was secured by me it would almost certainly follow my lead. I was confronted with the 'turkey voting for Christmas' scenario. Either I voted for the proposed CVA or I could be responsible for the club being liquidated.

By now I had accepted that I was never going to return to Selhurst Park and to be honest I wasn't desperate to hang on to some vestige of control.

What I didn't think was unreasonable was to expect a decent amount in the pound for the unsecured creditors, of which I and the bank made up 80 per cent, to allow me to leave this heartbreakingly difficult time behind me. I was advised that a deal of somewhere between 10 and 20p in the pound was what I could expect. Even the unsecured creditors at Portsmouth, which was universally accepted as fucked as a club, got 20p in the pound. What I was then told I had to vote for was half a penny in the pound, one of if the not the lowest ever CVA payouts. For the £35 million-plus I had put into Palace, I was going to get £175,000 back. My financial nightmare was showing no sign of subsiding, even now. But if I didn't vote this through the 'club's blood would be on my hands'.

Parish and his group were apparently the only bidders in town and apparently the administrator had limited funding and could not go on. Perhaps the fact he took his fees at the beginning rather than the end didn't help. He was in a hurry to sell, which suited Parish as he desperately wanted it. I wanted the administrator to have longer to market it and find a few bidders. Palace still had to survive relegation from the Championship, which meant no one would really bid until they knew what division the club was in.

All of this led, in my opinion, to a forced sale with propaganda abounding in the media about the impending demise of the club. The administrator's attempt to attract a buyer was pitiful. He engaged a sports agent to sell players and advertised the sale of the club in the *Financial Times* and that was about it. Guilfoyle was having a nightmare. He had Brajovic providing funding and screaming at him on a daily basis; he had Parish and his gang, the 'reluctant' but preferred bidders, playing hide and seek with themselves, and the problem of me as the biggest creditor.

The administrator refused to take time to find a better buyer so in the end I was forced into a corner. I had little choice but to vote for a CVA that, as I said, gave me virtually nothing. I could, of course, have played Russian roulette with the Parish consortium and the administrator and told them to liquidate, and, knowing how much Parish personally wanted some form of ownership of Crystal Palace despite his expressed reluctance, perhaps I should have done, but I didn't.

After nearly a year of purgatory I was almost glad it was over. At least I would have no more to do with people like the destructive Brajovic, disingenuous Parish, disappointing Guilfoyle and ultimately disloyal Phil Alexander.

Bitter? No, this is not me being bitter. For ten years I fought every battle and won most of them, except the most important one. I had lost a decade of my life and vast amounts of money and for what? The loss of a high-profile business in the public domain put every other facet of my financial life under scrutiny and set off a cascade of events that two years later is still causing me severe problems.

No. I am not bitter. I was complicit in my own downfall at Palace. They say that fortune favours the brave but I don't believe it extends to the foolishly brave. What I am is angry, angry with myself for putting myself in a position where people could take advantage of me.

I suppose I have to accept that people will try to take advantage of you or try to get what they want for as little as possible. I just would have preferred if they had been upfront about it, rather than show one face to me and another to the watching world.

Without a doubt, people's agendas were served and perhaps I got what I deserved for overextending myself or for being outspoken or whatever. But imagine how you would feel if you lost vast amounts of your money and ten years of your dreams and ambitions were taken away from you. How would you feel if you suffered damage to your reputation and put your own and your family's financial future in peril . . . Angry?

As for Agilo, did they get all their money? Despite all Brajovic's threats and bravado and extreme tactics, no, they did not – and without a shadow of a doubt they would have got it from me. Perhaps there is a god after all. I have to say that Milos Brajovic is one person I sincerely hope not to meet again.

The loss of a football club seems trivial compared to the scale of world problems but everything is relative. Life goes on, and perhaps writing this book has, in some way, closed this chapter of my life. This book was never meant to be an exorcism and certainly not a 'state of the nation' on football. I've tried to explain what my experiences of this world were like. Owning a football club is bloody hard work, extraordinarily expensive, and can be a thankless task.

The way I lived my life – professionally and personally – gave me so many experiences, good and bad, and something should be taken from both.

The multi-millionaire tag, as well as the benefits that went with it, may have gone for the time being and I suspect I will always carry a level of disappointment about the manner in which my ownership of the football club came to an end, but throughout life there are many challenges and how you approach the next raft of them defines you. After all, to paraphrase Kipling, with ambition often come both triumph and disaster and you have to treat both these impostors just the same.

I don't walk through life like a Monty Pythonesque character whistling 'Always Look on the Bright Side of Life'. But I do have an absolutely resolute determination to get myself back to a position where I can buy back my football club. Although, for God's sake, I trust that common sense would prevail. But who knows? Like the fable of the scorpion and the frog: I can't change my nature!

And as one philosopher said: winners are dreamers who never give up.

INDEX

CP indicates Crystal Palace Football Club. SJ indicates Simon Jordan.

Daily Mail 269
Daily Mirror 207–8
Dalien Shied 87
Dalli Brothers 252
Dammers, Jerry 193, 202
Danns, Neil 306, 382
Data Stream International 17
Davies QC, John 292, 293,
    296, 297, 299–300, 302
Davies, Billy 294
Davies, John 52
De Burgh Chris 118
De Rozario, Russell 312
Deane, Brian 201
Dein, David 88–9, 118, 219, 234
Dell'Olio, Nancy 157
Deloitte 356, 365, 368, 369,
    370, 371–2, 373
Demetriou, Andy 32–3, 34
Denton Wilde Sapte (DWS) 81,
    369, 371–2, 373, 374, 376
Derby County 167, 168, 253,
    300, 301
Derry, Shaun 160, 161, 322
Deutsche, Bank 335
Dickov, Jan 200
Dickov, Paul 199, 200, 321
Dillon, Matt 24
DLA 372, 377, 378
Doherty, Pete 308
Donn, Ivan 44
Dowie, Bob 215, 217–18, 223,
    224, 227, 230, 240–1, 243,
    252, 254, 255, 262, 263,
    264, 268, 274, 276, 279,
    290, 299
Dowie, Debbie 212
Dowie, Iain 187–8, 189, 190–1,
    194, 195, 200, 210, 211,
    212, 213–15, 217, 220, 223,
    224, 228, 230, 234, 239,

240–1, 243, 245, 246, 251,
    252, 253, 254, 256, 257,
    260, 262, 263, 264–5,
    266–73, 274, 275, 281, 291,
    292–304, 305, 316, 330, 341
Dragon's Den 285
Dressing Room 337–8
DTI 33
Dunstone, Charles 29, 30, 31,
    32
Durham, Adrian 146, 343
Dyer, Danny 307, 308

Earle, Robbie 384
Elliot, Ricky 27, 28, 30
Ellis, Doug 192
Ellis, Sam 184
Elton, Ben 43
England (national team) 7, 67,
    68, 76, 95, 102, 110, 114,
    118, 139, 142, 157, 175,
    178, 199, 221, 224, 226,
    236, 239, 253, 254, 259,
    275, 278, 280, 281, 363,
    376
Ericsson 237–41
Eriksson, Sven Goran 157, 228,
    229
ESPN 277
Eubank, Chris 156
Euro 2004 221–2
Evans, Roy 147
Eve, Edward 37–8
Evening Standard 117, 193,
    198–9
Everton 225, 228, 242, 256,
    274, 276, 308

FA Cup:
    1989–90 92, 263
    2002–03 164, 167, 168

393